Structure and Society
in Literary History

Structure and Society in Literary History

Studies in the History and
Theory of Historical Criticism

Robert Weimann

Expanded Edition, 1984

The Johns Hopkins University Press

Baltimore and London

Originally published by the University Press of Virginia, 1976
Johns Hopkins Paperbacks edition, 1984

The Johns Hopkins University Press, Baltimore, Maryland 21218
The Johns Hopkins Press Ltd., London

Library of Congress Cataloging in Publication Data

Weimann, Robert.
    Structure and society in literary history.

    Includes bibliographical references and index.
    1. Literature—History and criticism—Theory, etc.
I. Title.
PN441.W45   1984   801'.95   84-9706
ISBN 0-8018-3122-9 (pbk.)

Preface to the Original Edition

Although some of these essays are based on earlier versions in German, this book contains more than a translation of previously published materials. Taken together, these essays form a volume unlike any of my earlier books, which I have drawn upon either by way of translation or, more often, for inspiration. Very little, except for some basic practical experience in historical criticism, together with an occasional reference, has been taken from my books on Shakespeare and the Tudor and Stuart drama. But *New Criticism und die Entwicklung bürgerlicher Literaturwissenschaft* (1962; rev. ed., Munich: Beck, 1974) has provided me with a number of themes and a good many references, especially for the second section of the opening essay and the study of metaphor and historical criticism. More fully, my *Literaturgeschichte und Mythologie* (Berlin: Aufbau-Verlag, 1971) has contributed some basic ideas and materials to the essays on American literary history and structuralism, but the existing draft translations (by Jack Zipes, Mark Goldberg, and others) have been thoroughly revised and somewhat expanded. The essay on point of view is indebted to a more comprehensive German article of mine that first appeared in *Zeitschrift für Anglistik und Amerikanistik* (1962), but the present version has benefited from subsequent studies of point of view in Daniel Defoe (1964) and Thomas Nashe (1970) as well as from long reviews of books by Wayne C. Booth, also in *Zeitschrift für Anglistik und Amerikanistik* (1966), and Franz Stanzel, in *Sinn und Form* (1967). The nucleus of the chapter on tradition was first read as an address to the Fifth Triennial Meeting of the American Comparative Literature Association in Los Angeles (1974). An earlier version of this chapter has meanwhile been published in the *Yearbook of Com-*

parative and General Literature (Vol. 23, 1974). It draws chiefly on a collection of articles which I have edited and to which I have contributed under the title *Tradition in der Literaturgeschichte: Beiträge zur Kritik des bürgerlichen Traditions-begriffs bei Croce, Ortega, Eliot, Leavis, Barthes, u. a.* (Berlin: Akademie-Verlag, 1973), but in the process of incorporating new material, I have entirely rewritten it.

Three of the essays in their English version ("Past Significance and Present Meaning," "Structuralism and Literary History," and "Metaphor and Historical Criticism") first appeared in *New Literary History*. My thanks to the editor, Ralph Cohen, are most sincere. It was he who first suggested, and helped explore the possibility of, the present volume. He also helped in arranging for a draft translation of the essay on American literary history. Without his generosity and helpfulness, this book would not now be in print. All three of the essays from *New Literary History* have been revised for this volume and both the first and the last of these have been substantially expanded. An early version of the essay on point of view was first used as a lecture at Harvard University (1968), and that on metaphor was a contribution to a series of lectures at the University of Toronto (1971). The former essay was first printed in *Preserve and Create: Essays in Marxist Literary Criticism*, ed. Gaylord C. LeRoy and Ursula Beitz (New York: Humanities Press, 1973). I wish to thank the editors of this anthology as well as the editor of the *Yearbook* and of course the *spiritus rector* of *New Literary History* for kindly permitting me to use previously printed material here in a revised and expanded version.

My acknowledgment is due Faber and Faber Ltd. and Harcourt Brace Jovanovich, Inc., for permission to quote from T. S. Eliot's "The Function of Criticism," which appears in his *Selected Essays: 1917–1932*.

At this point I would like to express my appreciation and, indeed, my gratitude to the University Press of Virginia, especially to my copy editor, Gerald Trett, and to its printers.

Three of the essays as well as an early version of the Introduction have profited from discussions of Marxist alternatives to formalism in one of my graduate courses at the University of Virginia during the spring term of 1974. It is a pleasure for me to thank those of my students who generously offered to read and comment on manuscripts now included here. In particular I wish to thank Ann Hedin for her perceptive comments on the essay on point of view and Andrea Zapal for carefully reading and criticizing the manuscript on metaphor. Cordial thanks also go to Carol Dixon and Bill Marberg.

Various scholars kindly gave me the benefit of their criticism and advice. The Introduction was read by Peter Clecak, Arnold Kettle, and Annette Rubinstein and has much profited from their friendly counsel. Peter Clecak and David Peck also read, and made perceptive comments on, the chapter on American literary history. Years ago, when I had sketched an early version of "Past Significance and Present Meaning," Laurence Lerner was patient enough to read the essay and improve on some of its formulations. Cyrus Hamlin, who was my friendly host at Toronto, most helpfully read and commented on the study of metaphor which, in a somewhat later version, was also read and perceptively criticized by Norman Rabkin. It was a pleasure to have the criticism and advice of so many friends and colleagues. Vividly remembering their kindness and their generosity, I wish to express my sincere thanks to all of them.

Akademie der Wissenschaften der DDR
Berlin
9 May 1975

Contents

Contents

Structure and Society
in Literary History

Introduction

Toward a Theory of Literary History

IN the present state of English and American literary criticism, any new approach to literary history is bound to raise basic problems of theory and method for the study of literature at large. Perhaps it is not going too far to say that without a new and more profound understanding of the historical nature and the social function of literature, the most pressing problems of criticism cannot be coherently and systematically redefined; without a new awareness of history, the study of literature is unlikely to move beyond the confines of the intrinsic school of criticism. To say this is to point to the paradigmatic quality but also to the problematic assumptions of the historical perspective on literature, and it immediately involves a postulate of some theoretical and practical consequence. Above all, it involves an attempt to establish some reciprocal relation between a perspective on past history and an awareness of the social and cultural needs of the present. It is precisely the reciprocal quality in the relationship of "past significance" and "present meaning" that, in England and America, has become precarious. Here we have a problem so overriding that, upon inspection, it may well prove to be the most crucial single factor in the present crisis and the potential new growth of historical criticism.

There is a paradox involved in this: at the same time that the function of criticism in the present has become so problematic, much of the literature of the past has, at least potentially, gained new significance in the context of a rapidly changing society. Emerging out of the social protest and struggle of the sixties, a new consciousness of the need for a living and more truly democratic culture is being articulated in a number of ways. It finds expression in some of the more positive impulses in today's counterculture, in some popular and quite unliterary forms of song and music as well as in the new black writing, and in the growing theoretical stature of some of the New Left and radical liberal critiques of capitalist society. But the paradox of the situation is that there is hardly any point of fruitful contact or correlation between the new cultural and theoretical possibilities in the present and the historical approach to the literature of the past. And yet one would think that the new experience in the present must allow for and, indeed, demand such new perspectives on the literature of the past as cannot be achieved in terms of the traditional formalist methodology.

As far as academic criticism is concerned, this situation involves a good deal of frustration and uneasiness. For despite repeated and increasing protests against an excessively hermetic conception of literary criticism, it can still be said "that the intrinsic criticism of literature has been and still remains our most powerful programmatic idea." The same perceptive American observer goes on to characterize the paradox of this situation by saying that "academic critics have been asked to show more concern for historical and biographical contexts, for the social relevance of literature, and for our present cultural and psychological needs. Individual critics have followed these injunctions. . . . But the calls have not been answered on a big scale because so far they have not been followed by counterproposals that can compete with New Criticism in intellectual stature or practical effectiveness."[1]

If this is so, and if the tradition of formalism was, and is, so deeply ingrained that even now there are no mature foundations for an alternative paradigm in criticism, the present state of critical affairs calls for a radical critique and reassessment. In mid-twentieth-century England and America

---

[1]E. D. Hirsch, Jr., "Some Aims of Criticism," in *Literary Theory and Structure: Essays in Honor of William K. Wimsatt,* ed. Frank Brady, John Palmer, and Morton Price (New Haven, 1973), p. 44.

criticism has all too often provided criteria of reinterpretation that remained influential, not simply because
they were predominantly formalist, but because in their formalism they had developed a whole close context of categories and criteria by which their various assumptions and
procedures were reciprocally interlocked and hence fortified.
Thus, historical consciousness in literary criticism was im-
measurably depleted, and even historical-minded critics
found it difficult to move beyond formalism. Under-
standably, perhaps; for such a move involves a readiness and
an ability to challenge the whole context and system of intrinsic criticism. This was, and is, a formidable task; at any
rate, counterproposals that were designed to supersede individual positions or isolated aspects of its theory could not
seriously hope to achieve the "intellectual stature or
practical effectiveness" of the New Criticism.

Even more important, most of these counterproposals
were not based on a thoroughgoing break with the underlying ideology and cultural assumptions of formalism.
Such a break, if it were to lead to acceptable alternatives,
would have to embrace more than a recognition of the reciprocal quality of past history and present *Praxis*.[2] It would
have to involve the consciousness of a new and complex kind
of relationship between art and reality as well as between the
individual and society. But it was difficult to perceive even
the need for such a change. For was not the New Criticism
itself preoccupied with a more "autonomous," and hence
more objective, conception of literature as art? And did it
not, in contrast with the impressionism and subjectivism of

---

[2]Throughout I am using the concept of *Praxis* as denoting the total process
and activity by which men in society (as *Subjekt*) act upon and change the world
as their object. In this sense Marx and Engels, in rejecting Feuerbach's
mechanical materialism, emphasized the "active" and "subjective" dimension of
consciousness and society which, even while it reflects the material conditions of
its existence, helps to create them. For the epistemological significance of the rejection of "reflection" (contemplation) as an adequate mode of cognition and
source of knowledge, see the *Feuerbach-Thesen*, in Karl Marx and Friedrich
Engels, *Werke* (Dietz Verlag), III, 5–7.

the late romantics, plead for an impersonal, more rational definition of poetry? Certainly, it was not one of the least achievements of the New Criticism that its theories and interpretations were based, at least by implication, on a practicable critique of some of the most anachronistic and blatant assumptions of nineteenth-century bourgeois individualism. But this alone did not by itself promote a new sense of historical method. On the contrary, by discarding a subjective idea of poetry in favor of an impersonal one, these critics attacked not simply subjectivism but the very existence of the personality of the poet. They banished the author from both the texts and contexts of literary history. Once the intrinsic conceptions of verbal and semantic autonomy were established, language could be separated from consciousness. Now "meaning" was correlated with words, not with an aesthetic mode of weltanschauung. Most important, "structure" was divorced from both "genesis" and "effect," in other words, from the historical world of both the author and the reader. Since the structure of literature was so rigorously dissociated from its social functions, the whole question of function was reduced to the purity of an intrinsic problem and ceased to be considered as a "genetic" or an "affective" one. In sum, each of the terms and concepts became part of a self-contained world of poetics that shut out the world of history and thus became impervious to any objections short of a total critique and systematic refutation of the formalist aesthetic.

Counterproposals, if they hope to be effective, must go hand in hand with an alternative conception of literature. The new questions have to be asked in the process of refuting the old answers, and vice versa; both the critique of, and the alternatives to, formalism must be developed in terms of a new historical methodology. Naturally, such a task was, and is, not easy, and perhaps my own experience and anguish (as reflected in the use—for me—of an alien language in this book) can help illuminate some of the problems of terminology and conceptualization. As the title indicates, one of my basic theses is that the structure of literature is correlated with its function in society and that this correlation deserves to be studied in terms of both "genesis" (or *Entstehungsgeschichte*) and "impact" (*Wirkungsgeschichte*). The term *structure* presented relatively little difficulty, since it can serve simply as the most convenient and comprehensive concept to denote the art work's verbal and conceptual modes of organization, such as composition, plot, characterization, point of view, and imagery. But what about "genesis" and "impact" (or "effect")? Those cumbersome parentheses (*Entstehungsgeschichte* and *Wirkungsgeschichte*) seemed unavoidable so long as my conceptions of the genetic and effective (or functional) processes of literature go so much against the grain of most Anglo-American literary concepts and theories. This in itself made it difficult to find practicable semantic equivalents for more consistently historical concepts.

Perhaps "genesis" is an illuminating case in point. When I considered the most widely known and closely argued definition of genesis in American criticism, I was struck by a number of assumptions that a critic of the stature of William K. Wimsatt seems simply to have taken for granted. For him genesis is a category of biographical inquiry that seems somehow to contradict or to preclude "the public contexts of language and culture." Thus, in their earlier essay "The Intentional Fallacy" Wimsatt and Monroe C. Beardsley lump together and, of course, reject "the way of biographical or genetic inquiry," just as Wimsatt in his later essay "Genesis: A Fallacy Revisited" restates his objection to "the search for the author's generative intention." The implied equation between genesis and intention, or between the genetic and the biographical approaches, appears to me, however, profoundly misleading. The problem of genesis cannot be dealt with simply in biographical categories. It transcends the "private, individual, dynamic, and intentionalistic realm" of the art work and, of course, "its maker's mind and personality." Surely Wimsatt is justified in objecting to the limitations of this private realm, but his own definition of genesis is conceived entirely in terms of such individualistic categories. For him, the reconsideration of the problem of genesis (in 1968) is nothing but the intentional fallacy revisited. Together with many other critics, he ignores the fact that a writer's intention is only part (and not even the most important part) of that complex of historical origins by which the temporal complication of literary images, themes, genres, modes, and functions can be understood. But to ignore this is to remain entangled in the assumptions of individualism against whose aesthetic manifestations ("spontaneity," "authenticity," "genuineness," "originality") Wimsatt himself wishes to polemicize.[3]

Genesis, then, must be viewed as a more objective category, referring to the total context of which the individual "generative intention" is only a factor. For a fuller understanding of this context a more profound definition of the nature of the relationship of the individual and the social is needed. Perhaps Wimsatt's contradistinctions are here a little mechanical: the whole idea that the "private, individual" composition "enters a public and in a certain clear sense an objective realm" needs to be reconsidered. "If the art work has emerged at all from the artist's private world, it has emerged into some kind of universal world."[4] The emphasis on the public and objective realm is certainly laudable. But the artist's private world (let alone the art work's alleged genesis therein) cannot be defined in terms of any alternatives to society—unless, of course, the rationalizations of the alienated writer are taken at their face value. The artist's private world is not the opposite of society, any more than the recognition of the public world precludes a consideration of the creations of men as individuals.

Thus to challenge the intrinsic definition of genesis

[3] Both essays are conveniently available in *Issues in Contemporary Literary Criticism*, ed. Gregory T. Polletta (Boston, 1973); for these citations, see pp. 275, 206, 276, 255, 199.
[4] Ibid., pp. 255–56.

seemed impossible without, at the same time, redefining the relationship of structure and function in terms of a more profound dialectic of subjectivity and objectivity. To establish this dialectic is to conceive of genesis in such a way that both the full achievement of the artist's creativity and the whole context of the social function of poetry are involved. Once the achieved work of literature is seen as something that is subjective and objective at the same time, it can be more deeply understood as both an aesthetic mode of production and an aesthetic mode of "consumption" (or reception). By relating the activities of writing and those of reading to some comprehensive social context, we can view literature as both the (objective) product and the (subjective) "producer" of a culture. To differentiate the two aspects in this way is, of course, somewhat abstract, and such a differentiation does not define the ways and means by which the individual creation of the poet and the social function of poetry are interconnected. For such a definition there is no facile formula, and in any case the nature and the degree of the interconnection vary from age to age, from poet to poet. But these interconnections do exist and they are not external: they comprise the tension between the social and the individual perspectives on experience, including the experience of literature. Therefore, it is an oversimplification to say that the social perspective (or the element of tradition) can be associated with the reading of literature, whereas the individual perspective (or the element of originality) can be referred to the writing. It would be more helpful to observe that the inevitable contradictions and concurrences between the two inspire the modes of rhetoric and mediation (including the activity of reading) between the writer and his audience. But actually, and at the same time, the social and the individual perspectives on experience are *within* the poet and the creative process itself, just as they are *in* the reader and form part of the receptive process.

Structure is born out of this interaction by which the poet and his audience, and also the self and the social within the poet, are all genetically connected. When I say that "structure is born," I am using the metaphor to indicate not only the complexity but also the historicity of the origins of structure. In this sense structure is "historically given": it accommodates the traditional (or original) modes of rhetoric and mediation between the poet and his first audience, and it reflects or mirrors the form and pressure of the age in which the art work is created—whether the modes of structure are allegorical, symbolic, or representational. (These forms are by themselves related to a genetic constellation.)

However, to stress the historicity of structure, and to say that structure is objectively given, is not to *reduce* it to a category of *Entstehungsgeschichte*, or genesis. It is true that structure reflects the mode of representation of a given reality; as such it is related to both the expressive and mimetic dimensions of literature, which, necessarily, reflect the premises, needs, and perspectives of the age in which it is created. At the same time, structure is related to the complex process of mediation (between author and reader, but also between past writing and new writing), and it reflects the historicity of this process itself. In other words, the creation and the interpretation of structure are affected by the changing dialectic of tradition and originality that is characteristic of the writing as well as of the reading of literature. But whereas the process of writing is associated with the period of origins, the process of reception (or reading) is not so limited. Structure is born in the genetic process, but it *lives* in the process of reading and interpretation: it is *affected* by the social and individual perspectives of its readers and critics. Thus, it can be progressively explored and illuminated, though not created, by the reader in the process of its reception. In other words, though the impact and effectiveness of a particular poem may vary according to the context in which it is read, the poem as a structure retains a certain objectivity that nevertheless has to be seen in terms of history. Structure is a product of history; but at the same time it is also a producer of literary history: it is an objective outcome of a past *Entstehungsgeschichte*, but a subjective factor and potent inspiration of all *Wirkungsgeschichte.*

The reconsideration of the concept of genesis takes us directly into a discussion of some of the basic theoretical premises on which the following chapters rest. These premises should be made explicit, even though this (in the preliminary context of this brief introduction) necessarily involves some drastic and oversimplified abstractions. At the center of these there is, as indicated, the attempt to view aesthetic structure and social function as interrelated. Each is approached on two interrelated levels that, for the sake of convenience, I call "past significance" and "present meaning." The dialectic of past significance and present meaning relates genesis to reception, origin to effect. The structure of literature is correlated with its function in society; a fundamental connection is made between the writing and the reading of literature as a social activity. Such a connection is a historical one; and, at the same time, it is one that involves value, in the sense that writer and reader can potentially achieve a more profound apprehension and comprehension of the world and of themselves. This process of *Aneignung*, the imaginative appropriation of the world and the nature of one's own existence in it, is more than mere recognition. It embraces the imaginative experience of the unity (and the contradiction) between the self and the social; it involves, however tentatively and however momentarily, the socializing of the individual and the personalizing of the social. This is the function of most of the great writing of the past, and it is still the true function of reading in the present.

To use a phrase like "the true function of reading" is to point to the social context of literature and to view it as a context of value. It is to reopen the question of how literary value can be defined as functional and how function can be defined as valuable. The two aspects are complementary in any theory of literary history. But the main problem is not

simply how to understand literary values as both historical
and valid in the present, but rather how to perceive the value
of literature in history itself. If this can be done at all, the
only practicable frame of reference must be one that links
the writing and the reading of literature and recovers a sense
of the unity of man's activities in history, of which writing
and reading form a part. For a definition of such unity or
wholeness, the activities of the individual do not provide us
with adequate criteria. The understanding of the wholeness
of man's activity in history involves a sense of the ensemble
of physical and mental faculties, efforts, and achievements
by which—through their subjectivity, or *Praxis*—men in society first change and subjugate the world and finally come
to terms with the limitations of physical growth as a condition of their natural existence.

Such a view of history as a total process of social
change, struggle, and control involves not only the
subjugation and safeguarding of nature and the struggle of
classes and individuals but also the rise and development of
cultural needs and aesthetic faculties. In fact, there is an interrelationship between the physical appropriation of the
world (as an extension of objectivity) and the unfolding of
man's sensuous and aesthetic faculties (as a projection of his
subjectivity). It is by appropriating the outer world of
perceived objects that man can develop the versatility of his
sensuous perceptiveness; only by seeing, handling, and
listening to objects can the human eye, hand, and ear develop as a *Subjekt;* only by raising the standards of his own
needs can man find the means and capacities for satisfying
them and for creating new cultural needs and possibilities.
This interrelationship is vital: it points to the essential links
by which the rise and history of aesthetic endeavors can be
viewed as part of the larger history of human activities in society. Here, if anywhere, are the historical foundations on
which a reintegration of art into the social process of living
seems theoretically meaningful. In this sense, the history of
art and literature, from the early effective forms of magic

and ritual to the affective and ironic ways of aesthetic consciousness, constitutes a specifically imaginative mode of the appropriation of the world in its wholeness. By personalizing the social and by socializing the individual, art itself recreates the "I" in an ensemble that is larger than the self. The resulting imaginative experience of unity and contradiction is unique; precisely because its function is valuable, it cannot be replaced by another form of human activity. Thus, art was, and is, part of the more comprehensive dialectic by which the appropriation of objectivity and the realization of subjectivity are mutually intertwined.

Such a frame of reference is, finally, based on the recognition of the indivisibility of the activities of man as both the product and the agent of his own history, including the history of art and literature. In the process of the appropriation of the natural means and the social forms of human existence, labor and art and consciousness all interact. They are reflections of, and factors in, the never-ending endeavor of men to understand and control (and to affect by playing, and making images of) the destiny of their social existence. Art, much like some of the results of other types of creative labor, is both a force in history and a source of value that can survive the changing conditions it originally reflected. Thus, the most fundamental concepts of historiography can best be derived from the fact that "the whole so-called history of the world is nothing but the begetting of man in the process of human labor, the transformation of nature for mankind."[5]

This points to the overriding context of history, in which "art" is "one of the specific modes of production" as well as a form of consciousness and is thereby linked to a great variety of social activities—economic, political, philosophical, and psychological. So viewed, art is part of the humanizing process of working and living and feeling that provides us with the only comprehensive frame of reference within which the functional and the structural aspects of any

---

[5] Marx and Engels, *Werke* (Dietz Verlag), Ergänzungsband, I, 546.

aesthetic activity can be correlated in terms of a potential connection of history and value. To say and to do this is not to blur the essential difference between the material and the artistic forms of creation. For even when it is a highly specific mode of production, art is also play and game. Once we really overcome the nineteenth-century romantic conception of art as distinct from the ordinary things in life, it will be easier to understand the *specific* ways and means by which art and literature are related to the most *basic* civilizing activities of man in society. Then it will be possible to conceive of both the unity and the division of labor and art as the basis on which modern conceptions of history can be fraught with value, just as aesthetic values can then be seen as part of the history of man's appropriation of nature and society and of the corresponding unfolding of his own consciousness. Thus, there could result historical standards of evaluation that are neither relativistic nor absolute, neither pragmatic nor out of time and space. The terms of value must rather be linked conceptually with the principles of historiography itself. In other words, the contribution of the art work to the real world of history (its contribution to our standards of value) and our theory of literature must be connected conceptually. As a result, the creation and study of value could itself be conceived and practiced as a mode of historicity.

This brings us back to the point of departure: once literary history has reintegrated both its historical and its evaluative frames of reference, it can hope to achieve at least some rudimentary basis for interrelating the social function of literature and the structure of its artifice. In terms of the methodology of literary history, this involves more than a necessary plea for the general integration of historical analysis and critical judgment. It calls for an interconnection between the study of literary origins (the *Entstehungsgeschichte*) and the aesthetics of representation or structure (the *Darstellungsästhetik*), on the one hand, and the study of the impact of literature (the *Wirkungsgeschichte*) and the aesthetics of reception (the *Rezeptionsästhetik*), on the other. To realize all these points of reference may be more than one literary historian can hope to achieve, but to be aware of the full context of their interconnection is not quite so difficult. This is more than just a methodological postulate. It is based on the actual complications inherent in the process of literary history, which involves the history of the writing as well as the history of the reading (and the new writing) of literature. Between writers and readers, origin and reception, structure and function, there is a vital and very real relation that the literary critic and historian ignores at his peril. To stress only the *Darstellungsästhetik* leads to a formalized or absolute treatment of structure and abstracts the work from the history of its readers and the process of its communication and survival into the present. Merely to stress the *Rezeptionsästhetik* leads to a pluralistic kind of relativism that abstracts the work from the history of its creation; it ignores the fact that the structure of the work (though affected and permanently redefined by readers and critics) is historically given. It is in this sense that structure and function, as well as genesis and reception, may be viewed as complementary objects of historical criticism.

The six essays contained in this volume do not attempt to develop these suggestions toward a theory of literary history systematically but proceed empirically. That is to say, the chosen subjects and themes themselves have provided me with more specific frames of reference within which I have attempted to reconsider such concepts as tradition, *le système*, metaphor, and point of view. With the exception of the opening essay, which does retain a more purely systematic and theoretical approach, the treatment is, wherever possible, historical in the simple sense that it observes and respects the chronology of things and ideas. Thus, the emergence of the modern theory and language of "tradition," the rise and the development of critical approaches to American literary history, and the changing modes of the criticism of imagery are each traced as a temporal process in connection with which the theoretical positions and counterproposals can, I think, best be analyzed and elaborated.

But although the texture of these essays is thematic and historical, the structure of the book as a whole reflects a somewhat more systematic concern with its subject. At this point a brief overview of the argument of the book may help the reader more easily to follow the links connecting the individual essays and their wider contexts. The opening consideration of the relationship of past significance and present meaning provides a general outline of methodology that leads to a critique and reconsideration of the concept of tradition. In terms of the relationship of past writing and present reading (and new writing), tradition can be viewed as a concept that links the genesis and the structure of past creations to their present functions, origins to reception. In more than one respect the study of both the process and the concept of tradition can trace not only the continuity but also the discontinuity and the crisis in the interrelationship of past values and present evaluations. As outlined by T. S. Eliot and, more recently, as appealed to by Northrop Frye,[6] the problem of tradition is deeply involved in changing historical perspectives on the literary and cultural past. As an examination of some of the underlying assumptions of method and ideology in American literary history reveals, the context of this change is related to growing contradictions between past origin and present function, as well as to tensions between past reception and present interpretations.

If this points to the central methodological problem of literary history today, then the two most influential schools of criticism in the West, the structural and the mythological,

---

[6]Northrop Frye, *The Critical Path: An Essay on the Social Context of Literary Criticism* (Bloomington, Ind., Midland Books, 1973), p. 139. At some earlier date, Frye had dismissed "the magic word 'tradition' " as providing "coherence . . . by sheer sequence" (*Anatomy of Criticism: Four Essays* [Princeton, 1957], p. 16). For discussion of this contradiction, see below, pp. 63, 142–44.

can be viewed as obssessed with the difficulties arising out of this dilemma. Their most basic conceptions involve rejections of the temporal process which, in the words of Northrop Frye, is dismissed as "the principle of chronology" and that of "sheer sequence." But is chronology or sequence really the "one organizing principle" that "has so far been discovered in literature"?[7] Is literary history no more than that? Some of the most influential approaches to past literature seem to imply as much: T. S. Eliot's concept of tradition as some ideal order and the spatial approach of critics such as Wilson Knight and Joseph Frank have, each in its different way, anticipated Northrop Frye's attempt to view literature, not as a temporal complication of writing and reading, but "as spread out in conceptual space." But the question is how to write criticism that includes a historical dimension; how to relate literary history to the process of history when the basic order is seen (in Frye's words) as "an order of words," or a "relatively restricted and simple group of formulas."[8]

Even more than myth criticism, structuralism has attempted to provide an elaborate mode of rejection of the temporal dimension ("ce grand obstacle à toute rationalité," as Viggo Brøndal once said). And yet, faced with the widening chasm between the idea of history and the concept of *le système*, a number of structuralist critics have developed a *méthode structuraliste génetique*. Similarly, just as H. R. Jauss in his *Rezeptionsästhetik* has attempted a synthesis of sociology and Russian formalism, so, more recently, Northrop Frye himself has reconsidered the social context of literature and what he used to dismiss (in the *Anatomy of Criticism*) as "the magic word 'tradition.'" But is it possible from here to proceed to a new synthesis between the formalist (and structuralist) idea of literature as "an order of words," on the one hand, and a view of literary history as a

---

[7] Frye, *Anatomy*, p. 16.
[8] Ibid., p. 17.

temporal and functional complication of structures, on the other? In particular, has the structuralist interest in genesis produced any workable correlation between structure and function, origin and effect?[9]

For English-speaking readers such concepts of history and methodology may sound somewhat abstract—indeed, it is no easy matter to render them in English. In order to particularize the abstractions, I have followed up the more general studies in the theory and history of historical criticism with some specific applications. If, as two examples, I take metaphor in poetic drama or point of view in prose fiction, the justification, I hope, will become obvious: metaphor, especially in the interpretation of Shakespeare's imagery, and point of view, especially in the study of the modern novel, have established themselves as critical concepts of central significance in the definition of literary structure. Nonetheless, they have rarely been integrated into a coherent theory of the historical process of literature. Their historical modes and changing functions have been left largely unexplored, and their usefulness as concepts of historical criticism has consequently been diminished.

These, then, are some of the questions that I reconsider with a view to suggesting some counterproposals based on a conviction of the need of an approach to criticism that is both historical and dialectical. The reconsideration attempts to take into account the fact that historical criticism of literary form, even after the decline of the New Criticism, has all too often remained in the hands of formalists, whereas the reawakened interest in history and society has

[9]For a more extended critique of H. R. Jauss and the more recent directions in the work of Northrop Frye, I must refer the reader to two articles in German: "'Rezeptionsästhetik' und die Krise der Literaturgeschichte," *Weimarer Beiträge*, 19 (August 1973), 5–33, and "Literarische Wertung und historische Tradition: Zu ihrer Aporie im Werk von Northrop Frye," *Zeitschrift für Anglistik und Amerikanistik*, 20 (1973), 341–59. The latter continues a critical discussion of Frye's work that I first published in *Literaturgeschichte und Mythologie*, 3d ed. (Berlin: Aufbau-Verlag, 1974), pp. 342–63. There is an English translation of the former which is forthcoming in *Clio* (Fall 1975).

more often than not been impoverished, either by the failure to view the problems of structure in correlation with the process of social and cultural history or by the refusal to see in the study of the structure of past literature anything more than a preoccupation with bourgeois ideology. Against these tendencies, I suggest that the study of basic literary figures, forms, techniques, and genres can be meaningful in terms of a new historical criticism, a criticism that relates the history of writing and reading and the history of social and economic activities to that tertium quid which (quite schematically) I have called the process of the appropriation of the world and the whole nature of man in society.

I
Past Significance and Present Meaning in Literary History

WITH the decline of the New Criticism, an exploration of the idea of literary history is the most urgent task confronting the student of literature today. But it is a difficult task, and it involves problems whose solution is directly and indirectly linked with an awareness of crisis in both criticism and society. If, in England and the United States, the historical study of literature is to achieve a new sense of direction and purpose, it must first be prepared to face (with all that this implies) the full extent of the crisis of its discipline. This crisis is in many ways a symptom of the larger crisis of Western society, in which the revolutionary idea of change, organic and dialectical concepts of evolution, and the liberal and humanist traditions of progress are all, in various degrees, affected. Following the academic rebellion of the sixties, the consciousness of this wider background of crisis seems once more to be gaining ground; perhaps one may hazard the conjecture that a new interest in historical method can only benefit from an awareness of its present background. In fact, such awareness has already facilitated the first steps toward reopening, in the realm of literary history, the question of method and purpose from an angle that points, at least in several important aspects, beyond the assumptions of formalist criticism.

Contradictions beyond Formalism

The need for theory and method is usually felt most acutely when, in a time of rapid changes, the object of theoretical inquiry no longer functions in its traditional context. It seems significant, therefore, that there has recently developed a new consciousness of the need for historical theory, historiography, and hermeneutics which, in England and North America, was formerly an almost unheard-of phenomenon. This consciousness, as expressed in the work of Stanley Fish, Geoffrey Hartman, E. D. Hirsch, Jr., Paul de Man, Hayden White, and others, has provided some new and welcome perspectives on the current discussion of the aims and methods of literary criticism—perspectives which, at least by implication, point beyond the ahistorical orientation of the New Criticism. But for all their advances beyond some of the programmatic ideas of the intrinsic school of criticism, the outcome and the overall results of these new departures seem strangely tentative, incoherent, and, finally, disappointing. The reason is not primarily that some of the most basic questions, such as the relationship of text and context or that of literary structure and social function, have been left vague or have not been systematically explored. Nor can it be said that some of the new positions are not solidly developed and admirably argued. In fact, most of these new departures are, each in its own direction, profoundly searching, and they certainly constitute highly intelligent reflections of a transitional situation in American literary criticism and theory. However, taken together, they fail to provide a new paradigm consistent and coherent enough to supersede the ahistorical orientation of the formalist school of criticism.

The charge of failure, inconsistency, and incoherence is, of course, a grave one and needs to be substantiated. Let us, therefore, briefly refer to some of the new positions that, over the last eight or ten years, have emerged in varying contexts. There is (to begin with what may well be the most sustained theoretical contribution) the renewed emphasis on the author as an element in the relationship between the meaning of a text and that "person," or "conception," or "situation" to which that meaning is (in historical criticism and judgment) related. In this sense there has been established a methodological difference "between the meaning of a text (which does not change) and the meaning of a text to us today (which changes)."[1] From a vastly different position, the reader, who in formalist criticism was excluded by legislation, has been reconsidered "as an actively mediating presence." Along these lines, the "meaning of an utterance" has been redefined as, simply, "its experience": the sentence or the utterance "is no longer an object, a thing-in-itself, but an *event*, something that *happens* to, and with the participation of, the reader."[2] More generally, there is the search for "a larger conception of literary form" that attempts to go beyond "formalism, structuralism, and myth criticism" because "the structuralist science of myth does not allow us to cross over from its theory of form to a descriptive or critical account of the artist's historical consciousness."[3] Among the attempts to work out a "theory linking the form of the medium to the form of the artist's historical consciousness," attention has been drawn to the artist's struggle with his vocation as "a version of a universal human struggle: of genius with Genius, and of genius with the *genius loci*."[4] Thus, the new interest in method has led to a call for a new "metahistory" by which "the explanatory and the interpretative aspects of the narrative tend to be run together" in such a way that the distinction between "proper history" and "metahistory" has no longer any "adequate theoretical justification."[5] Such a broad perspective is finally corroborated when the expressed "need to revise the foundations of literary history" is seen in

[1] E. D. Hirsch, Jr., *Validity in Interpretation* (New Haven, 1967), pp. 8, 255.

[2] Stanley Fish, "Literature in the Reader: Affective Stylistics," *New Literary History*, 2 (1970/71), 123, 160, 125.

[3] Geoffrey Hartman, "Toward Literary History," *Daedalus*, 99 (Spring 1970), 357, 362.

[4] Ibid., pp. 364, 369.

[5] Hayden White, "Interpretation in History," *New Literary History*, 4 (1973/74), 282, 309.

connection with the "disquieting" assumption that "literary history could in fact be paradigmatic for history in general."[6]

This brief and purely descriptive (and highly selective) summary of some of the new departures must here suffice to convey an idea of the various directions from which recent scholars and critics have developed suggestions toward a new historical perspective in criticism. But this perspective remains fragmentary, spontaneous, and unstable because none of these contributions has developed a comprehensive consciousness, let alone a methodology, of the full correlative connections between literature and history. For although the author has been reconsidered as against the formalist theory of authorial irrelevance and although the reader has been vindicated as against the intrinsic assumption of the affective fallacy, the theoretical and practical framework of these extensions—and, above all, the methodological connections between author and reader, structure and function—have not been developed historically. But the failure to connect these most basic points of reference reflects more than some necessary (and provisional) division of interest and labor among scholars. Even the most systematically elaborated positions reveal a deliberate abstention from, or lack of awareness of, the need for a more sustained and coherent methodology for historical criticism.

To illustrate, I can here refer only in passing to the assertion of "the timelessness of understanding" that is a major premise even in the most impressive recent American contribution to hermeneutics.[7] To "disregard the historicity of understanding," however, raises some fundamental methodological questions as to the validity of historical generalizations at large. For instance, do the differences among individual perspectives on art and society, from the

---

[6] Paul de Man, "Literary History and Literary Modernity," *Daedalus*, 99 (Spring 1970), 403.
[7] Hirsch, *Validity*, p. 137.

point of view of historiography, have priority as against the differences between the social perspectives associated with changing historical eras? Can literary history be based on the assumption that "the real ontological gap" is "the one that subsists between persons, not the one that subsists between historical eras"?[8] From a position like this the rationale for an approach to the changes and temporal complications in literary writing and reading might more easily be found in psychology and anthropology than in sociology and history. Thus, even the most cogent hermeneutical refutation of the theory of semantic autonomy does not by itself help to constitute the basis on which a new methodological perspective in literary history can be reestablished.

The recent approach to "the reader as an actively mediating presence" in literature presents similar problems. It is of course true that a study of the reader in *Paradise Lost,* for instance, may be profoundly rewarding in terms of an understanding of the experience (and the structure of the response) that literature can actually provoke.[9] But as soon as this approach tends to limit itself to a study of "the developing responses of the reader in relation to the words as they succeed one another in time,"[10] it has surrendered the full field of *Wirkungsgeschichte* to a much more narrowly conceived "Affective Stylistics." Again, stylistics can provide a very meaningful "bridging of life and art" in the sense that it establishes not only "the continuing presence of the author in the work" but also that of the reader "as created and creating power in the poem."[11] But as long as the reader's responses are studied intrinsically (exclusively "in relation to the words"), the reader himself can hardly be defined historically, as a changing *ensemble* of social and

[8] Ibid., pp. 256, 258.
[9] Stanley Fish, *Surprised by Sin: The Reader in Paradise Lost* (New York, 1967).
[10] Fish, "Literature in the Reader," p. 139.
[11] Joan Webber, "Stylistics: A Bridging of Life and Art in Seventeenth-Century S' dies," *New Literary History,* 2 (1970/71), 294.

aesthetic values, attitudes, and forms of consciousness. Instead, the reader is defined as "a construct, an ideal or idealized reader," and the structure of his response is viewed primarily in terms of "linguistic experiences."

On what grounds, then, can it be said of this type of stylistics that the "method will obviously be radically historical"?[12] Such a claim, if it does not remain completely unjustified, amounts to an unconscious apology for the unhelpful relativism ("The meaning of an utterance . . . is its experience") in accordance with which criteria of critical evaluation as well as standards in aesthetics are *expressis verbis* rejected. (This "method allows for no such aesthetic and no such fixings of value: In fact it is oriented *away* from evaluation. . . .")[13] But to dismiss "the objectivity of the text" as "an illusion" is as problematic as it seems unnecessary from a position which, for all its concern with "language as an experience," still approaches the text (as a perceptive commentator remarks) "as an autonomous structure of internal relationships."[14] In the last resort it is this lingering hermetic conception of literary structure that leads the new stylistics (if not to the idea of "the timelessness of understanding") to the postulate of the timelessness of reading and an ahistorical conception of the reader and his responses. For it is precisely the implied timelessness of reading that makes it difficult to conceive of the activity of the reader as some form of social and historical activity

---

[12] Fish, "Literature in the Reader," pp. 145, 159, 146. Michael Riffaterre ("The Stylistic Approach to Literary History," *New Literary History*, 2 [1970/71], 39–55) betrays a comparable lack of awareness of the degree to which the concept of "the reader" is an abstraction from cultural activities in history, as when he completely ignores the changing social and ideological contexts and functions of reading (see, e.g., pp. 46 f.). Based on such premises, the "contribution of stylistics to diachronic analysis" (p. 52) amounts to no more than a reaffirmation of the principle of verbal autonomy: "Literary history should therefore be a history of words" (p. 55).

[13] Fish, "Literature in the Reader," p. 146.

[14] Hayden White, "Literary History: The Point of It All," *New Literary History*, 2 (1970/71), 177.

involving the changing nature and the reciprocal quality of the relationship between the past world of the art work and the present world and mode of its reception.

If, judged by the requirements of historical method, the most important contributions to the rehabilitation of both the author and the reader prove vulnerable, it is perhaps not surprising that the more general recent reorientations "toward literary history" also leave a number of questions unanswered. It is certainly noteworthy when (writing under that title) a distinguished American scholar-critic urges the "importance" of literary history and deplores "the absence of methodological thinking in that area." It is indeed interesting to read that in reference to a phrase used by Werner Krauss literary history is understood as "our 'historical duty' because it alone can provide today a sorely needed defense of art."[15] Here the implied emphasis on a larger historical conception of literary form is related to a new sense of the public function of art. But in contrast to Werner Krauss's concept of *geschichtlicher Auftrag*, the expressed need for a defense of art is conceived as pragmatic rather than historical: the postulate seems divorced from the more comprehensive process of history that links the past work of the artist and the present world of its historian.

It is true that there is no really satisfying English equivalent for the German term *Auftrag;* but the context in which *Auftrag* is rendered by "historical duty" turns the implied consciousness of historical function almost into a postulate of self-defense. For the advocated "defense of art" sounds more like a defense of art for its own sake than a defense of art in its relation to society. At this point to urge "the formality of art . . . as a central issue in any literary history" involves an emphasis that tends to predetermine the attempt "to bring together the form of art and the form of its historical consciousness." Again, it is true that the new con-

---

[15] Hartman, "Toward Literary History," p. 356.

ception of form is to be based on "a theory of *literary* as well as *functional* form" and that, in this connection, the "theory of literary vocation" definitely points beyond the hermetic conception of function as an order of internal relationships. Yet can the repeated emphasis on the vocational crisis of the poet and his rite of passage serve to integrate the new concept of function in a more comprehensive perspective on history? Does this provide a frame of reference large enough for both the genesis and the impact of literature? The question is at least an open one, since it is the individual poet's literary self-consciousness and self-objectification that are taken to furnish criteria for the identification of, or conflict between, "genius" and "Genius," or "genius" and *"genius loci."*[16]

Although such categories and such a relationship do point to important manifestations of the growth in, and crisis of, historical consciousness, they still reflect the same preoccupation with *literaturnost'* ("literariness") that is revealed in the work of another well-known critic and scholar when, in order to underline the essential unity of history and literary history, he postulates "that the bases for historical knowledge are . . . written texts, even if these texts masquerade in the guise of wars or revolutions."[17] To view literary history as a paradigm "for history in general" points to an altogether larger dimension of methodology. But the question that has to be asked is, Can the nature of the *sources* of history and literary history be made to provide a basis for the paradigmatic quality of the latter? Here, to point to written texts as presumably the only, or major, source for historical knowledge seems to disvalue the practical experience of living in society (in a society that reflects and promulgates the very outcome of wars and revo-

[16] Ibid., pp. 356, 361, 364, 365 ff.
[17] De Man, p. 403. The original version of the text has (wrongly, I suppose) "wars or evolutions." I have corrected this after consulting the reprinted version of the essay in de Man's *Blindness and Insight: Essays in the Rhetoric of Contemporary Criticism* (New York, 1971), p. 165.

lutions) as the crucial impulse and criterion of knowledge and insight. The written texts are taken to be both source and message, the actual process of history providing a mere guise, or costume.

This takes us very close to that metaphorical terminology according to which historical events are defined in terms of "scenario," "act," and "stage." The underlying ambiguities in the implied relationship between art and history seem significant. The function of art is not described and criticized in terms of the language of history; the function of history is described in terms of the language of art criticism. The resulting metaphors dramatize and formalize the modes of correlation between art and history (and in that they reflect some changing patterns of perception and expression that developed in the sixties). But as a basis for a methodology of literary history, let alone for one that "could in fact be paradigmatic for history in general,"[18] this provides a questionable frame of reference.

Although these new departures in historical criticism are too serious to be reduced to the level of a fashionable phraseology, the trend toward an *Ästhetisierung der Historie*, instead of a *Historisierung der Ästhetik*, seems to affect even the most carefully developed theoretical contributions to a new sense of historical method. Small wonder. For even the two most prestigious critics and theoreticians writing in the West at the present time, Claude Lévi-Strauss and Northrop Frye, have tended to view the modes and principles of interpretation in history not as historical but as mythical. It may seem highly tempting to many who now begin to grapple with problems of historical method and interpretation to take up these cues. We will take up only one (but the most brilliant) example.

It is possible to argue that "interpretation in history consists of the provisions of a plot-structure for a sequence of

---

[18] De Man, "Literary History and Literary Modernity," p. 403.

events so that their nature as a comprehensible process is revealed by their figuration as a *story of a particular kind.*" The suggested differentiation between "story" and "plot" and the resulting "Modes of Emplotment" (Romance, Comedy, Tragedy, Satire), together with corresponding "Modes of Explanation and Ideological Implication," amount to a triangle of quaternary forms that is as ingenious as, and possibly more fearful than, Northrop Frye's patterns of symmetry. And although the achieved complexity in the interconnections of the three basic modes of reference (aesthetic, epistemological, and moral) is certainly impressive, the final, though still tentative, definition of "interpretation" in historical thought leads the modes of conceptualization away from its objects in reality. For if historical interpretation is said to consist of "the formalization of the phenomenal field originally constituted by language itself on the basis of a dominant tropological wager," the present activity of the interpreter of past works and events finds itself at two removes from the historical process.[19] Consequently, the analysis of the modalities of historical interpretation becomes purely *geistesgeschichtlich* and breaks away from what that interpretation is all about. The present methods of historiography and the past objects of history seem so unrelated that the process of historiography itself can only be defined logically and poetically, but never historically. Thus, the modes of historiography are being established spatially, in an almost autonomous manner that ignores or contradicts (and is ignored or contradicted by) the mode of existence of its own object and content. Again, the reciprocal quality of the relationship between "past significance" and "present meaning," between historical structures and modern functions, seems to escape.

As this brief and highly selective survey of some of the new departures in literary theory and history indicates, there

---

[19] White, "Interpretation in History," pp. 291, 307, 312.

have emerged a number of fresh and genuinely stimulating perspectives on historical criticism, but a more comprehensive functional attitude toward both the objects and the interpretations of literary history has, in practice, failed to develop. For all the increased consciousness of "the need to revise the foundations of literary history," such revision is slow to move beyond the limitations of formalism. If the formulated task is considered, again in the words of Paul de Man, "a desperately vast undertaking,"[20] then the task seems so formidable partly because there has not developed a unifying methodological perspective in accordance with which the various aspects of the history of both reading and writing might be organized and interrelated under an integrating idea and method of history and criticism. Such a view of the whole is sorely needed; without it, the limitations of formalism (and the more recent contradictions beyond formalism) cannot be overcome. So long as some of the most distinguished critics of formalism are still haunted by an increasingly blurred and ambivalent concept of autonomy, the process of literary history is still, historically and categorically, dissociated from the worlds of both its creation and reception.

It is true, at this date, that the concept of autonomy is hardly used any more in the sterile sense of the intrinsic school of criticism, but it still involves some of the old ambiguities and it already reflects new uncertainties. How do we view "literature in history without denying its autonomy"? is the sort of question asked by even the most historical-minded of the newer critics.[21] But is this not a question that recalls the old, sterile dualism of the "intrinsic" and the "extrinsic," as well as the older postulate of a "literary" or "inside" history of literature? What exactly is the meaning of autonomy in a context like this? Has it simply come to

[20] De Man, p. 403.
[21] Hartman, "Toward Literary History," p. 356.

stand as a synonym for a (justified) demand that we observe the specific nature and function of poetry? This seems to be contradicted by the general trend toward an *Ästhetisierung der Historie*, which I have observed above.[22]

The paradox of the situation is perhaps best expressed by Geoffrey Hartman when he in an essay with the programmatic title "Beyond Formalism" writes: "To go beyond formalism is as yet too hard for us; and may even be . . . against the nature of understanding."[23] Indeed, the heritage of the New Criticism is a burden for critics still. This holds good more or less for most of these counterproposals, be they hermeneutical or stylistic, on the relation of form and consciousness or on that of history and literary history, or, finally, on the modes of historiography itself. Wherever we look there is some remnant, however hidden, of some of the

[22] On the other hand, if "this characteristic autonomy of literature" is understood as the "'capacity of art-forms to outlast the destined hour'" (ibid.), then it must be pointed out that the very process of survival witnesses the historical *functioning* (which is highly specific) of the art work, i.e., a continued mode of social, not autonomous, existence. It is curious to find that, at this late date, Hartman and scholar-critics like Paul de Man persist in an increasingly vague conception of "the autonomous domain of literature" (de Man, p. 401). But in the same book in which de Man still writes in seeming approval of this concept (*Blindness and Insight*, p. 162) he can already demand "a long overdue re-examination of the assumptions on which the position of autonomy was founded" (p. 22); indeed, he does so himself mainly (and in a characteristically limited manner) by questioning the new critical "rejection of *intentionality*" (p. 25) and the related notion "that literature is a privileged *Language*" (p. 12; again my italics). Thus, there results the ambivalent charge that formalist ideas of autonomy "may very well have been founded on preconceptions that were themselves derived from non-literary models" and that (consequently, one assumes) the concept of autonomy "has to be redefined" (p. 22; but see p. 21). In a totally different context, where the concept *is* redefined (James S. Ackerman, "Toward a New Social Theory of Art," *New Literary History*, 4 [1972/73], 330) "autonomous" merely seems to emphasize an objective mode of existence, as when it is said that "a work of art has an autonomous existence (since, whether or not it communicates, it is still there)." But is not communication (function) an implicit condition and a constituting (structuring) factor of "existence" (genesis)? It would be easy to trace several more versions of autonomy, but the conceptual content of this semantic confusion seems to reflect at least some of the contradictions in current attempts to move beyond formalism.

[23] Geoffrey Hartman, "Beyond Formalism," in *Issues in Contemporary Literary Criticism*, ed. Polletta, p. 162.

ahistorical ideas and concepts of formalism. Perhaps it is not saying too much to suggest that it is the lingering impact of the formalist aesthetic which, more than anything else, stands in the way of a more functional and comprehensive integration of the new perspectives on the author and the reader. Thus, genesis and impact, the approaches to the structure of, and the response to, style remain fundamentally dissociated.

What, then, accounts for the hold that the intrinsic school of criticism has even over its critics? To answer this question historically is to inquire into the function of ideology as it affects the needs and perspectives of literary criticism as a social and academic institution in the United States today. Although since the fifties the function and status of the university has been involved in struggle, controversy, and recession, there is an obvious element of continuity. And even though it can be said that the academic rebellion in the sixties witnessed significant and, indeed, radical changes in the social role and class alignment of many students and professors, the social and cultural context and, together with it, some of the most basic problems that challenge literary study and the literary profession have largely remained the same. As some recent radical critics of society have observed, these problems (which arise "from the roles culture and its bearers have played in bourgeois society") persistently affect not only the study of literature but the most general assumptions about the practical uses of literature as an agent of social change and consciousness. Criticism reflects this situation by skepticism and retreat; it no longer fulfills the cultural needs and expectations of society: it has become "related to the institutional procedures of education rather than to the education of a social class." In other words, so much academic criticism is written to fulfill professional requirements that it is possible to say that the "primary function of writing literary criticism has . . . become certifying college and university teachers of literature."[24] If this seems an exaggerated statement, it does point to a social and ideological context which is radically different from that of the past, in which criticism was more intimately bound up with the whole business of living in the present. But whereas critics like Johnson, Diderot, Lessing, or Belinski made a point of relating literature not to the professional specialists but, rather, to the intellectual and practical needs of the whole of their readers' lives, Western academic critics have largely abandoned this broadly civilizing function of criticism.

In a subsequent chapter I shall return to the narrowing scope of the function of criticism (and discuss at greater length the consequences for the modern ahistorical conception of tradition). Here it must suffice to suggest that the rise and success (and the survival) of the intrinsic idea of the autonomy of literature is, at least indirectly, connected with the social and cultural dilemma of a society where the professionalized use of criticism is alienated from the practical concerns and the culture of the majority of the people. As a matter of course, the institutional function of criticism (as against its civilizing role in society at large) tends to encourage the approach to literature as a formal discipline. As a mere body of formalized knowledge, the object of study and the purpose to which it can be put become more and more unrelated. The correlation between knowledge and education becomes precarious. There is a dissociation between the self-contained needs and standards of the discipline (and the corresponding emphasis on formality, autonomy, on internal relationships and demonstrably "written texts"), on the one hand, and the role that the discipline (and the use of its results) can play in the lives and the society of those who practice it, on the other. And since the objects of the discipline are usually taken from the literature of the past, the

[24] *The Politics of Literature: Dissenting Essays on the Teaching of English*, ed. Louis Kampf and Paul Lauter (New York, Vintage Books, 1972), pp. 7, 18 f.

dissociation tends to disturb, or leave undeveloped, the reciprocal quality of the most basic historical relationship between the past significance of the work and the present meaning of its revitalized use and interpretation.

The methodological dilemma of the new historical criticism, then, is also, and perhaps even primarily, a cultural one. This is not to say that the outcome of the recent methodological debate is predetermined by the type of social relationships that it, among other things, reflects. (If this were so, any discussion of method and principle would, in this context, be a futile waste of time.) But if the prolonged influence and the lingering impact of the intrinsic approach to literature as an autonomous object of formal knowledge is to be understood, this social background must be taken into account. Here, finally, are the cultural conditions which, through schools and publishing houses, have been instrumental in creating a situation in which the reading of literature and the understanding of history are not self-evident (and mutually intertwined) modes of social activity for the majority of citizens. It is a situation in which "people are not participants in a cultural enterprise but spectators at a performance."[25] The achievement of the literature of the past and the participation in, and control of, the civilization in the present appear (to the ordinary reader) as unrelated as the world of beauty and the world of labor or (for the formal critic) past aesthetic structure and present social function.

The ultimate contradictions, then, are to be found in the relationship between work and leisure, social facts and artifacts. In the last analysis, they cannot be resolved without a reconsideration of that larger question of the relationship of social history and cultural (or aesthetic) value that I have raised in the Introduction. The reader does not have to accept my own position in order to understand that a

[25] Ibid., p. 46.

theoretical challenge (not to say solution) of the problem is possible not on the basis of some partial revision or some single specific counter-suggestion but only in the full context of a new literary theory and history that attempts to recover a sense of the unity of man's activities in society, of which writing and reading form a part. So long as the specific modes of art and criticism are conceived as categorically and historically unrelated to the process of the more basic and ordinary civilizing activities of man, the burden of formalism is likely to remain heavy, and the methodological alienation of art from the history of society cannot finally be overcome.

New Criticism and Historical Philology

If, under these circumstances, the intrinsic approach to literature is still "the most powerful programmatic idea" in American criticism, the relationship between the New Criticism and the traditional modes of literary history needs to be reconsidered more closely. The ahistorical orientation of formalism is well known; but while it is impossible not to reject this orientation, the New Critics' objections to traditional literary history did raise a number of very important questions. There is no need to oversimplify their critique or to reject it out of hand. Now that the New Criticism has itself become part of the history of criticism, the neohumanist and formalist revolt against positivism, as well as its consequences, can more nearly be seen in perspective. At this date there is no need to go back to the nineteenth-century tradition of historical philology. To criticize the New Criticism involves no apology for the uncritical study of sources, influences, and biographical data as an end in itself. To ignore the fact that the formalist critique of literary history involved areas of strength and consistency as well as limitations is not helpful; to do so does not allow us to focus on and confront the complexity of those premises, both

theoretical and practical, on which the historical approach
to literature was bound for crisis.

This is not the place for a full survey of the theoretical
positions from which the New Criticism challenged the
methods of traditional literary history, but perhaps a few
illustrations will suffice to bring out its main direction and
emphasis. Even when, with some effort, the New Critics
would retain a grudging modicum of respect for the "intense
and precise labors of the Victorian philologists in the service
of authenticity and other forms of factuality," their rejection
of historical antiquarianism was as consistent as it was complete. If this had entailed a formulated alternative in historical method, there might have been more to be said for
their polemics, especially for their attacks on the academic
accumulation of unrelated historical facts, and even their
scarcely concealed scorn for those mechanistic "exercises relating literature to various kinds of influence—social,
political, economic, climatic, national, regional, traditional,
psychological, and genealogical."[26] Such polemics, of
course, were almost as vigorous in Britain and Europe, as in
F. R. Leavis's protests against "the usual compilation . . .—
names, titles, dates, 'facts about,' irrelevancies, superficial
comments, and labour-saving descriptions."[27]

These attacks (which were also aimed at "the verbose
inanities of tendencies," zeitgeist, and the like and which
were echoed by a good many liberal critics) are too
well known to call for further documentation. They were all
more or less explicitly based on certain theoretical assumptions which, reduced to their common denominator, can
perhaps best be phrased negatively: they saw "the great mistake of the scientific-historical scholarship" in the fact that it
"had allied itself with the physical sciences of the nineteenth

[26]William K. Wimsatt, Jr., and Cleanth Brooks, *Literary Criticism: A Short History* (New York, 1957), pp. 537, 543.
[27]"Criticism and Literary History," *The Importance of Scrutiny*, ed. Eric Bentley (New York, 1964), p. 12.

century." The most disreputable symptoms of such mes-
alliance were diagnosed in "the whole underlying assumption that literature should be explained by the methods of
the natural sciences, by causality, by such external determining forces as . . . *race, milieu, moment."* Such "scien-
tism," it was argued, was behind both the "study of causal
antecedents and origins" and the use of "quantitative
methods of science: statistics, charts, and graphs."[28]

Again, this is not the place to open the vast question of
the relation of historical scholarship and natural science, and
in any case an answer to this question would have to show, as
many scholars and critics have done, that literary criticism is
not an exact science. But even though the early battle in
"the revolt against positivism" was in many ways justified,
later new critical polemics tended toward complacency and
ingenuousness. Even when the enemy was routed, the attacks continued to be directed at a straw man who supposedly still believed in the methodological identity of history and mechanical physics. Although positivism was dead,
its specter was not allowed to find rest. These polemics,
which served as a comfortable *alibi* to the antihistorical bias
of the New Criticism, were questionable in several respects.

In the first place, the attack against the mechanistic
aspects of nineteenth-century literary scholarship never
paused to consider that the tradition of historical inquiry was
much older than, and never solely identical with, the
pseudoscientific pose of some latter-day philologists. The
rise of historical criticism can roughly be traced in the decline of the social and theoretical presuppositions of natural
law, and dates from, say, Vico's *La Scienza Nuova* (1725),
the work of Leibniz, Shaftesbury, the French Enlightenment, and, in its fully developed form, from Herder's *Ideen
zur Philosophie der Geschichte der Menschheit* (1784–91). It

---

[28] Lionel Trilling, "The Sense of the Past," *The Liberal Imagination*
(London, Mercury Books, 1961), p. 182; René Wellek, "The Revolt against
Positivism in Recent European Literary Scholarship," *Concepts of Criticism*, ed.
Stephen G. Nichols, Jr. (New Haven, 1963), pp. 256, 257.

finds its mature expression in Goethe's own "sense of the past and the present as one," for him a "powerful and overwhelming feeling," which could hardly "be expressed wonderfully enough." ("Ein Gefühl aber, das bei mir gewaltig überhand nahm und sich nicht wundersam genug äußern konnte, war die Empfindung der Vergangenheit und Gegenwart in Eins. . . .") This is a poet's statement that corresponds to Schiller's attempt, in his theory of *Universalgeschichte*, "to connect the past with the present" ("das Vergangene mit dem Gegenwärtigen zu verknüpfen"). From here, through Hegel, this tradition of historical thought branched off in two directions. On the one hand there was the *geisteswissenschaftliche* idealism of Dilthey and the later historians of *Historismus*, Ernst Troeltsch and Friedrich Meinecke, whose philosophy of history certainly contained elements of irrationalism, but not of mechanism. On the other hand it was, in the context of revolutionary materialism, carried on by Engels and especially Marx, who in his well-known comment on classical Greek art argued that certain great works of art can only arise at an early or undeveloped stage of social development and that "the charm of their art for us" is not opposed to their historical origins; so that the true "difficulty" of the historian's task lies not in the fact that "the Greek epic and Greek art are connected with certain social forms of development" but rather that these works of art "still offer aesthetic pleasure to us and in some respect serve as norm and unattainable standard." ("Aber die Schwierigkeit liegt nicht darin, zu verstehn, daß griechische Kunst und Epos an gewisse gesellschaftliche Entwicklungsformen geknüpft sind. Die Schwierigkeit ist, daß sie für uns noch Kunstgenuß gewähren und in gewisser Beziehung als Norm und unerreichbare Muster gelten.")[29]

[29] J. W. Goethe, *Dichtung und Wahrheit*, *Goethes Sämtliche Werke* (Jubiläums-Ausgabe), XXIV, 213; Friedrich Schiller, *Was heißt und zu welchem Ende studiert man Universalgeschichte?* 2d ed. (1790; rpt. 1953, ed. F. Schneider), p. 36; Karl Marx, "Einleitung zur Kritik der politischen Ökonomie," Marx and Engels, *Werke* (Dietz Verlag), XIII, 641.

It was an illusion, therefore, to assume that the indictment of philological positivism could refute the tradition of historical inquiry at large. At the time when Hippolyte Taine was developing his determinism in terms of the *moment,* the *race,* and the *milieu* (1863), the more dialectical concepts of historical criticism were perhaps overshadowed by what Nietzsche contemptuously called the reign of "that blind force of facts" ("jene blinde Macht der Fakta"),[30] but they certainly had not ceased to be available. There was, from the point of view of method, a tradition in which "the past and the present" could be considered "as one" and in which the present "charm" (and meaning) of great art, its norm and standard, might well be reconciled with a thorough understanding of its past genesis.

If it was undiscriminating to charge the historical approach with the abuse of "the methods of the natural sciences," then it was no less questionable, in the fourth decade of the twentieth century, to conceive of these methods solely or mainly in terms of nineteenth-century ideas of causality and such mechanistic assumptions as "that the world was reflected with perfect literalness in the will-less mind of the observer."[31] Again and again the literary historian was warned to keep away from the methods of science—but of a science that was hopelessly out of date. Nor was there, on the side of the critics, any curiosity as to whether the method of historiography itself had not (like that of modern science) developed considerably. By now to condemn the writing of history on the charge that it adopts the methods of the natural sciences (*which* "natural sciences"?) has become meaningless, if not downright complacent. At any rate (and this is not the place to say more), it ignores a great deal in modern physics; for instance the tendency among physicists in recent years to speak of their

[30] Friedrich Nietzsche, *Vom Nutzen und Nachteil der Historie für das Leben* (Leipzig, Kröners Pocket Edition [1933]), p. 70.
[31] Trilling, *The Liberal Imagination,* p. 182.

science in terms which (as a distinguished historian notes) suggest an "identity of aim between scientists and historians" and even "more striking analogies between the physical universe and the world of the historian."[32] It may be that in the light of such statements and recent insights into the nature of "the two cultures" (and how "dangerous" it is "to have two cultures which can't or don't communicate"),[33] the responsible literary critic will have to be more and more wary of stressing the irreconcilability of the two disciplines.

To say this is not to minimize the basic differences in method, and is emphatically no apology for positivism, but it may help us to recover a more sober perspective, from which the nineteenth century's "serene unification of scientific conscience" can be viewed with less ambiguity (than Cleanth Brooks betrays in the context of this phrase). Whatever its shortcomings, historical philology was intellectually the most coherent movement in nineteenth-century scholarship, and it is with some feeling of respect that one would wish to see *the necessary criticism* be based on more facts and less arrogance. It would take more detailed investigation into the method and practice of nineteenth-century literary history to assess the degree to which the attempts at historical syntheses were actually thwarted by the pseudoscientific pose. Not that the "blind power of facts" can ever be admired again, but on the basis of a recent study of traditional literary history in America, one is inclined to think that the really important works are less

---

[32] E. H. Carr, *What Is History* (London, 1962), pp. 80, 66. Contrasting modern and nineteenth-century assumptions of method, Carr writes: "Nowadays both scientists and historians entertain the more modest hope of advancing progressively from one fragmentary hypothesis to another, isolating their facts through the medium of their interpretations, and testing their interpretations by the facts; and ways in which they go about it do not seem to me essentially different" (pp. 77–78).

[33] C. P. Snow, *The Two Cultures: And a Second Look* (New York, Mentor Books, 1964), p. 90. Snow raises a vast question which has been asked, independently, in the distinguished work of Jacob Bronowski (see, e.g., *Science and Human Values* [London, 1961], p. 50, et passim).

seriously affected by the mechanism of uncritical research than is commonly assumed by the critics of positivism.[34] A sober reassessment of these works (some of which, by the way, are eminently readable) would, among other things, reveal a startling contrast to the much more analytical and experimental prose of the New Criticism.[35]

If the new critical attitude toward historical scholarship was somewhat ambiguous, it was also, of course, not uniform. The various critics reacted rather differently, and there were quite a number of protests (some of them undoubtedly sincere) "that the literary historian and the critic need to work together" and that both functions should, ideally, be united "in one and the same man."[36] But, as the main works in the tradition of historical inquiry were generally treated with more condescension than knowledge and as their results were, in the practical business of criticism, usually ignored, such protests often rang hollow. So whereas the critics did not offer any theoretical alternative, there developed and spread a climate of critical opinion in which historical scholarship per se seemed hostile to critical evaluation; likewise, the genetic approach per se seemed to be an expression of relativism; the study of the writer's background and biography per se seemed to be a symptom of the "intentional fallacy." As the New Criticism reaped its academic triumphs in the forties and early fifties and one scholarly journal after the other thinned the volume of its historical contributions, it must have appeared to many that the study

[34] See my comments on the work of Moses Coit Tyler, pp. 99–100.

[35] Ironically it "was precisely this scientific pose, conscious or unconscious, that constituted one of the main strengths of the New Criticism" (J. H. Raleigh, "The New Criticism as an Historical Phenomenon," *Comparative Literature*, 11 [1959/60], 23). The irony of it was noticed by at least one critic who—finding in Allen Tate's work "a rage, so deep a hatred of science and positivism, not to say democracy"—saw "a certain irony in his position, since the very textual analysis he defended was an aping of scientific method and rigor" (Alfred Kazin, *On Native Grounds* [New York, Overseas ed., 1942], p. 361).

[36] Cleanth Brooks, "A Note on the Limits of 'History' and the Limits of 'Criticism,'" *Sewanee Review*, 61 (1953), 132.

of literary genesis could only detract from, and never add to, the critical approach to literature as a serious art form. Small wonder, when even the most thoughtful observers approached the relations of history and criticism as "something unavoidably problematic, part of a troublesome opposition which runs through all our experience."[37] Such an opposition was in many quarters not merely taken for granted; it was justified by, and elaborated into, the theory of "absolute" criteria of evaluation. It was an "absolutism" by which the (undoubted) "relativism" of the traditional literary historian was, unfortunately, not overcome but relegated to a series of opposites, among which change and value, development and order, history and aesthetics, past significance and present meaning appeared more irreconcilable than ever before.

Criticism and Present Meaning

However, it would be a gross oversimplification to imply that the new critical view of traditional literary history was entirely based on a series of formalist fallacies. Nor would one wish to minimize the extent to which the virtue of close textual analysis can survive the decline of the dogma of the autonomy of literature, thereby making a very considerable contribution to the more recent rapprochement of literary criticism and historical scholarship. And in the work of critics such as F. R. Leavis, Yvor Winters, and Kenneth Burke, these possibilities reach as far back as the thirties and forties. For whatever the degree of the failure of the New Criticism in the field of literary history, even in its heyday it raised a number of serious issues and asked several very penetrating questions that a new approach would not wish easily to dismiss.

[37] W. K. Wimsatt, Jr., "History and Criticism: A Problematic Relationship," *The Verbal Icon: Studies in the Meaning of Poetry* (Lexington, Ky., 1954), p. 253.

Among them, the question of relevance was foremost. Inspiring the attack on historical antiquarianism, it asserted the need for a new consciousness of "the relation between antique fact and poetic value." The simplest and the most straightforward form in which the problem was posed was one in which the purpose of literary history was defined from the angle of the present. A history of English literature, F. R. Leavis wrote, "will be undertaken because the works of certain poets are judged to be of lasting value—of value in the present." From this position, which may be said to stress one aspect of one basic truth, the need for evaluation was articulated with a new sense of urgency: if the criteria for a history of literature somehow correspond to a living system of values, then an awareness of these values would indeed seem to be *one* prerequisite for historical studies. F. R. Leavis (without bothering much about the emphasis carried by my cautious italics) put this quite bluntly: "Such a history, then, could be accomplished only by a writer interested in, and intelligent about, the present. It would, for one thing, be an attempt to establish a perspective, to determine what of English poetry of the past is, or ought to be, alive for us now."[38]

The strength of this position consisted in the fact *that* (not in the method *how*) the literature of the past was related to what was felt to be "alive" in the present. When the interests of contemporary literature can find an echo in the literature of the past, then there needs must exist some community of poetic values (and, we should add, of historical moments). Even when this community was defined solely in terms of "modern" values, it comprised, and had to be defined in terms of, a sense of tradition. But then, again, "tradition" was taken as a mode of relating (rather than *correlating*) past poetry to present practice. F. R. Leavis and most of the New Critics still behaved as if their literary his-

[38] Wimsatt and Brooks, *Literary Criticism*, p. 537; Leavis, "Criticism and Literary History," pp. 13, 14.

tory virtually had the choice between past significance and present meaning—*their* choice being, of course, in favor of the latter.

The result, even though it satisfied current aesthetic assumptions, was not very helpful in establishing criteria by which a new approach to literary history might have prospered. F. R. Leavis's *The Great Tradition* (1948) and Cleanth Brooks's *Modern Poetry and the Tradition* (1947) yielded the proof that by and large the historical community of values had been defined solely in terms of "modern" meaning. Here were two accomplished critics, both of them certainly "interested in, and intelligent about, the present" and both venturing into literary history, but with a result that somehow defeated the very aims and functions of this discipline. To be sure, neither critic had intended to write anything like a history of the English novel or a history of English poetry—as they are, "or ought to be, alive for us now." But the historical elements of tradition that they recommended were so much at odds with the history of English literature as an actual process of possibilities (a process, that is, of both developments *and* values) that not even the rudiments for a future synthesis of history and aesthetics were laid. (In this, Leavis and Brooks followed the critical theory and practice of T. S. Eliot, who, however—interestingly enough—had defined the idea of tradition more generally and less exclusively when he said that tradition involves "the historical sense" with its "perception, not only of the pastness of the past, but of its presence."]³⁹

To take up only one example, the criteria by which Leavis defined the great tradition of the English novel were not merely narrow and exclusive, but also confusing. To dismiss, usually in form of a footnote, Defoe (without mentioning *Robinson Crusoe*) as well as Thackeray, Scott, and

---

³⁹T. S. Eliot, "Tradition and the Individual Talent," *Selected Essays: 1917–1932* (London, 1932), p. 14. But see my critique of Eliot's definition in the following chapter.

Hardy may perhaps be legitimate for one who wishes to bring out the undoubted greatness of George Eliot, Henry James, and Joseph Conrad. But in this context to introduce such concepts as "historical importance" or "the important lines of English literary history" is entirely to beg the question, not merely of literary history, but of a workable synthesis of criticism and history. If Leavis states his "reason for not including Dickens in the line of great novelists" and then proceeds to assure us that he is "a great genius and is permanently among the classics," if he gives a mere "note" to Emily Brontë "because [her] astonishing work seems to me a kind of sport" and then continues to say that "out of her a minor tradition comes . . .;" if Fielding is rejected as "simple" and then is said to have "made Jane Austen possible by opening the central tradition of English fiction"—then there must be something wrong with a criticism that conceives of tradition not historically, not as a process of both developments and values, but in terms of three or four major modern novelists. Again, the complex relationship between past significance and present meaning is overlooked. It is ignored or replaced by a concept of tradition which can conceive of no unity and of no living interplay between the past world of the English novel and its present reception, but which judges everything in terms of "the significant few" major novelists. (Leavis touches on the real problem, which he prefers not to go into, when he says: "To be important historically is not, of course, to be necessarily one of the significant few.")[40]

But to raise these objections is not to dispute the relevance of a concept of value, which (for Leavis) is seen "in

---

[40]*The Great Tradition* (Harmondsworth, Penguin Books, 1962), pp. 29, 38, 11. There seems to be a similar contradiction, of which Cleanth Brooks is probably unaware, when he says "that we need to revise drastically our conventional *estimate* of the *course* of English poetry" ("Criticism, History, and Critical Relativism," *The Well Wrought Urn: Studies in the Structure of Poetry* [New York, Harvest Books, 1947], p. 224; my italics). At any rate, this is too facile a way of correlating value ("estimate") and development ("course").

terms of that human awareness . . . of the possibilities of life."[41] Nor can such a concept of value be anything but critical. That is to say that it will evaluate the literature of the past not "as a record of past customs, past habits, past manners, past fashions in taste,"[42] or anything that is in the nature of a museum. If, as the New Criticism was perfectly justified to insist, literature is properly understood as literature and not as a medium of sociological reference and exemplification, then indeed the poetic value of a work of literature is not to be easily abstracted from its ideological or biographical significance. To elucidate the latter is not in itself identical with an awareness of the former. And to achieve this awareness, it is certainly not enough to assume "that the specific problem of reading and judging literature is completely met in the process of learning the meaning of words, the political and philosophical allusions, the mental climate in which the poem originated, etc. etc."[43]

The most valuable contribution of the New Criticism, then, was to raise (if not to answer) the question as to the function and the criteria of literary history. To stress the need for evaluation involved an awareness of both, the necessity of selection and the importance of achieving a point of view from which to select and hence to evaluate. In the words of W. K. Wimsatt: "We are bound to have a point of view in literary criticism, and that point of view, though it may have been shaped by tradition, is bound to be our own. . . . Our judgments of the past cannot be discontinuous with our experience or insulated from it." The realization of one's own point of view as both distinct from, and shaped by, the past finally called for a recognition that the object of evaluation was (just like its "subject," its ego) part of a more

---

[41] Leavis, *The Great Tradition*, p. 10.

[42] Cleanth Brooks, "The Quick and the Dead: A Comment on Humanistic Studies," in *The Humanities: An Appraisal*, ed. Julian Harris (Madison, Wis., 1950), p. 5.

[43] Cleanth Brooks, "Literary History vs. Criticism," *Kenyon Review*, 2 (1940), 407.

comprehensive process of tradition and experience. Such an approach could conceive of history not only "in its several antecedent or causal relations to the writing of literature" but it could also raise the question "whether antecedents themselves, if viewed in a certain light, do not become meanings."[44]

But to answer this question already involved a break with the formalist dogma of the autonomy of the work of art. This paved the way toward the more recent synthesis between literary criticism and historical scholarship that reveals the extent to which the virtues of close textual analysis can survive the decline of formalism. In subsequent chapters I shall return to the inevitable compromises so characteristic of the late fifties and the sixties. For obviously there were plenty of ways and means through which historical concepts such as, say, the author as "the necessary stylist" (Mark Spilka) could be reintroduced, and the whole question of rhetoric be used to overcome the frustrations of the formalist approach to the novel. Once the "implied author" was conceived as a "core of norms and choices," a "choosing, evaluating person" who attempts "consciously or unconsciously to impose his fictional world upon the reader," the "strategy of point of view" (Percy Lubbock) could no longer be entirely divorced from the world of history and sociology. This was a far cry from the formalist ghost of "the affective fallacy"; and even though *The Rhetoric of Fiction* still neglected the "social and psychological forces that affect authors and readers,"[45] it again pointed to what is potentially the historical meaning in the narrative structure of point of view. Similar tendencies have for some time been noticed in the interpretation of imagery, another domain of formalist interpretation, where

[44]Wimsatt, "History and Criticism," pp. 258, 254.
[45]Wayne C. Booth, *The Rhetoric of Fiction* (Chicago, 1961), pp. 74, [ix]. See also Mark Spilka, "The Necessary Stylist: A New Critical Revision," *Modern Fiction Studies*, 6 (1960/61), 285.

we shall note a tendency to widen the scope of the term *image* and to stress its subject matter, or "tenor," as opposed to its "vehicle"—the real subject of the discourse as opposed to the adventitious and imported image.[46] It surely was a sign of the times when a critic like W. K. Wimsatt produced a historical monograph on the portraits of Alexander Pope or when Cleanth Brooks, former explicator of paradox and irony, began to write at great length on the geographical theme and background of Yoknapatawpha County. To recognize "that a writer's choice of a subject is an aesthetic decision" prepared the way for a deeper understanding of history as part of the literary theme.[47] The renewed interest in thematics, like that in poetic personality and rhetoric, was an indication of far-reaching transitions and changes in critical doctrine. By reopening the neglected dimensions of change and society, the work of these critics began to move toward, and raise, those authorial, functional, and metahistorical contexts that, as I have noted above, the literary criticism and theory of the late sixties and early seventies has begun to discuss in what is still a somewhat fragmentary, spontaneous, and, finally, ahistorical manner.

Toward a Dialectic of Genesis and Function

A dialectical approach, which is conscious of its own social function, will wish to consider the problem of literary history from an angle where literature *is* history, and history is an element of literary structure and aesthetic experience. What is needed is not simply an act of combination between the literary historian's approach ("A is derived from X") and that of the critic ("A is better than Y"). It is not good enough to have—in F. W. Bateson's sense—a "more intimate co-

---

[46]See chapter 5.
[47]Harry Levin, "Thematics and Criticism," in *The Disciplines of Criticism,* ed. Peter Demetz et al. (New Haven, 1968), p. 145.

operation" of their efforts or anything less than an integration in method and purpose. To say that the historian is concerned with a task like "A is derived from X" is in itself a somewhat superficial formula; but even if this is read as a symbol of the genetic approach, it will not do merely to combine or to *link* the study of genesis with the critical evaluation of the art work. One has to be contained in the other, and the historical sense of the critic needs to be quite indistinguishable from the critical sense of the historian.

A postulate like this may sound presumptuous and, perhaps, overoptimistic, but the object and the function of literary history can demand no less. Let us for a moment ask the question, What *is* the object of the literary historian as critic? Is it the work of art as it is experienced today? Or is it the work of art in *statu nascendi,* in the contemporary context of its genesis and original audience? To ask the question is to draw attention to both the unity and the contradiction of the past world of the art work and the present world of its reception; or, in other words, to suggest that the historian's task (and the pastness of the work) cannot be separated from the critic's task (and the work of art as a present experience). Obviously, we cannot afford to isolate these two necessary aspects: merely to do the former is to fall back into some kind of antiquarianism; merely to do the latter is to run all the risks of misunderstanding and distortion that the New Criticism was guilty of so often. The one alternative will finally reduce literary history to a study of origins and influences, a mere *Entstehungsgeschichte;* the other reduces the discipline to a series of modern appreciations, a mere *Wirkungsgeschichte.* Neither is (as an alternative) acceptable: in the last resort, for literary history to study past significance makes no sense without an awareness of present meaning, and an awareness of present meaning is incoherent without the study of past significance.

Thus the object of the literary historian as critic is necessarily complex. It involves both genesis and value, development and order, the work of art as a product of the past and the work of art as an experience in the present. To stress these two dimensions of the art work in terms of their interrelationships is to argue for more than just expediency (in the sense that an awareness of history might prevent us from making a mistake or overlooking an anachronism in interpretation). The point that has to be made is not that the historian (or the critic) had better do his job thoroughly. The point is that these two dimensions are *inherent* in the work of art and that the study of genesis and the pursuit of evaluation find an equivalent in the similar relationship, which is a historical *and* an aesthetic one, between the mimesis and the morality of the work of art itself. Or, to make this point from a somewhat different angle, one might refer to two basic functions of literature; on the one hand, the work of art as a product of its time, a mirror of its age, a historical reflection of the society to which both the author and original audience belonged. On the other hand, it is surely no idealism to assume that the work of art is not merely a product, but a "producer" of its age; not merely a mirror of the past, but a lamp to the future. Incidentally, it was Karl Marx who pointed out that art is one of the "besondre Weisen der Produktion"—one of the "special forms of production"—for instance, in the sense that the work of art can produce its audience and influence their attitudes and values.[48]

In order to distinguish these two basic functions of literature one might call them, although this is to oversimplify, the mimetic and the "moral." (The oversimplification does not reveal that each is, indeed, correlated with the other: the moral element is implicit in mimesis as representation, just as the sensuous nature of representation points to the only process through which morality can be translated into art.) But if, for the present purpose, we accept this provisional distinction of terms, it may be said that

[48] Marx and Engels, *Werke*, Ergänzungsband, I, 53 f.

the mimetic function results from the artist's holding "a mirror up to nature." The world that is reflected in the mirror is, inevitably, the contemporary world: the past world at the time of the composition. In this sense the mimetic function of *Tom Jones* is related to an eighteenth-century world, just as the mimetic dimension of *Hard Times* reflects nineteenth-century society. But whereas the study of mimesis points back to origins and genesis, the interpretation of "moral" and artistic meanings (while it cannot disregard the mimetic dimension) is concerned with the art work as a living presence, its ever-changing impact on the reader and society. Critical value judgments as to the literary quality and, of course, the "morality" of the work of art cannot be conceived in disregard of the present world in which these aesthetic and "moral" qualities are judged and experienced. So if for the moment we ignore the oversimplification involved in so schematic a distinction, it may be said that some of the basic functions of literature itself call for the twofold activity of the historian as critic and of the critic as historian. Once the work of art is seen as both imitation and creation, it must be conceived as not merely a product of the past but also as a "producer" of the future. And while the former function is involved in the genesis (and is rooted in the past world of the art work), the latter function is realized in both the past world and the present world of its reception: it is rooted in a creative capacity for "production" which transcends the very time and age that are the object of the mimesis. Thus, the "mimetic" (the historical) and the "moral" (the ever-present) functions interact: the literary historian as critic approaches an object in which *Zeitlichkeit* and *"Überzeitlichkeit,"* discontinuity and continuity, can be fused into one.

This is the very stuff that literary history is made of. The past significance of the work of art, its background and origins, is ultimately indivisible from its present meaning and its survival into the future. The literary historian is confronted with more than the coexistence of these aspects: he has to face both their contradiction and unity. But to say this is not to make a new and particularly sophisticated demand on the historian of literature. Eventually, this is the same problem that, some three hundred fifty years ago, Ben Jonson faced when he paid his highly complex tribute to his dead rival's work as "a Moniment, without a tombe"; Shakespeare's work, he said, was "for all time," but at the same time (or even before this) he also remarked that Shakespeare was the "Soule of the Age."[49] Jonson's epitaph can hardly be said to anticipate the systematic approach of a modern literary history, but the basic problem, which is a dialectical one, is there quite clearly. It is the problem of origin and survival or, in a different light, of a great work as the product of its age and the "producer" of its future. For the modern literary historian to grasp the dialectics of *Zeitlichkeit* und *Überzeitlichkeit* calls for an awareness of the art work as having both a past and a present dimension (as well as a present and a future existence). And it calls for a perception from this awareness that, as an object of literary history, these dimensions are simultaneous in their interaction and tension.

The task of the literary historian, consequently, cannot be abstracted from either the genetic or the functional aspects of literature. For the historical study of origins helps to assess the continuity of, or the degree of change in, its social functions; while the study of its present functions can, in its turn, help us to appreciate the potential richness of the conditions presiding at its origin. In this sense history can be studied as meaning: the structure of the work of art is potentially inherent in its genesis, but in society it becomes functional only through its effect in terms of a human and social experience. Structure is intimately linked up with,

---

[49] I use the text in E. K. Chambers, *William Shakespeare: A Study of Facts and Problems* (Oxford, 1930), II, 208 f.

though not determined by, either its genesis or its affective relations. It is correlated to both its past genesis and its present functioning; for the critic to understand the full measure of this correlation is to become conscious of the necessary complexity of structure as history.

Past and Present Correlated: The Case of Shakespeare Criticism

To discuss this correlation in terms of history and aesthetics yields only very general results, which do not by themselves suggest a more practical application of theory. In order to illustrate some of the issues involved, I propose to raise the problem in the more practical context of the historical, critical, and theatrical interpretation of Shakespearean drama. Although here the gulf that separates the critical and the historical approaches has in recent years been considerably narrowed, there still exist an astonishing number of conflicting assumptions as to the aims and methods of literary inquiry into a great work of the past. Among these, the unresolved tension between past genesis and present function looms large, although as a problem of method it has hardly been perceived or discussed.

At the risk of repetition, the basic problem may perhaps again be phrased in terms of the question asked above: What is the object of a historical and critical approach to Shakespeare? What does the literary historian as critic mean when he refers to *Hamlet?* Presumably the answer would still be quite different according to whether the person in question would wish to stress the importance of historical research or the priority of critical judgment. On the one hand (in terms of historical research), the answer would preferably be "the Renaissance play." Hamlet, according to this approach, will be a historical figure, the play's message an Elizabethan one in the sense that its past significance is to be explored without implicit reference to its modern meaning. On the other hand (and this would be the more critical approach), the answer would involve a different object, one primarily related not to the Elizabethan theater or even the Elizabethan text but to the modern sensibility that it is meant to evoke. From this angle an interpretation (or a theatrical production) would be authentic so long as it achieves the tone and tenor of our own age: Hamlet will be a modern symbol and the play's message a contemporary one in the sense that in the last resort its present meaning has priority over its past significance.

Actually, the two points of reference may not be so diametrically opposed, but the contradiction involved is an objective one. No matter what the approach is, there remains a historical text for modern readers (or actors). On the one hand, there is the Elizabethan context and meaning, on the other, the modern understanding and interpretation. There is no getting away from this inevitable tension between the historical and the modern points of view, and no one-sided solution is feasible. The most learned and historical-minded scholar cannot physically become an Elizabethan; he cannot recreate the Globe or visualize the original production. Even if he conceived of Shakespeare's drama as being enacted in the theater, he would still be influenced by his own experience of the modern stage, its twentieth-century audience and actors and their social relationships, which are quite different from those that, in Shakespeare's Globe, then constituted part of the play's meaning.

The underlying contradiction is not an academic one, and the more we think of it in terms of practical interpretation (including the theatrical interpretation of Shakespeare on the modern stage) the clearer the theoretical implications will emerge. Since today it is just as impossible to understand Shakespeare without a modern interpretation as it is to have an interpretation without Shakespeare, we cannot proceed from either a genuine Elizabethan production (and this already contained an interpretation of the text) or from one that makes us believe that *Hamlet* is a modern play. Today *any* Shakespeare interpretation has to come to terms with the tension between historical values and modern evaluations. But this contradiction is not necessarily frustrating, and the way it is solved constitutes the most essential decision of both historical criticism and serious theatrical interpretation. Viewed from the angle of the drama as a work of the theater, this contradiction involves an inevitable tension between the mimetic (or expressive) and the affective aspects, between the significance of what Shakespeare's work reflected (or expressed) in plot and character and the changing impact of this on the contemporary spectator. To recreate the mimetic and the expressive dimensions is impossible without reference to Shakespeare's world and his intentions; to reassess their affective and moral effects is impossible without reference to our audience and our world.

For the literary historian and critic the question, then, is not *whether* to accept both worlds as points of reference, but rather *how* to relate them so as to obtain their maximum dimensions. To put it like this may appear provocatively superficial, but to resolve the contradiction one cannot minimize the conflicting elements when each is—in its different world—so inevitable and necessary. The "maximum dimensions," then, can mean no more and no less than this: to have as much of the historical significance and as much of the contemporary meaning merged into a new unity. Of course there is no easy formula as to how this synthesis of historical values and modern evaluations can be achieved. But in order to grasp its dialectic, it is well to remember that it is not entirely a case of opposites. On the contrary, it would be a grave mistake to overlook those many points of contact and identity, where, say, Shakespeare's Renaissance values can today be considered valid. This area of identity or interaction, however, is not simply given; it will be enlarged from a contemporary point of view that can conceive its own social direction as historical in the sense that it affirms both the revulsions and the links of contact between the past and the future. In the end this relationship involves a social and a methodological position from which both the change and the continuity can be accepted as part of a meaningful movement in history. In the present interpretation of Renaissance drama, therefore, the area of identity will radically differ between, say, a Marxist interpretation and one based on the premises of Jacques Maritain's neo-scholasticism. Where the Renaissance heritage is not repudiated, there is bound to be a wide range of living contact, in which the "historical" element can be viewed as part of a wider configuration in which the present reproduction of past art is one way of bringing about a meaningful future.

Thus, the "area of identity" between past significance and present meaning is a complex and changing one. Yet it has a certain amount of permanence which, among other things, has to do with man's anthropological status. (That is only one of the reasons why it is not confined to the Renaissance tradition.) We are all—the great dramatists of the past, their contemporary producers and critics—characters in history; our own points of reference are, like our predecessors', products of history. In this, our present values emerge from the same historical process that is both reflected in, and accelerated by, Shakespeare's contribution. This is quite obvious in the history of literature, which can only be written in reference to a scheme of values that (among other things) has to be abstracted from its great objects, including Shakespeare's dramas. Their greatness has been confirmed by the very contribution they have made in furnishing us with criteria by which to judge, and to judge not only modern plays but also the history of the drama as a whole.

Since such area of identity may be accepted as given, the relationship between Shakespeare's vision and its modern perspectives cannot simply be described as one of conflict or opposition. The difference between his world and ours is obvious enough, but it does not exclude some kind of concurrence. As Arnold Kettle has remarked, "The best way to emphasize the value of Shakespeare in *our* changing world is to see him in *his*, recognizing that the two worlds, though very different, are at the same time a unity."[50] This unity is at the basis of all our veneration for Shakespeare; without it, the impact of his work would not be possible. At the same, this unity does not preclude a contradiction that is at the basis of all our conflicting interpretations. In very much oversimplified terms: the unity creates the need of our interpretations of *Shakespeare;* the contradiction accounts for the need of our *interpretations* of Shakespeare. But actually each is contained in the other, and the interpretation as a whole can only succeed when these two aspects are inextricably welded into one. (By himself the modern historian can, as we have seen, either enhance or reduce the sphere of unity or the area of contradiction, but he can never entirely annihilate either.)

Once this relationship (although here still oversimplified) is understood more deeply, the historical study of literature has gained at least two negative standards of evaluation. These may have some practical use for judging not only the literary but also the theatrical interpretation of the great drama of the past. For in the theater as elsewhere, the modernized classic is no more acceptable than the museum version. This may not be saying anything new, but perhaps it helps to recover certain assumptions that might prove practicable to both the theater director and the historical scholar. If the rift between them could thus be narrowed, the present theatrical interpretation of Shakespeare need be neither academic nor irresponsible. In modern Shakespearean productions, then, Hamlet need not become a hippy in order to convince, nor would it be necessary, as

[50]*Shakespeare in a Changing World,* ed. Arnold Kettle (London, 1964), p. 10.

Martin Walser thinks it is, to produce "the old play" in order "to show us what things were like formerly" ("um uns zu sagen, wie es früher war"). If the past can be conceived, neither in its identity with, nor in its isolation from, the present, a historical perspective could evolve that might be both theatrically effective and convincing to the scholar. No topical effects are wanted, but a sense of history that can discover permanence in change but also change in seeming permanence; the past in the present but also the present in the past. Hence the "timeless" would result through a sense of time and history. It is in this sense that Shakespeare is "for all time" precisely because he was the "Soule of the Age." In this view, a historical vision can be made to yield a contemporary meaning. Its past significance was achieved because, at the time, it was contemporary and *then* incorporated the experience of the present. The meaning of literary history today can best be discovered through this past present, or that part of it which—although past—is still present and meaningful in a contemporary frame of reference. Thus, past significance and present meaning engage in a relationship which, in its interdependence, may illuminate either—the past work as against its present reception, and the contemporary interpretation against the historical significance of the work of art.

II
The Concept of Tradition Reconsidered

ONCE the relationship of past significance and present meaning is viewed as one involving both social function and literary structure, the links between past writing and present reading (and new writing) need to be considered more closely. Obviously, such links, if they are sought for on historical and aesthetic planes, must be conceived in the complex terms of literature as an aesthetic mode of social activity involving individual sensibilities as well as social attitudes, craftsmanship and ideology, originality and "influence." The study of these interrelations is a more comprehensive task than can be summed up by any one critical term or postulate; but a reconsideration of the concept of "tradition" may help provide us with some idea, or even a paradigm, of the nature of the links between past writing, present reading, and new writing. For a dialectical theory of literary history to ignore the *process* that sustains and informs these links is not possible. If this process is seen as a historical one, the concept of tradition, which I propose to use in this connection, will have to be redefined. The reason is obvious; the most widely shared and well-known definition of tradition in English and American criticism, that of T. S. Eliot, provides us with a singularly unhelpful category for historical criticism. Judged by the needs and perspectives of literary history, this definition has failed to come to terms with tradition as the temporal and functional process of handing down, through writing, reading, and new writing, ideas and literary values in history.

Again, as in the case of "genesis," any counterproposal worth making must be prepared to challenge a close context of terminology and methodology. In Anglo-American criticism the theory and the language of tradition may of course easily be criticized for its underdeveloped modes of abstraction or lauded for its empirical flexibility and elegant lack of pedantry. But at this point neither a conventional acceptance nor an offhand dismissal of the existing language can be helpful. Rather, what is needed is a thoroughgoing critique of the underlying modes of conceptualization, for these reflect not simply the verbal idiosyncracies of Anglo-American criticism but the more general (though not necessarily explicit) interconnections between critical method and social consciousness. It is through a critique of these largely unformulated assumptions that eventually the concept of tradition can perhaps be rehabilitated as a useful agent in the business of historical criticism.

Thus, to reconsider the concept of tradition is, first and foremost, to revisit the historical and ideological context in which the formalist idea of tradition first emerged in the early criticism of T. S. Eliot. At the same time, this context is an international one: it is characterized not only by the antiromantic direction of modernism in England and America but also by that wider revaluation of the heritage of liberalism and positivism that is associated with Nietzsche's influence in Germany, Croce's work in Italy, or Ortega y Gasset's in Spain. To be aware of this wider background helps to place in perspective the consistency, but also the limitations, of the modern Anglo-American definition of tradition. It seems never to have occurred to Eliot and his followers that the revaluation of tradition, at least in the second quarter of the twentieth century, had become a worldwide phenomenon. The leading critics who used the concept in England and America seemed unaware of comparable modes of revaluation in Italy, Spain, and Germany. And their ethnocentrism (not to say parochialism) was such that they quite ignored the entirely different aims and methods of the Marxist approach to tradition, or *Erbe*, which was so much in the center of the Brecht-Lukács debate and has recently become a source of renewed discussion and considerable controversy.[1] There is some irony in the fact that while the issue of tradition, with its profound cultural and political implications is being more widely discussed the world over, the question of tradition in English criticism (which found such noteworthy early answers) has never really been reopened. At a time when the nature and the function of tradition has been a central issue in several of the cultural revolutions of our time (the recent Chinese one included), the idea of tradition has for the past two decades, in England and America, been either neglected or ignored, rather than reconsidered and investigated. To say this is not to plead for the Red Guards' approach to the cultural heritage but is one way of providing a badly needed perspective on the excessively hermetic dimensions and categories of the Anglo-American language and theory of tradition.

It had best be said at the outset that the use of the term *tradition* has up to this day remained deeply affected (positively or negatively) by the conceptions of formalist criticism. During the heyday of the New Criticism, Eliot's definition, as outlined in his early essay "Tradition and the Individual Talent," was of course widely taken for granted. In this sense F. R. Leavis proposed his early *Revaluation: Tradition and Development in English Poetry* (1936) and Cleanth Brooks his *Modern Poetry and the Tradition* (1947). Even before Eliot (especially in *After Strange Gods* [1934]) turned to an orthodox idea of tradition and stressed "the Christian faith and the classical languages,"[2] and even be-

---

[1] For the continued impact of the Brecht-Lukács debate on the problem of tradition, see Werner Mittenzwei, *Brechts Verhältnis zur Tradition* (Berlin: Akademie-Verlag, 1972); for a vehement critique of both Mittenzwei and Brecht, see Hans-Heinrich Reuter, "Die deutsche Klassik und das Problem Brecht," *Sinn und Form*, 25 (1973), 809–24. See also Hans-Dietrich Dahnke, "Sozialismus und deutsche Klassik," *Sinn und Form*, 25 (1973), 1083–1107. My own paper on tradition, in *Literaturgeschichte und Mythologie* (pp. 47–128), must be referred to the context of this debate.

[2] T. S. Eliot, "The Classics and the Man of Letters," *Selected Prose* (New York, Penguin Books, 1953), p. 238.

fore he arrived at a broader understanding of the social nature of tradition (in *The Use of Poetry and the Use of Criticism* [1933] and *Notes towards a Definition of Culture* [1949]), the poet-critic had, for many in England and America, provided a definition and, by implication, some suggestions of method and approach. It was the work of the early Eliot (the author of *The Sacred Wood* and *Selected Essays: 1917–1932*) and his early attitude and approach that proved seminal. As the work of F. R. Leavis, Cleanth Brooks, and others witnessed, his definition was almost taken as established; it was elaborated and applied rather than critically examined or challenged.[3] If in later years objections were raised by historical scholars, such as Rosemond Tuve, they were directed against the modernist reinterpretation of Renaissance and metaphysical poetry, that is, against the content rather than the concept of tradition as a category of historical criticism.[4] This was equally true of the critique voiced from liberal positions like that of Stanley Edgar Hyman, who attacked Eliot's "doctrine of tradition" as a reactionary "weapon."[5] In this respect the most consistent way to challenge the whole modernist line of tradition was to submit some historically based counterproposals, as did Marxist critics like Alick West, Arnold Kettle, or Annette Rubinstein in *The Great Tradition in English Literature from Shakespeare to Shaw* (1952).[6] But when new dissident voices in the sixties called for the exploration of a "new literary past," the whole concept of tradition was completely and

---

[3]See, e.g., the introduction to F. R. Leavis, *Revaluation: Tradition and Development in English Poetry* (New York, 1947): The critic's aim "is to define, and *to order* in terms of *its own implicit organization*, a kind of *ideal* and *impersonal* living memory" (p. 2; my italics). Cf. the quotation from T. S. Eliot, p. 76.

[4]Rosemond Tuve, *Elizabethan and Metaphysical Imagery: Renaissance Poetic and Twentieth-Century Critics* (Chicago, 1947).

[5]*The Armed Vision: A Study in the Methods of Modern Literary Criticism*, rev. ed. (New York, 1955), p. 72.

[6]See, in addition to Annette Rubinstein's book, the introduction to Alick West, *The Mountain in the Sunlight* (London, 1958) and Arnold Kettle, "The Progressive Tradition in Bourgeois Culture," *Radical Perspectives in the Arts*, ed. Lee Baxandall (Harmondsworth, 1972), pp. 159–75.

violently rejected as a "fraud," designed, as Jonah Raskin wrote, to emphasize "conservatism, continuities" and to "smother upheavals, innovations, revolutions."[7] The New Left mood, as John Allen noted, was bent "on scrapping all our traditions," and even the more serious new radical theory from Marcuse to Louis Kampf was inclined to dismiss, rather than critically consider, the problem of tradition.[8]

To summarize thus the discussion of the concept of tradition in England and America involves, of course, some sweeping generalizations and, among other things, ignores a good deal of the implicit use of tradition in practical criticism and interpretation. If here, too, the application of the concept of tradition remained indebted to Eliot, it was used with less dogmatism and exclusiveness than had been the case in the work of Leavis, Brooks, or the New Critics. Perhaps it was Eliot's repeated reference to "the historical sense" as "a perception, not only of the pastness of the past, but of its presence," that proved stimulating. Here, at any rate, was a formula that some of the leading critics and scholars hailed as liberating them from the more mechanical procedures of purely factual studies of influence and sources.[9] Perhaps it is not going too far to say that it was this larger view of tradition as "the unified vision of a

---

[7] *The Mythology of Imperialism* (New York, 1973), pp. 5, 32.

[8] John Allen, "On Scrapping All Our Traditions—In Favor of Older Ones," *Arts in Society*, 7 (1970), 157–59. There is, however, at least one remarkable New Left anthology which defines a "counter-tradition" as "not 'that which opposes tradition,' but 'the tradition which opposes'" (*Counter-Tradition: A Reader in the Literature of Dissent and Alternatives*, ed. Sheila Delany [New York, 1971], p. 4). Delany rejects the "confusion of relevance with up-to-the-minute modernity" and remarks that the striving for such "'relevance' paradoxically shows itself to be of a piece, after all, with the conservative past" (p. 3). But whereas Kettle has argued "that the greatest art of the bourgeois period is the *least* bourgeois" ("The Progressive Tradition," p. 167) those who speak of a counter-tradition would presumably insist, as Louis Kampf and Paul Lauter have done, that high culture is apologetic and reflects the interests of the ruling classes then and now (*The Politics of Literature* [New York, Vintage Books, 1973], p. 8).

[9] René Wellek sums this up by saying that "Eliot's view of tradition has been followed by almost all recent English and American critics" ("The Concept of Evaluation in Literary History," *Concepts of Criticism*, ed. Stephen G. Nichols, Jr. [New Haven, 1963], p. 47).

literature" which, being fully developed by 1932, not only became a constituent element in the rise of the New Criticism but seems to have survived its decline remarkably well.[10]

For that, the reason is not hard to find. Had not Eliot in connection with his emphasis on "the historical sense" of the poet stressed a more objective and impersonal approach to poetry? And had he not argued against an inflated sense of romantic genius and originality? So he had indeed, but in a highly contradictory manner. At some basic level his recommendation of "the historical sense" and his suggestion for an "extinction of personality" were at odds with each other. Once the "personality" of the artist was said to be extinguished, or reduced to a rather technical "medium," the relationship between the individual poet and his audience could hardly be defined in terms of any meaningful cultural (or historical) relationship. Was there, in this view of tradition, any room at all for the ordinary reader as a factor in the handing down of the literature of the past? And if there was, was the reader's personality to be considered as a medium of the poetry, or, rather, was not the poetry to serve as a medium of the growth of the *reader's* personality?

To ask these questions in retrospect is to submit that the concept of tradition should not, and cannot, be abstracted from the practical concerns of today's culture and society. After the sixties it is becoming increasingly difficult in England and North America to ignore the fact that what is involved in recent social and cultural changes is not merely the concept, but also the practice, of tradition, not merely its theory but also its function. If, in the third quarter of the twentieth century, Eliot's dislodgment from a position of critical preeminence was effected with remarkably little fuss, that is by itself a token of what, in present popular phraseology, is called "The Times They Are A-Changin'." I

[10]Sean Lucy, *T. S. Eliot and the Idea of Tradition* (London, 1960), p. 8.

quote the idiom of popular entertainment, not to be picturesque, but to suggest that a more wide-ranging consciousness of tradition in today's society would be ill advised to ignore such phenomena as, say, the revival of free verse in the fifties or, for that matter, the changing adaptations of the folk song tradition from Pete Seeger and Woody Guthrie to Bob Dylan with corresponding developments in the mass culture of Western Europe.[11] To point to such popular and unliterary artists is, quite deliberately, to stress the wider cultural and social areas that today confront the idea and practice of tradition. It is also one way of suggesting that far more is at stake than questions of literary theory and methodology. More than ever before, the idea and the function of tradition are deeply involved in the widely felt need for a reordering of values and a reassessment of the problems and directions of the present in relation to a past which, to some of the most vocal sections of Western society, has ceased to serve as an available means of self-identification. What is involved is a dilemma Northrop Frye is aware of when, in *The Critical Path,* he remarks that "for people on this continent at least, the real cure for the identity crisis . . . is the recovery of their own revolutionary and democratic myth of concern."[12]

[11]See Gene Bluestein, "The Poetry of Rock: Folk Tradition and the Individual Talent," *The Voice of the Folk: Folklore and American Literary Theory* (Cambridge, Mass., 1972), pp. 141–50.

[12]*The Critical Path: An Essay on the Social Context of Literary Criticism* (Bloomington, Ind., Midland Books, 1971), p. 139. After Frye had completely rejected "the magic word 'tradition'" (*Anatomy of Criticism: Four Essays* [Princeton, 1957], p. 16), he more recently began to stress the prophetic, utopian, and revolutionary elements in the romantic tradition (*The Stubborn Structure: Essays on Criticism and Society* [London, 1970], pp. vii, 179, 200 ff.). But he can stress these values only in accordance with a principle of social function and critical evaluation that (in the *Anatomy*, pp. 6 ff., 20 ff., or in *Fables of Identity: Studies in Poetic Mythology* [New York, 1963], p. 8) he himself had previously rejected as being incompatible with "the autonomy of criticism." It is a principle that (in *The Stubborn Structure*, p. 66) he still rejects as "an individual, unpredictable, variable, incommunicable, indemonstrable, and mainly intuitive reaction to knowledge." These seem highly characteristic contradictions between the present critical methodology and a new awareness of cultural function.

This may point to the wider background against which the problem of tradition can today be reopened. But traditional values cannot be revitalized through recommendations; nor can any "myth of concern" be recovered by some purely intellectual activity. For a living tradition would presuppose some more comprehensive intellectual *and* practical correlation between the achievements of the past and their changing functions in the present and the future. What is at stake is not simply a verbal redefinition of tradition, but the contemporary confrontation of both a historical past and a historical future by a consciousness capable of correlating them in the *Praxis* of the present. It is this historical function of consciousness that is in trouble: the vision of its prehistory has become blurred to the same degree that its posthistory is steeped in uncertainty. But if the nature of this dilemma is such that it affects the concept of tradition, then the resulting contradictions are of a historical, rather than a logical, order. Consequently, no purely theoretical critique of the modern concept of tradition can be satisfactory unless, first of all, the modernist idea of tradition itself is viewed historically, in terms of its prehistory and its nineteenth-century antipodes, against which the early T. S. Eliot reacted so violently.

The Liberal Tradition from Milton to Arnold

The difficulties in defining, with any precision, the nineteenth-century liberal sense of tradition are inherent in the positive and quite varied social modes of reception by which the great nineteenth-century critics and historians approached and estimated their literary past. If any generalized statement about figures such as Sainte-Beuve in France, Gervinus and Hettner in Germany, De Sanctis in Italy, Belinski and Dobrolyubov in Russia, Macaulay and Matthew Arnold in England is at all possible, it will probably point to the fact that they were all, more positively than negatively, related to the revolutionary and history-making forces in the sixteenth, seventeenth, eighteenth, and early nineteenth centuries, including the Renaissance, the Enlightenment, and romanticism. These were the traditions whose continuity in, and adaptation to, the later years of the nineteenth century they helped to promote. In doing so, most of them were highly conscious of the historical and literary heritage of the nation in which they lived, so much so that in the German, Italian, and Russian traditions, the history of literature was conceived of as either anticipating or consummating a social history and a national destiny that was politically retarded or thwarted.

In England, where the bourgeois revolution had occurred so early and insured such an exceptional continuity of institutions and ideas, it was possible for a liberal historian and critic like T. B. Macaulay to define the culture of the present as a legitimate and almost inevitable outgrowth of the past. In underlining the connection between the two, he chose as his most relevant (and yet traditional) point of reference the political settlement of the seventeenth century, as when he remarked, not without some complacency, that the "highest eulogy which can be pronounced on the revolution of 1688 is this, that it was our last revolution. . . . It is because we had a preserving revolution in the seventeenth century that we have not had a destroying revolution in the nineteenth. It is because we had freedom in the midst of servitude that we have order in the midst of anarchy."[13] From a position like this, the direction of past events could be taken to correspond to the future goals that England and the English-speaking world had set for itself in the present.

Small wonder, then, that where tradition, both as a concept and as a term, could so much be taken for granted, it was so little developed. As Eliot noted in the opening

[13]T. B. Macaulay, *The History of England from the Accession of James II* (London, 1906), II, 214.

sentence of his early and most seminal essay, "In English writing we seldom speak of tradition"; but the reason was not that tradition, in the Victorian era, was remarkable by its absence. If the phrase or concept was little used, the matter itself could be solidly relied upon. Again, if the consciousness of being part of a tradition of liberalism and individualism was not articulated, the reason was that the very nature of the liberal tradition, its ideological structure, was not favorable to an articulation of such consciousness. Originality and individuality were considered self-evident values in the still relevant process of the liberation of the bourgeois individual in the course of the political and industrial revolutions. Against this background the concept, or even the word *tradition*, seemed hardly usable, "except," as Eliot noted, "in a phrase of censure."[14] But a tradition it nevertheless was, and part of its strength consisted in the fact that the relation of the nineteenth-century consciousness to the past comprised literary as well as social and political levels of contact and confirmation and that these levels were mutually linked and intertwined. This was so not only in England and, in a different way, in France, but also in Germany, Russia, and Italy, where the absence of a bourgeois revolution, or the failure in the struggle for national unity and independence, had resulted in periods of setback and discontinuity. And yet in these countries a more complex and less inflexible idea of cultural progress allowed the liberal conscience to readjust its version of the past in terms of the social, political, and literary experience of the present.

To illustrate that point, I can only hint at the way in which Belinski read the work of Pushkin and the activities of the *decabristy* in terms of mid-nineteenth-century developments to whose outcome both politically and culturally they are seen to contribute. Or let us take the very different

[14]T. S. Eliot, "Tradition and the Individual Talent," *Selected Essays: 1917–1932* (London, 1932), p. 13.

tendency in De Sanctis's literary history of the Italian Renaissance, where an overriding frame of reference is established by both the contribution made by the literature of the Renaissance and the standards of its nineteenth-century reception and evaluation; this provides some sense of coherence, and it points toward a comprehensive idea of literary and national culture. Similarly, the German historian of the European Enlightenment, Herrmann Hettner, was concerned to describe and estimate the origins of the tradition of free inquiry and rational discourse, especially in seventeenth- and eighteenth-century England, in terms of both the social and cultural needs of the emancipation of the nineteenth-century German bourgeoisie. Discussing the revolutionary movement in France in terms of its European significance, Hettner concludes the introduction to the first volume (1856) of his *Literaturgeschichte des achtzehnten Jahrhunderts* by relating the revolutionary struggles of the seventeenth and eighteenth centuries to the basic needs and issues of mid-nineteenth-century culture and society: "Even today we are in the midst [of these struggles.]" ("Noch heute stehen wir mitten in ihnen!") For whereas "some of us endeavor to carry on and adapt the leading ideas of these struggles" so as to realize and transform the age of Enlightenment into "an age of universal and complete education permeating all sections of society," others tend "now more than ever to question the legitimacy (*Berechtigung*) of these struggles and to throw back the currents of history for centuries" ("die strömende Geschichte . . . zurückzutreiben"). Those are the words of one of the greatest German literary historians; they reflect a sustained and profoundly functional nineteenth-century sense of tradition as expressed in the need for an appropriation and a continuation, on a more democratic plane, of the social and cultural achievements of both the English and French Enlightenment and the German *Klassik* of Herder, Goethe, and Schiller. And even though the watershed of 1848, especially in Germany, led to a new phase of reassessments and regressive withdrawals into either positivism or irrationalism, for Hettner, as for all those unaffected by the subsequent impact of Nietzsche and Schopenhauer, the inevitable readjustments were made in a way that allowed for a subdued but still, in many ways, functional use of the culture arising out of the revolutionary struggle of the past.

But it was in England, even more than in France, that the continuity in the process of the political and industrial revolutions created the most consistent and positive need for the handing down of those achievements that so directly and visibly seemed to provide both present standards and future directions of cultural activity and literary excellence. Here, such diverse critics and thinkers as Macaulay, Carlyle, Ruskin, William Morris, and, of course, Matthew Arnold could positively elaborate their own position in functional reference not only to a literary but a social and cultural past. This, indeed, is the first and most striking difference between the critics of the nineteenth century and those who followed Pound and Eliot: the achievements of the postrevolutionary settlement of the late seventeenth and eighteenth centuries are so received that the direction of past events is taken to support the present orientation of culture and society toward the future. It is in this sense that Macaulay finds reason to celebrate the "preserving revolution" of the seventeenth century as "our last revolution." The degree of preservation provides an index to the validity of a tradition which, because its historical direction is so obvious and alive, is neither questioned nor defined.

The nineteenth-century liberal reception of John Milton is a case in point. Perhaps Macaulay himself took the most characteristic stance when, "in all love and reverence," he approached "the genius and virtues of John Milton, the poet, the statesman, the philosopher, the glory of English literature, the champion and the martyr of English liberty." What the liberal critic finds especially fascinating in Milton is "a powerful and independent mind, emancipated from the influence of authority." In other words, it is Milton's originality, his personal independence, and, even more, the process of his emancipation from "authority" that are seen as his most distinctive heritage. It is his Protestant rejection of an older tradition that makes it possible for him to constitute a new tradition. For him, to be "emancipated from the influence of authority" is to achieve the true authority and contemporary relevance of a great nineteenth-century model. In this sense Macaulay views Milton as ranking "with those great men who, born in the infancy of civilization, supplied by their own powers the want of instruction and, though destitute of models themselves, bequeathed to posterity, models which defy imitation." In this view Milton has almost become an autodidactic genius; he is celebrated as a founder of the new tradition of self-made authority. What is more, Milton's self-made authority (or, in Macaulay's terms, his "want of instruction") provides a model for all those who, "destitute of models themselves," yet create a great work that defies imitation. It is the tradition of those who (it is thought) have no tradition except the "Inner Voice."[15] The poetics of inspiration are here intimately linked with the Protestant emphasis on the individual's "calling," or "election," which, as Eliot later noted, denies "the existence of an unquestioned spiritual authority." For Eliot (we note his consistency) this was only another name for "Whiggery."[16]

But for the liberal critics the correlation between the social and moral values of the English Revolution and their renewed function in the nineteenth century is obvious enough. Certainly, there was as marked a difference in response between the liberal and the not-so-liberal positions, as, on many other issues, between Benthamites and con-

---

[15] T. B. Macaulay, "Milton" (1825), *Essays Historical and Literary* (London, n.d.), p. 2.
[16] Eliot, "The Function of Criticism," *Selected Essays*, p. 29.

servatives. Yet in making this correlation, Macaulay, that "Philistine of genius" (as A. L. Rowse calls him), is not so far removed from Matthew Arnold. It is true that even when he considers Macaulay's essay "brilliant," Arnold finds an "unsoundness" in what he views as a mere "panegyric on the Puritans." But even though he disapproves of "Milton's asperity and acerbity, his want of sweetness of temper," he stresses his "importance to us Englishmen" as being based on some "unsurpassable grandeur" in both the man and the poet.[17] What is more, Arnold calls attention to Milton's "discipline of respect for a high and flawless excellence" as "the most salutary influence" amidst "all the flood of Anglo-Saxon commonness." With changing emphasis, he again stresses the greatness of his "vocation" as well as the originality and independence of his inspiration: "Nature formed Milton to be a great poet." And Arnold concludes his tribute (for a tribute it is) by acknowledging the Puritan poet's genius in terms of the identity of Milton's seventeenth- and nineteenth-century meanings within the same nation, language, religion, and morality: Milton, says Arnold, is "one of our own race, tongue, faith and morals."[18] The surprising thing is that Arnold, for all his increased awareness of what he calls the "commonness" of the middle classes and the anarchy of the working class, can find in Milton a heritage with a changing but no less urgent function and significance. When, therefore, the changing emphasis on the more abstract and refined ideals of discipline and excellence is allowed for, the Milton tradition is equally confirmed and reconfirmed in the unity of its more comprehensive political, cultural, religious, and literary functions.

It is in this sense that the criticism of Milton can serve as a paradigm for the nineteenth-century mode of reception

---

[17] Matthew Arnold, "A French Critic on Milton," in *Selected Criticism*, ed. Christopher Ricks (New York, 1972), pp. 312, 315.
[18] Matthew Arnold, "Milton," *Essays in Criticism* (London, 1911), pp. 61, 64, 67.

which, by correlating the literary *structures* of the past with
the *functions* of literature in the present, best helped to turn
the great poet of the seventeenth century into a cultural acquisition of the nineteenth-century reading public.

The Modernist Revaluation: Past Structure
versus Present Function

When we turn to the modernist revaluation of the literary
tradition, it is at once clear that the nineteenth-century
liberal sense of tradition provides so much more than a mere
background. It is probably not saying too much to suggest
that the very strength of the Milton tradition in the nineteenth century was one of the reasons why, in the criticism of
the early T. S. Eliot and F. R. Leavis, the rejection of the
great Puritan poet was so violent and so hostile. And the
crisis in the reception of Milton involved more than just a
dismissal, on aesthetic grounds, of the poetry of *Paradise
Lost*. The whole Protestant humanist and revolutionary
background was rejected as the ultimate source of what T. E.
Hulme considered the mistaken romantic notion of man as
"an infinite reservoir"; it was repudiated as an early expression of what Eliot called Whiggery, the position of
"doing as one likes."[19]

But the crisis of liberalism was not merely of an
ideological order. With the decline of the economic foundations of laissez-faire and the ensuing transition from the capitalism of free trade and competition to a new type of mo-
nopoly economy, some of the most basic nineteenth-century
social conditions and assumptions of culture began to appear
untenable. Now the writer and critic was faced with a rapidly
changing world in which the traditional premises of his rela-

---

[19]T. E. Hulme, *Speculations: Essays on Humanism and the Philosophy of
Art*, ed. Herbert Read (London, 1924), pp. 116 f.; Eliot, "The Function of
Criticism," *Selected Essays*, p. 27.

tionship to the middle classes were becoming increasingly problematic. Facing new divisions in class and education, the breakdown of the international economic and political balance of power, a new type of chauvinism, and a more vulgar and pervasive kind of commercialism, artists and intellectuals reacted against the cultural standards of the middle classes and the bourgeoisie. There developed a feeling of crisis and a sense, as Irving Babbitt put it in *Rousseau and Romanticism* (1919), "that we are living in a world that has gone wrong on first principles." In this connection the cultural history of the nineteenth century was radically revaluated. During that century "men were moving steadily towards the naturalistic level where the law of cunning and the law of force prevail, and at the same time had the illusion—or at least multitudes had the illusion—that they were moving toward peace and brotherhood."[20] The ideas and postulates of the bourgeois revolution in France and elsewhere had resulted in "vague emotional intoxications" which, economically and politically, were accompanied by an "everlasting expansion." In the twentieth century "to continue indefinitely the programme of the nineteenth century" seemed dangerous, especially in the economic, political, and cultural spheres. The expansion was to result, as Babbitt had predicted in *The New Laokoön* (1910), in "a concentration that will not be humane, but of the military and imperialistic type peculiar to epochs of decadence."[21]

The liberating potential of the ideology of individualism and romanticism had finally been exhausted. The "decline and fall of the romantic ideal" signaled the decline of a cultural tradition by which poets, critics, and their audiences had all shared some common bearings toward a common cultural past. Once the modernist spokesman of the new poetry, like Ortega or Eliot, had rejected the romantic

---

[20] *Rousseau and Romanticism* (Boston, 1919), pp. 373, 374.
[21] *The New Laokoön: An Essay on the Confusion of the Arts* (Boston, 1910), p. 241.

tradition as the heritage of the masses or as symptomatic of those who "ride ten in a compartment to a football match at Swansea,"[22] the isolation and alienation of the artist came to be compensated by a new elitism. But since the modernist poet or critic tended to reject the liberal and, sometimes, the humanist heritage, the cultural achievements of the past and the cultural needs of the present—romantic structure and modernist function—had become so incongruous that tradition as a meaningful point of contact and interaction ceased to operate spontaneously.

Now Milton's nineteenth-century function as a model of the emancipation from authority appeared no longer usable. If, in the view of the new critics of liberalism, man appeared as "an extraordinarily fixed and limited animal" and if it was only by discipline, organization, and authority that (in Hulme's words) "anything decent can be got out of him," then Milton's model of self-made authority clearly could no longer function. And the crisis in the functioning affected the estimate of the poetry. Milton no longer appeared as "the glory of English literature" but as a symptom of an irretrievable loss and damage which, according to Eliot, "happened to the mind of England between the time of Donne or Lord Herbert of Cherbury and the time of Tennyson and Browning." That, of course, was "the dissociation of sensibility," aggravated by the influence of Milton and Dryden, "from which we have never recovered." The dismissal of Milton after two centuries of preeminence became the center of a far-reaching revaluation that, as F. R. Leavis noted, was effected by "the force of a whole close context."[23]

This is not the place to follow the process of that extraordinary revaluation or to trace the gradual steps of its re-

[22] Eliot, "The Function of Criticism," *Selected Essays*, p. 27.
[23] *Speculations*, pp. 116 f.; Eliot, "The Metaphysical Poets," *Selected Essays*, p. 273; Leavis, "Mr. Eliot and Milton," *The Common Pursuit* (Harmondsworth, 1962), p. 12.

vision. But when Eliot in 1936 persisted in saying "that Milton's poetry could only be an influence for the worse, upon any poet whatsoever," or when, in his 1947 British Academy lecture, he took up "the case against Milton," his position toward the seventeenth-century revolution emerged more clearly. Eliot then said that "the Civil War of the seventeenth century, in which Milton is a symbolic figure, has never been concluded. The Civil War is not ended. . . ." That the issue of the civil war was a living one and that for Eliot at that late date it seemed desirable and possible to approach it from some kind of counterrevolutionary position had already become apparent in the late twenties in his essays on Bishop Bramhall and Bishop Andrewes. In the former Eliot professed to find "a fundamental unity of thought between Bramhall, and what he presents, and ourselves." And at the same time—and in the same essay, where he so conspicuously stood up for the High Church party—he rejected "a philosophy so essentially revolutionary as that of Hobbes, and so similar to that of contemporary Russia."[24]

But I do not point to these political and historical affiliations in order to underline their ideological quality (which is, in any case, familiar). Rather, let us examine the entirely different premises on which, methodologically, the new concept of tradition was based—premises that are usually overlooked when the revaluation in question is considered merely as Milton versus John Donne. Here the first point that has to be made is that Eliot repudiated the nineteenth-century consciousness of the present as being part of a historical movement from the past to the future—a movement by which the direction of past history was believed to correspond to an awareness of the present as the fulfillment of the past. Ironically, the new attempt to define tradition was made when that tradition could no longer be taken for granted; for

[24]Eliot, "Milton II," *On Poetry and Poets* (New York, 1961), p. 168; "John Bramhall," *Selected Essays*, p. 336.

that was when a meaningful correlation between the direction of the historical process and the idea of cultural progress had become difficult or precarious. In these circumstances Eliot's theory of tradition was, first and foremost, a repudiation of the hitherto unchallenged *Praxis* of tradition; his call for a new tradition was a symptom of the crisis of the old one.

Eliot himself was deeply aware of the crisis. But although he brilliantly perceived the growing incongruity between past values and their present reception, he could not solve the underlying contradiction. He only formulated it on a different level; for his definition of tradition, on the one hand, and the handing down of culture in the historical process, on the other, were now set against each other almost in opposition. The process of handing down had become problematic in its results; it was becoming difficult or undesirable to define tradition historically, in terms of the movement of past structures fulfilling present functions. By abstracting the concept of tradition from the temporal mode of this movement, Eliot, it is true, arrived at some new and valid insights into the simultaneous presence and availability of past literature; and he also made the profound remark that the literary past could "be altered by the present as much as the present is directed by the past."[25] At the same time—and this was the price he paid for the abstraction—the acquisition and revaluation of past literature was quite divorced from other modes of consciousness and the cultural process in history. Consequently, the question of tradition became quite narrow; it was reduced to some finer concern of the individual artist. It was, finally, no more than the impersonal mode in the poet's personal perception of the simultaneous existence of the whole of the literatures of the world.

In order to understand the way in which this abstraction

---

[25]"Tradition and the Individual Talent," *Selected Essays*, p. 15.

was formulated and almost compensated for, let us remind ourselves of Eliot's original context, which was that of "the impersonal theory of poetry"—a theory directly and indirectly linked with what was to become the programmatic idea of the New Criticism, namely, that literature should be described and analyzed according to its own intrinsic and impersonal categories. Eliot's emphasis on the impersonal mode of creation and reception and the related idea of tradition as some ideal and impersonal order might have been designed to oppose and curb impressionism. But even though they certainly helped to do that, they retained a highly subjective point of reference: the focus on, and criterion of, the subjective needs of the individual talent. There was a contradiction between the emphasis on the subjective needs of the individual writer, on the one hand, and the more objective idea, on the other, of "the literature of the world," *not* as a collection of the works of individual poets, but as some impersonal system of verbal and literary relationships. This contradiction was symptomatic of a dilemma that is already conspicuous in Eliot's essay "The Function of Criticism," where, after citing his early "Tradition and the Individual Talent," he goes on to say:

I was dealing then with the artist, and the sense of tradition which, it seemed to me, the artist should have; but it was generally a problem of order; and the function of criticism seems to be essentially a problem of order too. I thought of literature then, as I think of it now, of the literature of the world, of the literature of Europe, of the literature of a single country, not as a collection of the writings of individuals, but as "organic wholes," as systems in relation to which, and only in relation to which, individual works of literary art, and the works of individual artists, have their significance.[26]

This is both a reconfirmation and a development of his previous position; in fact, it is a key passage that retains the justified reaction against impressionism and individualism but proceeds to develop the concept of tradition toward, and

[26]"The Function of Criticism," ibid., pp. 23 f.

in connection with, a new definition of the function of literature and the function of criticism. The connecting link between the sense of tradition and the function of criticism is the "problem of order." But this problem of order is defined as involving, for tradition, some purely spatial system and, for criticism, some purely structural activity. Such a definition anticipated what, in structuralist terminology, may now be called the syntagmatic dimension of literature. What Eliot in fact says is that he thinks of the literature of the past "as systems in relation to which, and only in relation to which, individual works of art, and the works of individual artists, have their significance." Thus, the significance of the relationship of a new work of art to the literature of the past is established intrinsically, and it is in this sense that, with some consistency, both tradition and the function of criticism are defined as "generally a problem of order."

In this definition "order" is a formal category; it involves, as Eliot says in the same essay, "the relation of the work of art to art, of the work of literature to literature, of criticism to criticism." But since this system of order is seen as a simultaneous and spatial, not to say autonomous, pattern, how can "the consciousness of the past" be received by the artist and criticized by the critic unless the actual process of this reception itself, the processing of the old and the new, of continuity and discontinuity, is held up to criticism? To subject this process to criticism would have forced Eliot to see it as involving personal decisions and temporal positions, that is, as some form of social and historical activity. Indeed, how could a writer, as Eliot postulated, "be most acutely conscious of his place in time, of his own contemporaneity," unless the relation of his present consciousness to that of the past were taken as the most basic and primary context in which the process of reception could be analyzed for its significance and value?[27] It was only by ignoring the actual

[27] Ibid., p. 25.

needs and modes of reception as a process of consciousness in history that Eliot could define the quality of the individual talent as formal and impersonal. But to do so was to disregard the relationship between the receiving consciousness and the received one, as well as the meaning involved in the encounter between past creation and present reception and recreation; it was to ignore the content (and its inherent tension) of the process of interaction that is at the heart of any creative influence. To abstract from that was to preclude any meaningful correlation between the mode of reception as some form of cultural activity and the artistic mode by which the structure of the present art work is both organized and jeopardized through the impact of tradition.

Beyond *Bildungserlebnis:* The New Function of Criticism

However, the fact that Eliot in so conspicuous and deliberate a manner connects the sense of tradition with a definition of the function of criticism is worth examining in a wider historical context. In terms of any intrinsic frame of reference, this connection must appear strange; but it is not so strange when viewed against the background of the nineteenth-century liberal correlation between the function of criticism and the function of tradition. Eliot himself invites us once again to take into account this background, in his own critical reference to Matthew Arnold, who (according to Eliot) "overlooks the capital importance of criticism in the work of creation itself."[28] This may be so; but Eliot ignores the fact that Arnold is keenly aware of the extent to which criticism can both precede and follow up the act of literary creation extrinsically, by helping, for instance, to bring about "an intellectual situation of which the creative power can profitably avail itself." But then Arnold defines

28 Ibid., p. 30.

criticism broadly as a cultural force; as "the critical power" operating "in all branches of knowledge." As such, it is very much part of what, in a telling phrase, he calls "the general march of genius and society." In this phrase the genius of literature and the movement of society are metaphorically linked, and the image of their "marching" together suggests that the temporal process of the one can be related to the advance of the other. No matter how naive or complacent the image may ring in a post-Victorian context, it is seriously borne out by Arnold's historical view of the temporal and progressive nature of the relatedness of the past to the present. For instance, Arnold can stress the meaningful role of the past, in particular "the achievements of Protestantism in the practical and moral sphere" which, "though in a blind and stumbling manner, carried forward the Renaissance." Or take his related estimate of what he calls the "prodigious and memorable course" of the French Revolution, which he considers as "the greatest, the most animating event in history"; for him "a unique and still living power." And that sums it up neatly: for Arnold, the revolutionary achievements of past history are a "still living power" that initiates a meaningful movement and constitutes a living process.[29] (This concern with the idea of process is reflected in the temporal quality of Arnold's verbal and metaphorical language, as when he says that the Reformation "carried forward" the Renaissance, or speaks of the "memorable" quality of the "course" of the Revolution as an "animating" event.)

In using this language of motion, Arnold established a correlation between the achievements of the past and their "still living," though changing functions that he defined as the task of criticism. "I am a liberal," he said in *Culture and Anarchy*, "yet I am a liberal tempered by experience, reflection and renouncement, and I am, above all, a believer in culture." But that culture, even when defined as "the

[29] Matthew Arnold, "The Function of Criticism at the Present Time," in *Selected Criticism*, pp. 95, 98.

study of perfection," was not the study of perfection for its own sake; it was envisaged in terms of some more general social and educational function. If this function can be expressed in a formula, it may be said that, for Arnold, it was the education of the middle classes as the most promising, if indirect, way to "a general expansion of the human family."[30] This formula, of course, provides only an inadequate summary and does not allow for the contradictions and the apologetic note inherent in Arnold's idealistic conception of the role of culture in society. (These contradictions are such that Arnold has to rationalize them in an almost paradoxical way, as when he says that it is "only by remaining collected, and refusing to lend himself to the point of view of the practical man, that the critic can do the practical man any service.")[31] Even so, Arnold's definition of the social function of criticism as the disseminator of culture and his idea of tradition as a comprehensive historical process can be seen to be theoretically as well as practically related. In his essay on Milton he evaluates the poet in terms of a "still living" excellence that is expected to assist in the refinement of that unpleasant "commonness" so characteristic of the "practical man" and those successful but vulgar middle classes.

This is worlds apart from T. S. Eliot. For Eliot, criticism is not designed to "do the practical man any service." The critic has moved too far away from the middle classes, and he is not close enough to the working class, to be in a position to wish to educate them. But since criticism has ceased to disseminate culture in society, what is left of the function of criticism? Eliot's well-known essay by that name provides no answer, except the one phrase in which, in passing, Eliot hints at "the correction of taste." But as soon as he proceeds to discuss "the chief tools of the critic," these

[30] Matthew Arnold, *Culture and Anarchy*, ed. R. H. Super (Ann Arbor, Mich., 1965), p. 88.
[31] Arnold, *Selected Criticism*, p. 107.

turn out to be, characteristically, "comparison and analysis," while interpretation is deliberately rejected and evaluation ignored or overlooked. Again, this seems perfectly consistent with Eliot's view (which he takes to be "natural and self-evident") of the fundamental relationship "of the work of art to art, of the work of literature to literature, of criticism to criticism." By taking this relationship to form the basis of both the sense of tradition as a sense of order and the function of criticism as a problem of order, too, Eliot relinquishes not only the spontaneous links between literature and history, inherent in Macaulay's and Arnold's more comprehensive perspectives on art and society, but he also surrenders the essential premises on which historical consciousness and literary sensibility could potentially be made to engage in some meaningful interaction.

To understand the measure of the difference between Arnold and Eliot is to be aware not only of the direction of the English modernist conception of tradition but also of an international complex of cultural crises, which is marked by an impoverishment in the definition of both the social function of criticism and the cultural uses of tradition, as well as by the changing nature of the connection between the two. But as soon as we view the redefinition of the English tradition in reference to this larger complex, the picture begins to look much more complicated. To sum it up at its most general level, one might say that in the various European countries the diminishing social function of criticism and the changing theory and practice of tradition are differently, and never mechanically, related, and the relationship is usually of a complex type, the one aspect being interrelated with, rather than determined by, the other.

Let us take, for example, the completely different situation in Germany, where it is possible to establish a comparable, though not identical, pattern in the changing reception of Goethe, from Wilhelm Scherer, Richard Meyer, and Albert Bielschowsky to Friedrich Gundolf and Josef

Nadler, in terms of the surrendering of an interest in
Bildungserlebnis ("educational experience") in favor of one
in *Urerlebnis*. The historical interest in Goethe's own
education gave way to an irrational fascination with the
qualities of some demonic, timeless genius. This changing
mode of reception goes hand in hand with a change and reduction in the social role of criticism, insofar as the historical
content of Goethe's own education had ceased to find a
functioning equivalent in the modern education of the
German middle classes. Goethe's *Bildungserlebnis* was no
longer usable; consequently, the mode of correlation and
the amount of concurrence in the relationship between the
received consciousness and the receiving consciousness had
been seriously reduced, if not destroyed. The post-Nietz-
schean structure of the modern consciousness, on the one
hand, and the structure of the traditions of the Enlightenment and the Weimar *Klassik*, on the other, had become so
incompatible that they could no longer be functionally related. The needs and dilemmas of the antiliberal education
were such that the process and the results of Goethe's own
education ceased to be satisfactory: Bielschowsky's family
Goethe, which catered for some *Bildungsbürgertum*, was superseded by the idea of Goethe as an aesthetic genius,
experiencing an irrational kind of *Urerlebnis*.[32]

Spatial Order: "Culture without Yesterday"

The differences in trend and emphasis between the English
and the German early twentieth-century revaluations of the
literary past are too obvious to need elaboration; but the
overriding connection between the changing definitions of
tradition and the changing social functions of criticism
reflects some common pattern of loss and revaluation that

[32]See Paul Rilla, *Goethe in der Literaturgeschichte: Zur Problematik der
bürgerlichen Bildung* (Berlin: Henschelverlag, 1949).

can perhaps best be characterized by saying that a temporal and progressive idea of the literary heritage is surrendered in the process of the diminution of its social and cultural functions. This generalization is abstract enough to cover at least part of the wider European process of the revaluation of the Renaissance and eighteenth-century heritage, reflected in the work of such major figures as Croce and Ortega y Gasset. Reacting against what R. M. Pidal was to call the *arte de mayoría* as the mainstream of the Spanish literary tradition, Ortega proposed an antiromantic and aristocratic redefinition of the literary past based mainly, though not entirely, on the definition of literature for an intellectual elite. It is interesting to note that such a revaluation, as outlined in the early *Meditaciones de Don Quijote* (1914), went hand in hand with the concept of a "culture without yesterday" ("la cultura salvaje, la cultura sin ayer, sin progresión, sin seguridad").[33] It was a culture that offered objects that could not but appear "libres del espacio y del tiempo." It was, like *Don Quixote*, a noble and heroic fiction, but one that was still, somehow, related to history as the destiny of the nation. But at this point where Ortega finally seems to overcome his own unhistorical vision of the nation's heritage, where he is most passionately concerned with a modern meaning of the cultural past, he finally despairs of any temporal concept of tradition. By definitely rejecting a correlation of past and present history, he pleads for an inverted, atemporal reading of Spanish history: "cantar a la inversa la leyenda de la historia de España."[34]

While Ortega was concerned with redefining the changing role of an inverted past, it was Benedetto Croce who first questioned the entire concept of function in

[33]José Ortega y Gasset, *Obras Completas* (Madrid: Revista de Occidente, 1962–65), I, 355. See Monika Walter, "José Ortega y Gasset und das Traditionsproblem in der spanischen Geschichte und Literatur," in *Tradition in der Literaturgeschichte*, pp. 73–127.

[34]*Obras completas*, I, 320, 363.

literature and literary criticism. It is interesting to note that the rejection of the idea of function goes hand in hand with the repudiation of the concept of tradition as a temporal process in the interrelation of past and present art and consciousness. Croce, in fact, anticipated Eliot in his conception of "past history" ("if it really is history") as "also contemporary."[35] And although Croce's idea of a *storicismo assoluto* is too complex to be explored here, it is tempting to underline the fact that there is a similar tendency to dismiss the concept of temporal sequence. In contrast to Eliot's impersonal theory of tradition, the subjective nature of this conception is more readily apparent, as when Croce traces the presence of the past in the mind of the observer and defines "real history" as "the history that one really thinks in the act of thinking."[36] The element of unashamed subjectivity may, perhaps, have to do with the fact that even when he attacks the methods of positivism, Croce is still vitally associated with a tradition of liberalism. (And as the course of Italian history in the twentieth century revealed, this tradition had quite a different part to play than, say, the liberal one in England or even in another Catholic country like France.) But for all these far-reaching differences, Croce at least in part anticipated both Eliot and Ortega in that he was confronted with a literary heritage that had lost a good deal of its former practical, national, and social significance. In these circumstances the new concept of *poesia* (as opposed to *letteratura*)

---

[35]Benedetto Croce, *Teoria e storia della storiografia* (Bari: Laterza, 1948), "Senonché, considerando più da vicino, anche questa storia già formata, che si dice o si vorrebbe dire 'storia non contemporanea' o 'passata,' se è davvero storia, se cioè ha un senso e non suona come discorso a vuoto, è *contemporanea*, e non differisce punto dall'altra. Come dell'altra, condizione di essa è che il fatto, del quale si tesse la storia, vibri nell'animo dello storico . . ." (p. 4).

[36]Ibid., "Se, invece, ci atteniamo alla storia reale, alla storia che realmente si pensa, nell'atto che si pensa, sarà agevole scorgere che essa è perfettamente identica alla più personale e contemporanea delle storie" (p. 5). This leads to Croce's distinction between *la cronaca* as "dead history" and *la storia* as "la storia viva" and "la storia contemporanea": "la storia e precipuamente un atto di pensiero" (ibid., p. 10).

and the ever-recurring idea of "lyrical" intuition as some form of a "pure" intuition cleansed of all historical reference to reality are symptomatic. They form a whole close context that deeply affects Croce's view of the history of *poesia*. This view anticipates Eliot's idea of tradition as a phenomenon which (in the words of Leavis) involves "a kind of ideal and impersonal living memory" that the critic is "to order in terms of its own implicit organization."[37] Such a definition is foreshadowed in the fourth chapter of the third section in *La poesia*, where Croce considers "the aesthetic judgment as the history of poetry" and, rejecting "judgment by any extraneous criterion," proceeds to speak of an atemporal "hierarchy." Such an intrinsic order, or "hierarchy," arises spontaneously, by the very qualities of each work which takes, "in the mind of its readers," a certain place. ("Ma, senza ricorrere all'arbitrio del criterio estraneo, l'importanza di ciascun'opera si determina in modo spontaneo, e spontaneamente la gerarchia si stabilisce, per il carattere stesso di ciascuna opera, che prende nell'animo dei lettori quel posto e non altro.")[38] The timeless presence of *poesia* in the "mind" of its readers anticipates the "ideal" and "living memory"; the concept of a "hierarchy" recalls Eliot's statement that "the existing monuments form an ideal order among themselves." In this sense Eliot regards the nature of tradition, much as Croce considers the history of poetry, *as the judgment of poetry itself*. On this assumption Croce's "hierarchy," much like Eliot's "ideal order" or Leavis's "implicit organization," involves both the function of criticism and the history of *poesia;* that is, the aesthetic judgment itself. This points to the central dilemma, which is cultural as well as methodological; for the impoverishment in the definition of the function of criticism is one way to reflect the process of the alienation of literature from its total social

---

[37]*Revaluation*, p. 2.
[38]"Il giudizio estetico come storia della poesia," *La Poesia*, 4th ed. (Bari: Laterza, 1946), p. 132.

context, marked by both creation and reception, genesis and effect. For the critic to ignore this context and reduce the concept of tradition (as the most comprehensive link between past creation and present reception) is consciously or unconsciously to apologize for the alienation involved. At the same time, the methodological foundations of historical criticism are surrendered in favor of the subjective notion of a "hierarchy," of the spatial idea of an "ideal order" and related structural, typological, or mythological systems, by which the loss of the present social function of past literature is theoretically justified.

With Croce, as with Eliot, the problematic nature of the new concept of tradition reflects what Ortega called "la cultura sin ayer, sin progresión, sin seguridad." Against the background of the crisis of liberal European middle-class culture, Croce, Eliot, and Ortega can be seen as perhaps the most influential representatives of the process of revaluation that finds its earliest expression in Nietzsche's passionate dissociation of the values of life from the values of truth, subjectivity from objectivity, experience from recognition. It is a process that leads up to the representatives of the *Frankfurter Schule*, with their elitist positions, their mere *Ideologiekritik*, and their dualism of the objective and the subjective. For the purely negative critic of bourgeois ideology, the connection (*Zusammenhang*) of man and time has become problematic, and the idea of "tradition, destroyed and manipulated by the bourgeois principle, is turned into poison."[39] But the rejection of the whole concept of a literary heritage as "anachronistic" reflects a basic disregard of *Praxis:* to speak of the classics as "affirmative" or apologetic ignores their past as well as their potential present dimension of function, including the revolutionary principle of refunctioning, or *Umfunktionierung*. Finding its point of orientation primarily in the critical consciousness re-

[39]T. W. Adorno, *Ohne Leitbild: Parva Aesthetica* (Frankfurt a.M.: Suhrkamp, 1967), p. 29.

sponding to today's manipulated modes of the reception of a commercial culture, this rejection has stimulated the new aesthetics of reception.[40] Today the failure of the modernist concept of tradition and the corresponding dissociation of literary sensibility and historical consciousness have become easier to recognize. With Eliot, as with Croce and Ortega, tradition was always conceived in terms of the artist, never in reference to his audience; always in terms of an ideal order, never with regard to temporal change and social movement. By rejecting the world of history, the modernist concept of tradition failed in its most essential task. Positively speaking, that task is to stimulate a *Praxis* by which the culture that we receive and the culture that we leave behind can be made to meet and engage in struggle through potent interaction. In this view, tradition is a product of the past that helps produce the present; it is—to adapt my previous phrase— past culture turned present function. As such, it is meaningful history in the process of its present regeneration, application, and modification. It is a phenomenon ever changing, ever in motion, on which the impress of the past and the impact of the present constantly interact. This interaction produces a meaningful point of contact between both the genesis of a living literature and its past and present *Wirkung* and reception. It is this capacity for relating the living past and the life of the present, the ability to interconnect them and make them interact, that constitutes the historical dialectics of tradition.

Thus, to link the practical and the conceptual aspects of tradition is, finally, more than a theoretical postulate. It

---

[40]H. R. Jauss, *Literaturgeschichte als Provokation* (Frankfurt a.M.: Suhrkamp, 1970), p. 183. In his "Nachwort über die Partialität der rezeptions- ästhetischen Methode" attached to his study "Racines und Goethes *Iphigenie*," *Neue Hefte für Philosophie*, no. 4 (Göttingen, 1972), Jauss has attacked my theory of tradition as "objectivistic," to which charge I have replied in " 'Rezep- tionsästhetik' und die Krise der Literaturgeschichte," *Weimarer Beiträge*, 19 (August 1973), 5–33.

reflects the basic fact that, in the final analysis, tradition provides an overriding perspective on both the directions of creative writing and the orientation of criticism. In effecting and, at the same time, reflecting a potential correlation between them, the sense of tradition is unique in its comprehension of creation and theory, sensibility and consciousness, image and idea. There is no modern redefinition of tradition that does not involve creative as well as theoretical efforts. In this respect the problem of tradition is one relevant to both the history of literature and the history of criticism. In other words, tradition provides not only an object for, but also a perspective on, historical criticism and scholarship, and as such it remains an indispensable concept in the present radical reconsideration of the aims and modes of literary history.[41]

[41]On "tradition" as a methodological concept, see my *Literaturgeschichte und Mythologie*, pp. 86–97, and the introduction to *Tradition in der Literaturgeschichte*, pp. 9–25.

III

Past Origins and Present Functions in American Literary History

AT a time when the formalism of the era of the New Criticism is being superseded by a new understanding of the "historical vocation" of literature, "the absence of methodological thinking in this area" has become in many ways an anachronism in North America.[1] It is an anachronism in the sense that the reawakened interest in literary history cannot for a moment hope to recapture the historical vocation of literature unless, at the same time, it revitalizes the historical vocation of criticism. Today a viable literary history has to recover both its object and its subjectivity, the works of the historical past and its own consciousness of history, and, most important, the interconnections between them. To be aware of these interconnections is to control, and to make meaningful, the ambiguity of the term *literary history* itself. For literary history denotes both the literary process in the past and the conscious result of tracing that process in the present; it is the sum total of the books of the past but also the summary contained in the one book about all those past books of literature. Seeing these two meanings together can contribute to the strengthening of a new sense of both the unity and the contradiction between the past work and its present perspectives. This is the essence of methodology: to explore the changing relationship between historical reality and historical consciousness, between past origins and present reactions and receptions, between the object of, and the *Subjekt* behind, the historical interpretation of literature. In the terminology of structuralism, it is not enough to relate the historical concept to *le signifié*. The signification itself

[1] Geoffrey H. Hartman, "Toward Literary History," in *Issues in Contemporary Literary Criticism*, ed. Gregory T. Polletta (Boston, 1973), p. 753.

needs to be considered: the historian of literature can no longer speak of his object as something entirely apart from his subjectivity as *Praxis*. Even as he produces a literary history (the one book as summary), he himself is also, in a sense, the product of literary history (as the sum of the books he has read). Thus, to write history is both to make history and to be made by history.

Raising these very general points is one way of introducing a methodological perspective on the history and the theory of American literary history and thus serves to prepare the ground for viewing its developments and contradictions in a new light. For instance, let us consider the protracted and quite fundamental opposition between what (for the sake of convenience) I propose to call the sociological and the mythological approaches to American literary history. Although to speak of an opposition between the two approaches may be an oversimplification, it is indicative of the considerable tensions between two major traditions in American literary history and criticism. On the one hand, there is the Progressive tradition of the sociological interest in history and literary history as represented by Frederick Jackson Turner, Charles Beard, Carl Becker, and Vernon Louis Parrington. Centrally concerned with the democratic values of the American Revolution and the experience of the West, these historians viewed the directions of social history in the twentieth century as offering meaningful patterns of social development and continuity. They believed in the possibility of resisting vested interests and warding off their economic and political encroachment on the democratic ideals of the past of which the antiorthodox heroes of progressive liberalism, figures like Thomas Jefferson and Andrew Jackson, were taken to be representative. In the field of literary history, similar (though not quite so progressive) positions were anticipated by Moses Coit Tyler, and in part still found a belated echo in the *Literary History of the United States*. In this tradition the work of

Parrington was the most direct link with, and perhaps the most characteristic achievement of, what Richard Hofstadter called the Progressive historians.[2]

On the other hand, there developed, around the middle of the century, liberal and not so liberal types of revisionism by which Parrington's concept of reality in America (as in the title of Lionel Trilling's essay) was reconsidered and new formulas of interpretation and new images of reality were developed. By way of a critique of the Progressive tradition, historians and literary historians like Daniel Boorstin, Marvin Meyers, Perry Miller, R. W. B. Lewis, Henry Nash Smith, and, of course, Hofstadter himself moved to a new attitude toward the American past, approaching it no longer in terms of "democracy," "progress," and "reaction" but through concepts such as "myth," "symbol," "paradox," "ambiguity," and "irony." As in Reinhold Niebuhr's *The Irony of American History*, the new reading of history amounts to an exploration of a basic "incongruity" between purpose and result, intention and consequence.[3] In this tradition, however, the ensuing relationship of past and present history is read in terms of "innocence" and "guilt" (or "experience"), "good" and "evil," and similar anthropological, symbolic, or mythical concepts, which replace the more strictly sociological and economic tools of analysis.

The dichotomy between the two traditions is, of course, not absolute. There were, and are still today, numerous tran-

---

[2] *The Progressive Historians: Turner, Beard, Parrington* (New York, 1968). See also Charles Crowe, "The Emergence of Progressive History," *Journal of the History of Ideas*, 27 (1966), 109–24; Arthur Mann, "The Progressive Tradition," in *The Reconstruction of American History*, ed. John Higham (New York, 1962), pp. 157–79.

[3] Trilling, "Reality in America," *The Liberal Imagination: Essays on Literature and Society* (London, Mercury Books 1961), pp. 3–21; Niebuhr, *The Irony of American History* (New York, 1952). The irony consists of incongruity, which is revealed if "virtue becomes vice through some hidden defect in the virtue; if strength becomes weakness because of the vanity to which strength may prompt the mighty man or nation; if security is transmuted into insecurity because too much reliance is played upon it" (p. viii).

sitional or intermediary positions, and, to be sure, the attempt to link the main tenets of both social history and literary history in terms of two (necessarily limited) formulas is admittedly not without danger. Furthermore, the opposition between these traditions was weakened by the fact that the course of development during the fifties allowed one movement to gain ground at the expense of the other, until the more recent reorientation toward a newly radical view of social and literary history began. But even though the New Left approach has brought some impressive results in economic and social history, it has—so far—produced less convincing contributions to a new literary history. Here, a good deal of the literary past has been rejected on the assumption "that high culture propagates the values of those who rule and therefore helps to maintain current social arrangements."[4] But it may be that assumptions like these (and the new radical attitudes behind it) reflect the fact that, as Christopher Lasch observed, the "history of American radicalism . . . is largely a history of failure and therefore not a source of comfort to those who look to the past to find ancestors and heroes."[5] In this sense it may be said that the New Left approach to the literature of the past is not unaffected by the crisis in historical consciousness that is one of the factors behind the dichotomy of the social and the aesthetic approaches to literary history.

These two traditions, together with the New Left revulsion against any Progressive or liberal consensus, constitute the major paradigms of twentieth-century American historiography; their unresolved tensions are symptomatic of

---

[4] *The Politics of Literature: Dissenting Essays on the Teaching of English,* ed. Louis Kampf and Paul Lauter (New York, Vintage Books, 1973) p. 8. See also *Counter-Tradition,* ed. Sheila Delany, and my comments above, chap. 2, n. 8. For some of the early departures of New Left political and economic historians, see *Towards a New Past: Dissenting Essays in American History,* ed. Barton J. Bernstein (New York, 1968), and Irwin Ungar, "The 'New Left' and American History: Some Recent Trends in United States Historiography," *American Historical Review,* 57 (1967), 1237–63, as well as the more recent work of Eugene Genovese, Gabriel Kolko, and W. A. Williams.

[5] *The Agony of the American Left* (New York, 1969), p. viii.

larger social and cultural antinomies. The present crisis in the relationship of art and society and the methodological difficulties in the relating of aesthetics and history are not two completely isolated phenomena. In order to understand the nature of some of these developments and contradictions within the more limited confines of literary history, I propose to ask some questions of methodology and suggest that the answers involve the historical vocation of literary history, the consciousness of the changing nature of the relationship between past objects and present interpretations. These are questions which, in North America, have rarely, if at all, been asked.[6] As may perhaps be expected, when the two dominant traditions as well as the New Left approach are coming to define their positions (and their differences) more sharply, the crisis in the relating of literature and reality will be seen to be at the very center of the conflicting methodological perspectives on structure and society in literary history. The following notes toward a dialectical reappraisal of these traditions do not attempt to give anything like a critical survey of the problems involved; rather, their aim is to raise (though not necessarily to answer) questions of method in such a manner that some of the governing problems and contradictions in the changing relationship between critical method, historical consciousness, and the literary heritage may more clearly be perceived.

Function and Evaluation: Moments of Early Correlation

The rise and development of early American literary history were rooted in the peculiar historical background of a nation

[6]There is, however, an increased awareness of the need for methodology, as articulated, for example, by Gene Wise, *American Historical Explanations: A Strategy for Grounded Inquiry* (Homewood, Ill., 1973), who attempts an analysis of the three historiographic paradigms (Progressive, "counter-Progressive," New Left) which is valuable despite "the book's underlying assumption—that a historical explanation is distinguished not so much by its content as by its form" (p. viii).

freeing itself from a colonial status through economic growth, political revolution, and intellectual secularization. The revolutionary achievement of independence was accomplished at a time when the Enlightenment in Europe had already produced concepts of bourgeois consciousness so effective that they needed merely to be taken over by American thinkers so as to meet the needs of the new nation. Small wonder, therefore, that the movement of ideas following national independence was so much in the European tradition. The recognition in literary history of an emerging national culture was retarded by nearly a century: it occurred at a time when the French Revolution had long become a fact in world history and when the late German *Klassik* had redefined some basic theoretical positions of the European Enlightenment, especially in the philosophy of history, through contributions of Herder, Goethe, and Hegel.

It is obvious from this situation, which was further enriched by the genius of Vico and the influence and mediation of the French (such as Madame de Staël and Sismondi) that the basic impulses in American historiography were of common European origin. Creative theoretical contributions were slow to develop. History, as far as it was written down, was limited to political history or to some topical mode of pamphleteering, and it was these that kindled the self-confidence of the emerging nation. An interest in literary history developed much later, the first work deserving to be mentioned in this connection appearing in 1829. The response to Bacon's call for "a complete and universal history of literature and learning" was delayed even more than in Europe. When, however, toward the end of the nineteenth century, American literary history finally matured, there was a belated consistency in the application of historical principles—this in one application surpassing the contemporary model of the English, as well as that of romantic and later positivistic philology in Germany and

France. For the more comprehensive and, from then on, dominant conception of American literary history was that of literature as the expression of the social and cultural history of the nation and its people. The focal question was, as Howard Mumford Jones notes, the question of "the relation of literature to society in the United States."[7]

As an example, let us consider the most enduringly valuable of early literary histories, *A History of American Literature: 1607 to 1765* (1878) and *The Literary History of the American Revolution: 1763 to 1783* (1897) by Moses Coit Tyler. In spite of some eclecticism in approach, both works (each in two volumes) show a basic "reference of historic fact to life and experience."[8] To be sure, the nature of this reference to the life of society is still quite traditional: climatic conditions and the specific milieu of Colonial literature, for instance, are taken into account, almost according to the principles laid down by Hippolyte Taine. At the same time, the overall conception of the literary process remains quite idealistic: with characteristic Victorian emphasis, the literary process is likened to a "majestic operation of ideas." Thus, the struggle for independence, which is related to certain social and economic interests, is viewed as a somewhat regrettable "race quarrel" between Englishmen and Americans.[9] Almost as a matter of course, the presentation for long stretches is purely descriptive, and the overabundance of anthological material and quotations prevents both an analysis of individual works and a synthetic view of the course of development.

Yet in spite of these and other weaknesses, literary phenomena are seen as having some distinctly social and temporal frame of reference: literature is viewed "chiefly as

[7] *The Theory of American Literature* (New York, 1948), p. 176.

[8] *A History of American Literature: 1607–1765*, ed. Howard Mumford Jones (Ithaca, N.Y., 1949), p. v; *The Literary History of the American Revolution: 1763–1783*, 2 vols. (New York, 1957).

[9] Tyler, *Literary History of the American Revolution*, I, vii, ix, 509; II, 421.

the expression of American society." Consequently, certain essential facts of literary development, such as the rise and reception of some genres, are derived from the social function of these particular works of literature and the changing social situation in North America.[10] What is more, such a rudimentary correlation of literature to society is not, as a rule, established mechanically, as merely a mirroring of historical facts in literature. Rather, the reciprocity of the correlations made by Tyler deserves to be emphasized. Authors appear, not as pawns on the chessboard of a predetermined play of historical forces, but *they themselves* are observed to have "nourished the springs of great historic events by creating and shaping and directing public opinion." It is probably true that Tyler's principle of method was formed on the model of H. T. Buckle and Hippolyte Taine; it is, however, not fortuitous that the principle was strengthened and affirmed in the course of a study of the literature of the American colonization and Revolution. The literary historian, explicitly and implicitly, understands his own position to be both the product and the extension of the very forces and trends of development described by him.[11] The historic *results of this development* have become part of the *method* of literary history and the *mode* of retrospective selection and evaluation. The values of the epoch of literary history described are affirmed as a meaningful premise of the point of view of the literary historian. Thus, the historical period directly and indirectly enriches the historiographic perspective of the observer; the process of literary history itself suggests the method according to which it is to be treated, and vice versa. Such a historical conception of literature provides not only the essential points of the se-

---

[10] Ibid., I, 29. Take, e.g., the genres of Colonial Literature (*History of American Literature*, pp. 8 ff.), but also those of the Revolutionary period (*Literary History of the American Revolution*, I, 12 ff.), in particular the predominance of satire (p. 407), especially in Freneau (pp. 415 ff.) and John Trumbull (pp. 428 ff.).

[11] *Literary History of the American Revolution*, I, vii, viii, 12, 456, 516.

lection of material but also criteria for evaluation. For instance, the affirmation of the Declaration of Independence springs from the gratitude felt for "the prodigious service rendered to us."[12]

This security in the correlation of past achievements to present needs and functions provides some basis for defining not only historical but also literary values, and for viewing them together. The (contemporary) standard of evaluation of a work is related to the measure of its (historical) effect: at least one essential criterion of evaluation is the degree of historic effectiveness of the work in question with regard to the American commonweal. Such a frame of reference is broadly based on the assumption "that literature has its full meaning in society, that it is written by men speaking to men, and that judgments to be passed upon it spring from its usefulness to the public weal." Though the limitations of this standard (which is, after all, a sociological and not an aesthetic one) are not discussed, its criteria are, nevertheless, practically defined. It follows from them, as Howard Mumford Jones notes, "that writing is good in proportion as it expresses, or influences, political (that is, public) values."[13] In this sense Tyler's efforts were aimed at a principle of evaluation in which the judgments of literary criticism are in part determined by the test of social function and success.

It is proper for us to remember that what we call criticism is not the only valid test of the genuineness and worth of any piece of writing of great practical interest to mankind: there is, also, the test of actual use and service in the world, in direct contact with the common sense and the moral sense of large masses of men, under various conditions, and for a long period. Probably no writing which is not essentially sound and true has ever survived this test.[14]

In considering the "actual use" and "service" of literature as criteria of evaluation, Tyler presupposes some

[12]Ibid., p. 516.
[13]H. M. Jones, Introduction, *A History of American Literature*, p. vii; *Theory of American Literature*, p. 106.
[14]Tyler, *Literary History of the American Revolution*, I, 515.

undefined kind of unity between social and aesthetic functions. He was probably not even aware of the fact that his standards of "use" and "service" can become aesthetically relevant only if the judgments of the receiving audience prove so unassailable and incorruptible that the quality and, indeed, the breadth of reception by itself attains aesthetic, and not only sociological, significance. If the greatness of a literature is determined by "the test of actual use" and if the "actual use and service in the world" depend, among other things, on the greatness of the number of its readers, then the *sociological* extent of the reception of a book can serve as an initial pointer to its *aesthetic* value, and vice versa. Social impact and aesthetic structure might then be studied in some correlation to each other: history in terms of aesthetic values and art in terms of history. (These assumptions, of course, are never formulated, and my formulation is an extrapolation that runs the risk of making them appear much more utopian than in fact they are; for American literature in the eighteenth century can indeed be more adequately submitted to the "test of actual use" than, say, American literature in the twentieth century. In any case, for Tyler this test was based on a mode of reception that, to a much greater extent, excluded the best-seller and the exploitation of commercialized and degraded standards.)

On the basis of such unformulated premises, it seemed possible to Tyler to postulate some rudimentary correspondence between the *historical* interpretation of the past as a temporal process and the *critical* evaluation of the works created in the course of this process. It was Tyler's conviction that he himself was part of the historical process; his affirmation of the continuing results gave his critical standards their robust assurance. This attitude both necessitated and made possible a temporal and, at the same time, a critical mode of literary history that allowed for historical generalizations as well as for some sort of evaluation. Thus, the achieved "fusion of critical evaluation and historical methodology" (to use Howard Mumford Jones's words)[15] reflects and sustains a relationship between the past and the present in accordance with which the past subject and its present view point attain a considerable degree of reciprocal relatedness.

The nature of this reciprocal relationship can best be understood from its methodological presuppositions. For Tyler the idea of historical development was taken for granted; this assumption helped him to understand the sequence of literary works as a more or less coherent and meaningful development. Although similar assumptions were of course characteristic of early English literary history, with Tyler the correlation of historical and literary development took on a double relatedness.[16] Not only did Tyler consider the past works of literary history themselves as a foundation for his own position, thus strengthening his present point of view through the consciousness of its prehistory, but he also related the historical work and the contemporary point of view in such a way that the study of the former serves as a confirmation (and apology) for the latter. Tyler's nineteenth-century liberalism becomes a potentiation of his own historical perception of the Enlightenment and the revolutionary past. The idea of historical progress, expressing itself in a peculiarly Anglo-Saxon, mechanical, and naive manner, is used by Tyler for a practical mode of interpretation that is both object-oriented and meaningful to the present. While the distinction between historical explanation and cultural acquisition is minimized, the one aspect is used to potentiate the other. Thus, the inevitable tension

[15] *Theory of American Literature*, p. 108.
[16] See René Wellek, *The Rise of English Literary History* (Chapel Hill, N.C., 1941): "The germ of the concept of historical development is in the idea of progress . . ." (p. 26), and see p. 38. See also Sigmund von Lempicky, *Geschichte der deutschen Literaturwissenschaft bis zum Ende des 18. Jahrhunderts,* rev. ed. (Göttingen: Vandenhoeck u. Ruprecht, 1968), pp. 228 f.: It is the "idea of progress" that makes it possible "to order the entire historical process according to a structuring principle."

between historical effect and literary evaluation is largely
relieved; the historical fact itself is elevated to the level of a
constituent element of the poetic standard: the history of
the impact of literature (the *Wirkungsgeschichte*) becomes
an integral part of the *critical* task itself, no matter how
perfunctorily, in Tyler's case, that task is fulfilled. The
potential for synthesis contained in this view and the liberal
historian's spontaneous confidence in the usable nature of
the past are remarkable. What is involved is the assumption
that the highest literary achievement entails the greatest
social impact or popularity, and vice versa. It is the conception, peculiar to early Victorian criticism and preserved
much longer in the United States than in Europe, that individual attainment and public acceptance somehow correspond (or ought to), so that the writer's *social* impact and
public reputation by themselves may serve to measure his
literary achievement.

Again, such principles of method are nowhere formulated by Tyler; they are neither consistently realized nor supported by any methodological consciousness, let alone
system. My generalized analysis, therefore, must not be
allowed to obscure the severe limitations inherent in Tyler's
approach. For one thing, his standards of criticism are basically undeveloped, contradictory, and sometimes complacent, and not merely because they reflect the robust,
rather than the subtle, temperament of Moses Coit Tyler.
From the point of view of historical materialism, his narrow-
mindedness is quite obvious, though never contemptible.
From his class position, there result a number of contradictory, essentially apologetic attitudes, such as that toward the
Declaration of Independence. Though in principle he
affirmed the Declaration of Independence, he showed a
certain ambivalence when he spoke of its "sweeping propositions of somewhat doubtful validity" and called the
preamble "that stately and triumphant procession wherein,
as some of us *still* think, they will go marching on to the

world's end." Such traces of uncertainty are founded on a
liberal claim to the traditions of the Enlightenment in the
age of their imperialist dissolution. The very process of this
dissolution, inevitable by 1897, even in the United States, is
dressed up by Tyler as an "appalling national temptation":
"we fell, as is now most apparent, under an appalling national temptation—the temptation to forget, or to repudiate, or to refuse to apply to the case of our human
brethren in bondage, the very principles which we ourselves
had once proclaimed as the basis of every rightful government, and as the ultimate source of our own claim to an un-
trammeled national life." [17]

Tyler's limitations in his mode of presentation are no
less obvious. There is an element of positivism, which hinders
meaningful analysis. This is reflected even in the external
form of organization, by which each subchapter is identified
by the name of an author. It is true that this ordering principle does not result from a conception of literary history as
the intellectual exploits of great men (and indeed, the sub-
sections usually follow an introductory socio-historical and
cultural survey that already places them within a larger
context). It is, however, difficult to justify the biographical
ordering of the literary works where the function of
literature as the expression of the individual is often insignificant (as in the Colonial prose) or where it is largely
subordinated to political and public issues (as during the
time of the Revolution).

A comparison of Tyler's literary history with that of his
German colleague Wilhelm Scherer would easily bring out
the empirical spontaneity of the American. At the same time,
such a comparison illustrates a characteristic direction of
American literary history. At the end of the century (1878–
97) Tyler is still closer to the Enlightenment spirit of such
democrats as Gervinus and Hermann Hettner than to the

[17]Tyler, *Literary History of the American Revolution*, I, 499, 508 (my
italics), 516.

later mode of academic philology. In Germany, Scherer's heritage was soon superseded by what Werner Krauss called the "rattling of typological antitheses" in the writings of Dilthey's and Wölfflin's disciples.[18] American literary history, however, did not at that date follow the path into irrationalism. For several decades to come, it took up critical positions that were concerned with a practical perspective on what, in America, was called a "usable" past.

Progressive Redefinitions of a "Usable" Past

During the twenties, when German *Geistesgeschichte* reached a climax in the works of Strich, Cysarz, Ermatinger, Korff, and others, American literary history also took a new start. Under the impact of the world war, economic monopolization, and cultural commercialization, it strove, under the leadership of John Macy (*The Spirit of American Literature*, 1913) and Van Wyck Brooks (*America's Coming of Age*, 1915), for a new orientation toward the changing social and artistic peculiarities of American literature. These, however, were not abstracted according to types of style but were developed from the new conditions of American society and were measured on a literary-critical scale of originality, relevance to life, and realism. These were the new emphases in selection, evaluation, and organization that were meant to provide the key to a retrospective understanding of the process of national literary emancipation as seen from a modern point of view. Previously celebrated poets who had drawn on European sources and New England intellectual attitudes, such as William Cullen Bryant, Henry Wadsworth Longfellow, and James Russell Lowell, were drastically lowered on the scale. The romantic direction of their poetry paled before the prose of the critical realists. However, the

[18]"Literaturgeschichte als geschichtlicher Auftrag," *Sinn und Form*, 2 (1950), 100.

new evaluation of Melville, Mark Twain, and Harte did more than compensate for their previous neglect. Here a protest was involved: it crystallized in the attack on the overpowering Puritan heritage and the genteel tradition, which now seemed less useful as a living heritage. This reevaluation, in which Van Wyck Brooks played a leading role, climaxed in the definitely present-oriented quest for a *usable* past—a national tradition that would promote literature as the democratic conscience of the nation and form a bulwark against the paleness and narrow-mindedness of New England, against the vulgar utilitarianism and puritanism of the petit bourgeois, but also against the interference and chaos of those enemies of art—capitalism and big government. It was reevaluation that immediately established a remarkable accord between the new literary historiography and the new literary realism of Dreiser and Sinclair Lewis.

The reevaluation of the American literary heritage modified the traditional relation between the historical object and the contemporary view point of literary history. The modern cultural critic recognized a contradiction between the direction, the movement, and the results of the historical process, on one hand, and the values and the future of literature with which he identified, on the other. The great writer, such as Mark Twain, wrote *in spite of* bourgeois society, not *thanks to* it: his unrealized artistic talent, "a certain miscarriage in his creative life," was ultimately attributable to "the obscene advance of capitalistic industrialism," to the "business regime" that was hostile to art, and to its "vast unconscious conspiracy . . . against the creative spirit."[19]

[19] Van Wyck Brooks, *The Ordeal of Mark Twain* (London, 1922), pp. 14, 65, 69, 64. In a detailed reassessment of Van Wyck Brooks, M. O. Mendelson also places his later work within this tradition; see "Van Wyck Brooks i democraticheskaya traditsia americanskogo literaturovedenia," *Sovremennoye literaturovedenie v SSA* (Contemporary Literature Studies in the USA), ed. M. O. Mendelson, A. N. Nikoljukin, and R. M. Samarin (Moscow: Nauka, 1969), pp. 159–229.

It was now no longer possible to achieve an accord between the historical activity of bourgeois society and
literary-historical development. The former had failed in its
task ("of leading the whole human race upward to all the
higher planes of culture and happiness," as Tyler still de-
manded),[20] and the latter, namely, literature, now wished to
have nothing to do with such failure. Once the most widely
read lyricist of the nineteenth century, Longfellow appeared
as an insignificant epigone of bourgeois Victorian Europe;
the congruence between public reputation and individual
achievement was jeopardized. The history of a work's reception and influence was no longer acceptable as a starting
point for critical evaluation. The effect on the audience and
the reception of the artist no longer pointed to a measure of
aesthetic value. On the contrary, since the danger of commercial temptation and artistic corruption had grown
stronger, these considerations could only serve as a negative starting point for criticism. No longer the basis of
evaluation, they were the possible cause of the *devaluation*
of the individual artistic talent. Thus, Mark Twain's most
popular dimension, the humorous, now appeared as a
destructive concession to the complacency of a "bourgeois
democracy" that was essentially hostile to culture: "the
making of the . . . undoing of the artist. It meant the su-
pression . . . of everything on which the creative instinct
feeds."[21] The *public* had wanted unproblematical humor *in
spite of* Mark Twain's creative talent. The "test" of
affirmation by the public, which was still possible for Tyler—
the relative identity of critical evaluation and public ac-
claim—is given up, and the creative power of poetry is
derived, not from its accord with bourgeois civilization, but
from a conscious or unconscious opposition to the hostility
surrounding the cultural status of literature.

[20] *Literary History of the American Revolution*, I, ix.
[21] Van Wyck Brooks, *Ordeal of Mark Twain*, pp. 215, 218; and see pp. 94 f.,
198, 219.

The methodological resolution of the growing contradiction was not superseded, as in Germany, by typological abstractions from the concrete works of literary history. On the contrary, the conditions and modes of literary development were put in a new historical perspective; artistic achievements were newly evaluated and accentuated from the point of view of contemporary social criticism. At first glance, this seemed to involve a complete break with the methods and standards of Tyler and the Victorians. In reality, however, the bourgeois-liberal position had become modified in the sense that the mode of concurrence with the literary past was radicalized; it had moved away from the practical, but not from the intellectual, consequences of its bourgeois existence. The traditional concept of a continuous reciprocal influence between art and life, which was confirmed as a basic premise in the literary criticism of William Dean Howells, had remained intact.[22] The idea of progress had undergone a change in its traditional content, but it had not been rejected as a basic postulate. The source of certain problematic developments was found not in the nature but in the inconsistency of the application of liberal democracy. The Progressive attack on the narrow-mindedness of the bourgeoisie and its hostility to the arts was aimed at industrial capitalism; it was aimed at the Victorians and their epigonal successors, rather than at the cultural ideas of the Enlightenment, which never experienced such condescending treatment as in Germany. The differences in methodology between Tyler and the Victorians, on the one hand, and Van Wyck Brooks and his generation (H. E. Sterns, Waldo Frank, Randolph Bourne), on the other, was

---

[22] Karl-Heinz Wirzberger, "The Simple, the Natural, and the Honest: William Dean Howells als Kritiker und die Durchsetzung des Realismus in der amerikanischen Literatur des ausgehenden 19. Jahrhunderts," *Zeitschrift für Anglistik und Amerikanistik*, 9 (1961), 5–48.

quite considerable but still did not exclude some basic area of a concurrence.[23]

To understand both the continuity as well as the discontinuity involved, let us here reconsider the Progressive reaction to the liberal tradition in a postliberal society. Against a background of far-reaching changes (the industrialization and monopolization of the economy, the United States entry into the ranks of expansive, imperialistic world powers, a new era of world economic crises, bitter class antagonisms and two world wars), the Progressive response to the liberal tradition gave birth to what has been termed the "greatest critical accomplishment of the period between the wars."[24] The work of the radical Jeffersonian democrat Vernon Louis Parrington, *Main Currents in American Thought* (1927–30), reflects both the triumph and the debacle of the Progressive resolution of the crisis of bourgeois liberalism. This crisis led him to question the idea of the economic freedom of the individual and resulted in a break with the philosophy of individualism and the principle of laissez-faire. Parrington turned to the study of economic and social forces, with results and conclusions that brought him close to historical materialism.[25] But the ultimate contradiction was still unresolved: was it at all possible to reconcile a socioeconomic conception of history with the platform of liberal radicalism?

[23] Howells, who had called for an "intimate dialectical connection of art and life" (Wirzberger, p. 23), thus identifying himself with the "great democratic task" of literature (p. 25), was more than the "arbiter of all elegances" (Van Wyck Brooks, *Ordeal of Mark Twain*, p. 19). In his conception of art Howells is much closer to Brooks himself than Brooks is to Allen Tate or John Crowe Ransom, for example. The underlying continuity between the Victorians and the Progressives of the twenties needs to be emphasized, even though critics such as Bernard Smith in his pioneering *Forces in American Criticism* (New York, 1939) tend to see *only* the differences and oppositions between Parrington and Tyler's "frankly idealistic" position (p. 262; and see p. 329).

[24] Henry Lüdeke, *Geschichte der amerikanischen Literatur* (Bern: Francke, 1952), p. 490.

[25] Granville Hicks, "The Critical Principles of V. L. Parrington," *Science and Society*, 3 (1939), 447.

As long as Parrington dealt with the literatures of the Colonial and Revolutionary periods, or even that of the frontier, such a reconciliation appeared possible, at least to a certain extent. The overcoming of the doctrinaire theocracy of the Puritans; liberation from the supremacy of the English; the acquisition of territory following the westward pushing of the frontier—all of these were historical situations in which the secular culture of the Enlightenment, the individualism of the Colonial revolutionary, and the utilitarianism of the settler did not run counter to the progressive course of history. Their idealized or stylized reflections in literature could still be evaluated in terms of the Jeffersonian ideal; thus, their position could be appreciated retrospectively—from the point of view of Dreiser's contemporaries— as history-promoting attitudes. Even the great figures of the Colonial period could be viewed as either pioneers or reactionaries in the social struggle for the liberation of the individual. It is for this reason that, to Parrington, the problems and themes of the literature of the Colonial period seemed by no means outdated; rather, they were felt to have relevance for America in the early twentieth century: "at heart they were much the same themes with which we are engaged, and with which our children will be engaged after us."[26]

However, when Parrington turned to the era of industrial and monopolistic capitalism, the Jeffersonian democrat placed himself in a contradictory and highly defensive position "against the plutocracy born of the Gilded Age." Criticism of the social and cultural consequences of "a dehumanized economics" became inevitable. Faced with the inferno of the Chicago "jungle" and the banality of a Babbitt-like existence, nineteenth-century liberalism had discredited itself: it had by itself refuted the principle of laissez-faire. As Parrington recognized, the reign of the

[26] Parrington, *Main Currents in American Thought: An Interpretation of American Literature from the Beginnings to 1920* (New York, 1927–30), I, i.

American "middle class" had had "unexpected consequences": "the passion for liberty is lessening and the individual . . . is being dwarfed; the drift of centralization is
shaping its inevitable tyrannies to bind us with."[27]

Parrington attacked such a tyrannical "drift of
centralization" in the economy and in society. He opposed
the "transformation of the democratic state into the servant
of proprietary interests" and the perversion of the "abstract
principle of democracy" into the "right of exploitation."
However, when criticizing the "unexpected consequences"
and the monopolistic outcome of a social order based on individual liberty and property, Parrington must have found
himself in an embarrassing position. He could not now have
recourse to the laissez-faire philosophy of industrial capitalism from which, after all, monopolism had sprung. The
idea acceptable to him was not that of freedom, as in English
liberalism, but the idea of equality in the French Enlightenment. It was not the established bourgeois parties of the proprietary "democracy," but the later political protest movements (the Greenback, Populist and Progressive parties)
which had carried on the true democratic tradition in America. And in modern literature it was not romanticism or the
heritage of the genteel tradition, but critical realism, such as
that in the work of Sinclair Lewis, which still promised an
echo of "Jean Jacques and the golden hopes of the
Enlightenment—thin and far off, no doubt, but still an
authentic echo."[28] The point of view of the critical realists
offered literary standards and a historical perspective that
seemed best suited to the usable values of the American
literary heritage. It was a contemporary point of view that
now seemed to allow for the greatest possible area of correlation between past structure and present function.

Thus, there emerged a contemporary position in historical criticism that, again, was able to look upon itself as

[27] Ibid., III, x and xv (E. H. Eby's Preface), xx (Parrington's Foreword).
[28] Ibid., pp. xxiv, 367.

the true continuation and affirmation of national history. Writing under the pressure of a new and frightening social experience, Parrington was faced with, and prepared for, the need for a radical reordering of values. Although he himself did not live to follow his own challenging postulate, the need for a historical reinterpretation emerges as the logical consequence of a remarkably consistent thought process. The limitations of his Jeffersonian point of departure are unreservedly admitted, when he writes in the unfinished introduction to the third volume of *Main Currents:*

Amidst all the turmoil and vague subconscious tendencies, certain ideas slowly clarified: first, that the earlier democratic aspirations had somehow failed, that an equalitarian philosophy adapted to frontier conditions could not easily be carried over into a centralizing and stratifying America and was doomed to eventual defeat; second, that even in the supposed heyday of our democracy, we had never achieved a democracy, but rather a careless individualism that left society at the mercy of a rapacious middle class; third, that we must take our bearings afresh and set forth on a different path to the goal."[29]

These conclusions pointed beyond the Progressive response to the crisis of the liberal tradition in a postliberal society, and it was Victor Francis Calverton, Granville Hicks, Newton Arvin, and the Marxist critics who, during the thirties, adopted the perspective of a radical democracy as a most consistent point of reference.[30] Thus, after Parrington the Progressive tradition in literary history either moved on to a Marxist position (though this turned out to be a somewhat ephemeral move) or it had to reaccommodate itself

<hr />

[29] P. xxvii.

[30] See Rudolf Sühnel, "The Marxist Trend in Literary Criticism in the USA in the Thirties," *Jahrbuch für Amerikastudien,* 7 (1962), 53–66. There is an as yet unpublished survey by David Peck of the Progressive literary tradition in the thirties, which, together with Eberhard Brüning's studies on the subject, is the best I have seen; see also David Peck, "'The Orgy of Apology': The Recent Reevaluation of Literature of the Thirties," *Science and Society,* 32 (1968), 371–82, which suggests that the thirties were approached with a "point of view which is basically antipathetic to many of the literary ideas and movements of the decade" (p. 372).

with a liberal (and increasingly eclectic) approach to the sociological definition of the national heritage.

As late as 1948 the *Literary History of the United States* attempted, with questionable success, to synthesize and adapt the various Progressive and liberal positions to the early postwar situation. On the one hand, it still clings to the social-historical interpretation of "American literature in its historical relation to the American nation."[31] On the other hand, the emphasis on the original American impulses (in Walt Whitman or Mark Twain) is complemented by a less partisan evaluation of the more European-oriented authors (from Edgar Allan Poe to Henry James), and Parrington's orientation, which tended more toward the history of ideas, is extended by a more complex, though less unified, approach to the relationship of literature and society. Literature is presented as a product but also as an expression and function of American society. It forms and represents the national character; at the same time it maintains a reciprocal relationship to the most basic ideological, political, and economic efforts of the nation. In this sense the title may be considered programmatic: the aim is no more and no less than a literary history of the United States.

This concept is based on an understanding of history which, although it questions the traditional idea of progress, is prepared to affirm it in a modified form.

Progress, for example, as a concept may have little general validity; but whether we call it progress, or change, or development, increasing power and vitality are extraordinarily characteristic of the American nineteenth century—with which so much of this book is concerned. Never has nature been so rapidly and so extensively altered by the efforts of man in so brief a time. Never has conquest resulted in a more vigorous development of initiative, individualism, self-reliance, and demands for freedom. Never have the defeats which preceded and accompanied this conquest of nature led to more surprising frustration, decadence,

---

[31] Hans Galinski, "Strömungen der neueren amerikanischen Literaturbetrachtung in der *Literary History of the United States (1949),*" *Die Neueren Sprachen* (1952), p. 195.

sterility, and dull standardization. All this is in American literature, and the causes of both our successes and failures are implicit, and often explicit, in our early national books.[32]

This shows how history-making *Praxis*, the activities of men, became a factor of historical consciousness, and much more so than in Western Europe. To be sure, the course of history is no longer considered as progressively rich in intellectual achievements. It is not culture, but initiative, that progresses. It is not the liberties that grow, but the demands for more freedom. Progress no longer is an unambiguous phenomenon; it is accompanied by "decadence, sterility, and dull standardization." It is, above all, material achievements that are unambiguous, the "increasing power" of America: the "nature" that has been so "rapidly and so extensively" conquered by man. Of course, there are also signs of "vitality," "self-confidence," and the "drive for liberty," but these are the tendencies which can easily be frustrated. Moreover, in the mid-forties, immediately after the historic victory over the antidemocratic alliance, it seemed possible to suggest, and to hope for, a solution of at least some of the contradictions. The modified idea of "progress, or change, or development" refers back to the "human" and "optimistic" qualities of American literature, and it derives its most original and valuable impulses from the "practice of democratic life" and from an awareness of the "needs of the simple people." These impulses do not yet find themselves in an irresolvable opposition to the image and the imagination of the "individual." Consequently, American literature is seen as "a literature profoundly influenced by ideals and by practices developed in democratic living. It has been intensely conscious of the aspirations of the individual in such a democracy as we have known here. It has been humanitarian. It has been, on the whole, an optimistic literature,

---

[32]*Literary History of the United States*, ed. Robert E. Spiller et al., 3 vols. (New York, 1948), I, xv (hereafter cited as *LHUS*).

made virile by criticism of the actual in comparison with the ideal."[33]

Thus, out of the contradiction between the ideal and the actual, social criticism is affirmed as a true impulse of American literary development. But the contradictions in question are not uncovered with the acuity of Brooks or the consistency of Parrington, and even the subdued optimism cannot quite conceal a certain apologetic tinge, appearing at times somewhat labored: "a sort of compulsory cheerfulness keeps breaking in."[34]

At the same time there appears a somewhat dubious new emphasis in historiographic method. Historical development is not considered in its full temporal complexity: it is supposed that beside and behind the social forces there is some organic principle at work that fulfills itself in cyclical evolution. The editors of the *Literary History* take a "cycle" to be "the social development beginning with territorial conquest and leading to the full realization of a firm social order which, at first confining creative literary activity to the form of political and religious documentation, gradually allows primitive and imitative poetry, and finds its own organic artistic expression only during the phase of completion."[35] Aside from these "cultural waves" there are two overlapping cycles: one, which takes its origin from the eastern settlement of New England and the merging of nationalities on the entire continent and climaxes during the period between the two world wars in an "era of complete national fulfillment"; and a second American "renaissance," which is, however, of world literary importance, its focal point being the symbolic-realistic works of O'Neill, Hemingway, and Faulkner.

---

[33] Ibid., p. xvi.

[34] Leslie A. Fiedler, "American Literature," *Contemporary Literary Scholarship: A Critical Review*, ed. Lewis Leary (New York, 1958), p. 166.

[35] F. H. Link, *Amerikanische Literaturgeschichtsschreibung: Ein Forschungsbericht* (Stuttgart: Metzler, 1963), p. 14; see *LHUS*, I, xviii, et passim.

This theory involves a contradictory methodology: on the one hand, there is the rational sociology and the history of social and economic development; on the other, there is a turning, articulated later by Robert E. Spiller, against the materialistic concept of history and against the rational view of history that for him (1955) appeared suspiciously close to a "Marxian formula." It is replaced by a biologically or existentially conceived principle of development according to which each distinguishable unit partakes of "the circular pattern of life": "it has a beginning, a life cycle, and an end." However, this view of history with its Spenglerian echoes provides for the study of American literature a pseudoexplanation in which apology and commonplace combine: "Every action has a reaction, every rise a fall, every radical movement an ultimate conservatism."[36] Instead of a philosophy of history we find the formula of the swinging pendulum.

Social History versus Aesthetic Structure

The *Literary History of the United States* appeared at a time when the bases of the Progressive approach to history were undergoing rapid changes, and new modes of criticism and ideology were beginning to dominate the literary scene. Against these, the "sociologizing liberalism"[37] of the *Literary History* found itself in a precarious position. So far, the editors had followed a traditional approach, but they had neglected (in their characteristically pragmatic stance) to put their historical approach to literature on solid theoretical

[36]Spiller, *The Cycle of American Literature: An Essay in Historical Criticism* (New York, 1955), pp. xiii, xii, xiii, 301. Interestingly enough, the idea of the "culture-cycle, as Spengler convincingly described it," crops up in the later writings of Van Wyck Brooks; see *The Flowering of New England* (New York, 1952), p. 539; also, his Introduction to *The Reader's Encyclopedia of American Literature*, ed. Max J. Herzberg et al. (New York, 1963), p. v.

[37]Fiedler, "American Literature," p. 167.

foundations. For example, the concept of literature (as we saw) had been defined in a manner as traditional as it was all-encompassing: "the record of man made enduring by the right words in the right order"; this involved "any writing in which aesthetic, emotional, or intellectual values are made articulate by excellent expression."[38] Such a definition was not far removed from the one assumed by Moses Coit Tyler. The lumping together of aesthetic, emotional, and intellectual values leaves no doubt that the appended standard of "excellent expression" was too naive and ill equipped to meet the much more sophisticated conceptions of the New Criticism in any but a desperately defensive way. To be sure, the formalist claim of the autonomy of art was itself incapable of both connecting, and at the same time differentiating between, the specific modes and values of the literary process and that of society and culture. What was needed was a historically founded theory of the aesthetic mode of literature which, on the one hand, would recognize and specify the unique quality and function of art but, on the other hand, would also be in a position to correlate the aesthetic mode to that context of nonaesthetic activities against which alone (and in reference to which only) the specific nature and the mode of literature could be defined in the first place.

If, in 1948, it was still possible for the *Literary History* to ignore such questions of literary theory, only a decade later its most prominent editor, Robert E. Spiller, had to concede the resultant problems and weaknesss. But the dilemma of the liberal position was even more profound: it was the dilemma of a literary criticism that had reemphasized the sociological dimension of literature without retaining the traditional concept of the unity of social function and aesthetic value. It is true that Parrington and the early Van

---

[38]*LHUS*, II, xvi. Unfortunately, connections are sometimes postulated theoretically, but not demonstrated practically. The verbal statement is not turned into a structuring principle.

Wyck Brooks, at least implicitly, had already argued against
the spontaneous congruence of social and aesthetic values;
but now the diverging modes of the sociological and the
aesthetic approaches were moving farther and farther apart.
The correlation between the factors of history and the works
of literature, which for Tyler had been a matter of course,
had meanwhile become a very precarious undertaking. The
unity of the two was replaced by a new kind of dualism that
Spiller (ten years after publication) recognized as a basic
methodological dilemma. And this dilemma, he remarked,
was central: "The development of a method for American
Studies is bound up with the effort to resolve the dilemma
posed by the dualism which separates social facts from
aesthetic values."[39] Spiller argued that the "dualism" of
"historical fact" and "aesthetic value" could only be miti-
gated by a "dynamic cooperation" between historical and
aesthetic studies.

But behind this ringing call for cooperation, there was
the defensive and eclectic position of the post-Progressive
literary historian. Such a call did not even aim at a workable
integration but contented itself with the plea for "a tolerant
relationship of cooperation between the two disciplines."
Instead of overcoming that deplorable "dualism," one had
to find satisfaction in a program of methodological compromise that was careful to constitute itself outside the pale
of a *Literaturwissenschaft*: the desired synthesis was called,
not literary history, but American Studies. It led to that
symbol-myth-image school of cultural analysis that reached
its peak in *The American Adam*. But that was, as a recent
critic remarked, "an ironic effort to salvage what's left of
Parrington after Trilling and Niebuhr had got through with
him." At the same time, American Studies helped to
constitute that vogue of a disembodied history of ideas
which, in its concern for consensus, perpetuated, as

[39]"Value and Method in American Studies: The Literary versus the Social
Approach," *Jahrbuch für Amerikastudien*, 4 (1959), 20, 21.

Christopher Lasch wrote, "a nationalistic myth of American uniqueness."[40]

In spite of all willingness to compromise, the desired "dynamic cooperation" between aesthetics and history appeared still in danger, and the future of literary history as represented by Parrington and the *Literary History* was still uncertain. Thus, Spiller wrote in 1959: "The irony of the present situation in social and humanistic scholarship in the United States is that the trend is counter to any such cooperation. . . . If this trend continues, American Studies may well become a branch of sociology and move with the purists in that field into severely limited and definable areas of research or it may dissolve with the New Criticism into the vacuum of pure literary analysis." This statement sharply defined the methodological dilemma of traditional literary history: the path between the extremes of sociology and formalism had narrowed. And the traditional methods of literary history still found themselves placed between the Scylla of the *nonliterary* and the Charybdis of the *purely literary*. These were problems that had not seemed to exist at the time of Tyler, or Parrington, or even in the early forties. In this sense the conjecture made by Howard Mumford Jones as early as 1948 had come true: the publication of the *Literary History of the United States* signified the end of an epoch in historiography.[41] Thereafter, American literary history not only had to seek new methodological foundations

[40]Wise, *American Historical Explanations*, p. 314; Lasch, "The Cultural Cold War: A Short History of the Congress for Cultural Freedom," in *Towards a New Past*, ed. Bernstein, p. 323. (The passage is deleted in the book version.) See also Ursula Brumm, in *Jahrbuch für Amerikastudien*, 6 (1961), 78 ff.; *Studies in American Culture*, ed. J. J. Kwiat and M. C. Turpie (Minneapolis, 1960); *American Studies in Transition*, ed. M. W. Fishwick (Philadelphia, 1964); Leo Marx, "American Studies: A Defense of an Unscientific Method," *New Literary History*, 1 (1969/70), 75–90, who while stressing "our notorious methodological deficiencies" refers to the existing distances from both the "physical sciences" and the "social scientific disciplines" (p. 76).

[41]Spiller, "Value and Method in American Studies," pp. 21–23; Jones, *Theory of American Literature*, p. 175.

but had to defend itself against a new ideology that provided the basis for a revision of both the Progressive and the liberal views of history.

Beyond Liberalism: The Nietzschean Revision

At this point an excursion into the wider areas and sources of this revision seems helpful. As I have suggested in regard to the crisis of the Victorian liberal sense of tradition, these areas cannot be seen as confined within national boundaries.[42] Rather, they are linked with those vast economic, social, and political changes from a laissez-faire economy to a monopolistic type of capitalism—changes that are reflected in that gradual reorientation of European social and historical thought ushered in by Friedrich Nietzsche and the antiliberal ideology in Western Europe.[43] With regard to the development of American literary history this means, among other things, that its crisis, although it occurred relatively late, is not an isolated phenomenon. But to view it in connection with the larger crisis in European historical thought is not simply to raise the question of influence. (Besides, the proposition "that the European and, above all, the German consciousness of crisis has influenced American thought" seems much less important than the fact that such an influence *could* be exerted.)[44] It is of course true that the essentially antihistorical impulses of Croce, Maurras, and

[42] See pp. 58, 82–88.

[43] See H. S. Hughes, *Consciousness and Society: The Reorientation of European Social Thought* (London, 1959); the following paragraphs take up a point that I first made in *New Criticism und die Entwicklung bürgerlicher Literaturwissenschaft* (Halle: VEB Max Niemeyer, 1962), pp. 119–30.

[44] Helmut Kuhn, "Krisenbewuβtsein in Amerika," *Jahrbuch für Amerikastudien*, 1 (1956), 54. But the influence was also the other way round: as early as 1929, E. R. Curtius dealt intensively with T. S. Eliot; see his essay "T. S. Eliot als Kritiker," *Die Literatur*, 32 (October 1929), 11–15. In *Europäische Literatur und lateinische Mittelalter* (Bern: Francke, 1948), Curtius uses some of Eliot's basic conceptions (for example, "For literature, all past is present" [p. 22]), and he quotes (p. 334) from the *Selected Essays*.

Hulme had an effect on T. S. Eliot and that it is difficult to underrate the impact of Eliot on American literary criticism. Yet the prerequisite for the rise and development of a new American approach to literary history was to be found in the American situation itself. This is the basis of all analogies between the European and the American developments—analogies that are based mainly on the common renunciation of the methods of positivism, historical philology, and related forms of the ideology of liberalism.

The crisis in historical consciousness has a history of more than a hundred years.[45] It is probably not fortuitous that it was in Germany, after the defeat of the bourgeois revolution of 1848, that the renunciation of the Enlightenment idea of progress set in so prematurely. It was here that, in the social sciences, the rejection of the concept of scientific law was so systematic and the turn to an irrational ideology took place so early and so unsettlingly. In this context, the main directions of a new type of antihistoricism began to emerge with Nietzsche. Nietzsche first recognized the new "contradition between life and knowledge," experience and weltanschauung. He saw the threat to that social order which, for all his critiques, he passionately defended. Thus he attempted to revise, and even to abolish, the concept of law in the social sciences, which he considered "true, but deadly," in favor of some vitalistic philosophy.[46]

In this connection it must be remembered that, when speaking of the "dangers of our life and our culture," Nietzsche did have in mind the "mass of the people and the working class" of *his* time. This is the case in the second of his *Unzeitgemäße Betrachtungen*, conceived shortly after

---

[45]See the wealth of material in I. S. Kon, *Die Geschichtsphilosophie des 20. Jahrhunderts: Kritischer Abriss*, trans. W. Hoepp, 2 vols. (Berlin: Akademie-Verlag, 1964).

[46]Friedrich Nietzsche, *Gesammelte Werke* (Munich: Musarion Verlag, 1920–29), VI, 317.

1871, the year of the Paris commune. Here, for the first time and quite deliberately, he turned away from the liberal ideology and the materialistic view of history, chiefly because such a view could make possible or cause "terrible eruptions of imprudent egoism" in the proletariat.[47]

Surely, this is an hour fraught with danger: mankind seems to have come close to discovering that the egoism of the individual, of groups, or of the masses was at all times the source of historical motion; at the same time, no one is in the least alarmed on account of this discovery; instead, one decrees: let egoism be our God. With this new creed one goes about intentionally erecting future history on the basis of egoism: only, let it be a clever egotism, one that will subject itself to a few limitations in order to make its position more permanent, one which will study its history for the purpose of learning about non-clever egoism. In this study it has been learned that the state has a very special mission in the world system of egoism to be founded: it is to become the patron of all clever egoisms in order to protect them with its military and police force from the terrible eruptions of not-so-clever egoism. To the same end, the teachings of history—as animal and human history—will be spread among the dangerous, because un-clever masses of the people and the working classes.[48]

In the age of the awakening and organization of the labor movement, the materialistic conception of history "from the point of view of the masses" had become unbearable. It produced that "contradiction between life and knowledge" behind which Nietzsche almost intuitively sensed an antinomy between self-preservation and consciousness, between class ideology and truth, between apologetics and science. Since "all clarity, all naturalness and purity in that relationship between life and history" seemed jeopardized,[49] the antiliberal philosopher rejected not only the popularization of history but the whole discipline of history as a science with its "laws" because to him it now appeared "worthless":

Go on . . . writing history from the point of view of the *masses* and searching it for those laws which derive from the needs of these masses,

---

[47] Ibid., pp. 310, 313.   [48] Ibid., pp. 312 f.   [49] Ibid., pp. 317, 257.

that is to say, from the laws of motion of the lowest loam and clay strata in society. The masses . . . for the rest, may the devil and statistics take them. What? Statistics proves that there are laws in history? Laws? Yes, it proves how common and disgustingly uniform the mass is: shall the effects of those forces of gravity, stupidity, imitation, love, and hunger be termed laws? Well, let us admit it; but then it also proves this: insofar as there are laws in history, the laws are worthless and so is history.[50]

Against this background Nietzsche's seminal attack on the "objectivity" of history and "the demand that history should be a science" acquires an entirely new emphasis that is not at all contradicted by his brilliant (and largely justified) polemic against positivists and cultural "philistines."[51] For Nietzsche did not simply reject the methods of positivism. He surrendered a rational methodology by which the direction of the events of the past could be functionally related to a consistently historical understanding of life in the present. The relationship between past history and the study of "history," on the one hand, and the practical needs of living, the "life" of the ruling class, on the other, had become problematic: all previous "clarity," the "naturalness," and the "purity" in this relationship were found wanting. The structure of the historical process in reality and the function of the historical consciousness had become unbearably incongruous. The new methodology was to eliminate the contradiction between "life" and historical "knowledge," and "life" was to be reasserted against the laws in history and *against* the very "knowledge" which "proves that there are laws in history."

The Nietzschean revision was followed and taken up by many disciples, particularly in Germany. Thus, Oswald Spengler maintained: "To want to treat history scientifically is in the final analysis always something contradictory . . . history should be the subject of poetry." Rudolf Eucken expressed himself in a similar fashion when he denied "any possibility of framing an over-all picture, of discovering a sense of the whole"; in his attack on the "advocates of a

---

[50] Ibid., pp. 310 f.   [51] Ibid., p. 258.

scientific world-view" he affirmed the antinomy advocated by Nietzsche between (contemporary) "life" and (historical) "law" and arrived at the conclusion "that science cannot grant knowledge in our sense and cannot bind man and the world together." The philosophical idea of the German *Klassik* of the identity of the human and the historical was thus revoked. Whereas the *Geistesgeschichte* following Dilthey was still looking for the neo-Kantian compromise, it had already—with Rickert and Windelband—taken its direction from the opposition to natural science and had postulated as an alternative to the "explanatory science of laws" a vitalizing "science of events."[52] The recognition of objective connections was replaced by the "supra-rational act of true understanding which by nature demands that the possibilities for a real enactment have to be present in the experience, in the subject." This theory of understanding developed by Dilthey, Spranger, Rothacker, Bollnow, and others "does not seek the most accurate statement of a situation," but involves an irrational "synthesis of two life-forms."[53] In order to understand a historical phenomenon in this sense, it was not necessary to relate it to existing historical processes but to the inner experience of the observer and to the timeless, given "forms of life" of man which "are now to be applied to the phenomena of historical and social reality" as "timeless ideal types" or "normal structures." Thus, typological formulas had been found which, in combination with Wölfflin's psychology of style, "soon became a deadly Procrustean bed for historical life."[54] These were for-

---

[52] Spengler, *Der Untergang des Abendlandes*, 6th ed. (Munich: Beck, 1920), p. 139; Eucken, *Erkennen und Leben* (Leipzig: Quelle u. Meyer, 1912), pp. 12 ff.; Wilhelm Windelband, *Geschichte und Naturwissenschaft*, 2d ed. (Straβburg: Heitz, 1900), p. 12.

[53] Hanns Haeckel, "Das Problem von Wesen, Möglichkeiten und Grenzen des Verstehens für den Literarhistoriker," *Deutsche Vierteljahrsschrift*, 27 (1953), 439, 438.

[54] Eduard Spranger, *Lebensformen*, 6th ed. (Halle: Niemeyer, 1927), p. 114. "Thus, typology is the last grimace with which a fettered historical consciousness takes its revenge" (Werner Krauss, "Literaturgeschichte als geschichtlicher Auftrag," p. 100).

mulas of abstraction from real, historical processes that in some respects anticipated the later abstractions of the mythological and the more irrational types of the recent hermeneutic approaches to literature in America.

A Revised American Past: The Dichotomy of Impact and Evaluation

Even though the modes and methods of German *Geistesgeschichte* were at first rejected unambiguously, even contemptuously,[55] the new postwar American historical consciousness developed along lines that at least in part are comparable to the direction of the vitalistic idea of history. In both instances the development leads to a revision of the eighteenth-century heritage and a reduction in the consciousness of the links between a revolutionary past and a conservative present. To understand these postwar developments is to realize that behind (and beside) the analogies there are, in America, also impulses of a different nature at work whose confusing diversity must not be brought under one rubric, any more than the social and institutional context in which they are rooted. Even so, it seems possible to generalize the existence of a "consciousness of crisis" that, as Golo Mann observes, is above all the "crisis of the optimistic American belief in progress." This, of course, has roots in earlier twentieth-century history, such as in the Great Depression; still, it can be directly related, as Mann suggests, to the more recent emergence of "new relationships with a larger, more self-willed world outside." If we assume that North America (which was, after all, "so much accustomed to controlling its own destiny") is now faced with a "world full of resistance . . . engaged in the most far-reaching

---

[55] R. S. Crane speaks of "analogizing devices" (*Philological Quarterly*, 14 [1935], 154); René Wellek refers to those "fantastic, quibbling, pseudo-mystical, verbalistic productions" in Cysarz, Deutschbein, Meissner, and Stefansky (*Theory of Literature* [London, 1949], p. 117).

changes in the history of mankind," then this may well account for that "element of the unpredictable, terrifying, alien" which abruptly breaks into American historical thinking.[56]

The point made by European historians, such as Golo Mann or Herbert Butterfield, namely, that the historical conscience in America is profoundly affected by the "revolutions" of our time, is borne out by American historians themselves.[57] Looking back at the period I have discussed above, Robert L. Heilbroner writes:

No more than thirty years ago, the United States represented a form of economic and political society whose prospects and permanence were unquestioned. Today we find ourselves in a position of defensive insecurity. Who would have denied the brilliance of the outlook for the United States during the first quarter of the twentieth century? Who can confidently assert as much in the century's middle years? . . . We feel ourselves beleaguered by happenings which seem not only malign and intransigent, but unpredictable. We are at a loss to know how to anticipate the events the future may bring or how to account for those events once they are happened. The future itself is a direction in which we look no longer with confidence but with vague forebodings and a sense of unpreparedness. . . . At bottom our troubled state of mind reflects an inability to see the future in an *historic* context. If current events strike us as all surprise and shock it is because we cannot see these events in a meaningful framework.[58]

Small wonder, then, that historians like Heilbroner or Henry Steele Commager diagnose symptoms of intellectual "uncertainty," "doubt," "insecurity," and "disorder."[59] As

---

[56] *Vom Geiste Amerikas*, 2d ed. (Zurich: Europa Verlag, 1955), pp. 172, 47, 21.

[57] Herbert Butterfield, *History and Human Relations* (London, 1951), p. 160.

[58] *The Future as History: The Historic Currents of Our Time and the Direction in Which They Are Taking America* (New York, 1960), p. 15. In his more recent essay "The Human Prospect" (*New York Review*, Jan. 24, 1974, pp. 21–34), the dilemma is even more strongly generalized: "The values of an industrial civilization, which has for two centuries given us . . . a sense of *élan* and purpose, now seem to be losing their self-evident justification" (p. 22).

[59] Commager, *The American Mind: An Interpretation of American Thought and Character since the 1880's* (New Haven, 1950), p. 407.

key words of the new postwar intellectual climate, "surprise" and "shock" become the expression of a "disorientation before the future," of an uncertain relationship to the future that now, for the first time in North America, can no longer be considered as a predictable extension of the present: "If the future seems to us a kind of limbo, a repository of endless surprises, it is because we no longer see it as the expected culmination of the past, as the growing edge of the present."[60]

All this points to the changing premises of historical thinking. The history-making values of the past find a changing response in the present. The leading social and intellectual forces of American history, expressed in the rationalistic and democratic ideas from Jefferson to Parrington, the spirit of the American Revolution, and the Declaration of Independence, are no longer *usable* in the same way that they were for Moses Coit Tyler. Since the present is seen no longer as the "expected culmination" of the past, the past itself cannot so easily be construed as an inevitable or meaningful condition of the American present. There is lacking that "meaningful framework" comprising past events and present perspectives that was still available for American historians from Tyler to Parrington. Now the past fails to anticipate and to confirm the directions of the present, and vice versa: today's historian has a hard time affirming the rationalistic and optimistic heritage of the past which, he may feel, is not so much affirmed and enhanced by the present but, rather, revoked and frustrated. Consequently, the correlation between past achievements and present functions becomes more and more difficult, and the methodological unity of object-directed standards and those expressive of the *Praxis* of the present is seriously endangered. The alternative is an evaluation of the past in terms of the standards of the past (that is, a new relativism) or a distortion of

[60]Heilbroner, p. 15.

the past by the standards of the present, which are no longer congenial to the values of that past.

To speak of such an alternative is, of course, a considerable oversimplification, but it points to a methodological dilemma which, in Western literary criticism, amounted almost to a "disintegration of historical consciousness."[61] As early as the late forties and early fifties two tendencies developed: on the one hand, there occurred a more or less consistent turning away from the historical view of literature altogether (on the grounds that such a view had less educational value than the aesthetic view); on the other hand, there developed a new revisionism involving reinterpretations of American history and literary history that tended to be based on anti-Enlightenment or antiliberal points of reference, but also on mythological or anthropological concepts or on Freudean or Jungian psychology. These revisions by themselves reflect the crisis of *Wirkungsgeschichte* as the crisis of a tradition that was becoming paralyzed or demoralized by the sense of its own loss of social function and consequent ineffectiveness.

As an example of the revised conception of the course of American history, let us have a look at the works of Daniel J. Boorstin which appeared in the late forties and fifties (among them *The Lost World of Thomas Jefferson*, 1948; *The Genius of American Politics*, 1953; *The Americans: The Colonial Experience*, 1958). These attempted no more and no less than a consistent reinterpretation of the early history of the American nation. Without wishing to suggest an altogether too direct connection between the revisionism in political history and the reinterpretation of literary history, I

[61]Max Wehrli, *Allgemeine Literaturwissenschaft* (Bern: Francke, 1951), p. 133; for a broader view, see Kurt Sontheimer, "Der Antihistorizismus des gegenwärtigen Zeitalters," *Neue Rundschau*, 75 (1964), 612; or, as one among many American voices, G. J. Roush, "What Will Become of the Past?" *Daedalus*, 98 (1969), 641–53; Jan Brandt Corstius sums up a widespread feeling when he says, "It is beyond doubt that today the historical sense is weakening" ("Literary History and the Study of Literature," *New Literary History*, 2 [1970/71], 65).

believe that we can observe how Boorstin prepared the way
for two emphases which, in a different and somewhat
weakened form, can be traced also in the contemporary re-
cantation of the liberal and Progressive perspectives on
literary history. These were, first, a new interpretation of the
American Revolution and the European Enlightenment, as
well as their reciprocal relationships; second, and in connection with that, a new emphasis on the "American frame
of mind" and its role in the course of national history, especially with respect to the frontier.

The new perspective on the Revolution and the
Enlightenment involved the kind of revision that faithfully
reflected the era of the Cold War and the period of Mc-
Carthyism: the American Revolution was really not a revolutionary act at all, but rather the conservative victory of
constitutional right—that is, it was "a pretty technical legal
problem." Says Boorstin: "It has never been quite clear to
me why historians would not have found our revolution
significant enough merely as a victory of constitution-
alism."[62] The question why in the past a so potentially sub-
versive interpretation of the Revolution (namely, as a
political revolution) was at all seriously entertained was
answered by Boorstin with a new thesis no less revisionist:
the Revolution had up to now always been considered in the
light of the ideas and goals of the European Enlightenment
and had thus been profoundly misunderstood. The European
Enlightenment and other "such abstract, systematized, and
cosmopolitan notions" had sprung from the minds of radical
intellectuals—as had originally the entirely "un-American
demand for a philosophy of democracy."[63] For this reason
the Enlightenment had accomplished little, almost nothing
for the American nation, and a methodology working from
Enlightenment concepts of philosophy and history could

[62] *The Genius of American Politics* (Chicago, 1953), pp. 76, 68.
[63] Boorstin, *The Americans: The Colonial Experience* (New York, 1958), p.
394; *Genius of American Politics*, p. 184.

only betray a lack of understanding of American history. And the Declaration of Independence with its postulate that all men had been created equal? The Declaration of Independence, says Boorstin, is a constitutional revocation of the Colonial state, and the postulate of equality is not to be seen as a political statement.

Though the ideological raison d'être of this reinterpretation hardly needs any comment, the mode of reasoning deserves to be noted.[64] The rejection of the Enlightenment (so typical of postwar America) was based not simply on a new interpretation of constitutional history and the history of ideas but also on much less tangible cultural and psychological considerations: the lack of interest in Enlightenment ideas, which in turn had resulted from the Colonial experience, and the struggle against the wilderness of the American frontier. The overwhelming experience was one of the worthlessness of theory, ideology, and utopia. Hence developed the kind of national temper and the practical attitudes that determined the American frame of mind, which by its own nature turned out to be impervious to the reception of a social and political philosophy. But in referring to the (admittedly) huge importance of the westward-moving frontier, Boorstin did not simply paraphrase the well-known ideas of Frederick Jackson Turner. Whereas Turner sought to base the native sources of the American character on strictly historical foundations, Boorstin reduces the entire history itself to a function of national character. The uniqueness of the national temper is taken to constitute a historical experience in terms of a quest for identity and a manifest destiny. As a Western European historian puts it, such concepts become both "the navel of history and the principle of its explanation." They come

---

[64]F. H. Tenbruck, "Geist und Geschichte in Amerika," *Jahrbuch für Amerikastudien*, 4 (1959), 107–42. For criticism of Boorstin's conception of the Enlightenment, see Henry F. May, "The Problem of the American Enlightenment," *New Literary History*, 1 (1969/70), 203 f.

fatefully close to the typological and nationalistic concepts of German *Geistesgeschichte:* these, too, were concerned with the presentation of national characteristics as more or less incomparable and unchangeable, to be understood only from within themselves. In both cases social schisms are covered up by anthropological conceptions of cultural unity that facilitate the "renunciation of rational understanding."[65] Ultimately, there is a similar apotheosis of experience, an almost Nietzschean glorification of the vital as opposed to the intellectual ("it was life, and not thought, which would excel here") and a comparable rhetoric that substitutes biological metaphors for analytical concepts, as in Boorstin's rejection of "the *cancers* of European life (and especially of European political life)."[66]

This is not the place for tracing the antiliberal revision of political history in any detail; nor can I here do justice to the much more sober and self-critical positions in Boorstin's later writings. Yet Boorstin's early work may serve as a representative instance of the new conservative attitude forming part of the ideological background against which the mid-twentieth-century break in the main currents of American literary history can profitably be understood.

However, to illustrate this break in the more specific terms of a revised literary history calls for an example; Randall Stewart's study *American Literature and Christian Doctrine* (1958) may perhaps best serve. In reconsidering this book, let us first of all note the author's undisguised distaste for the traditional standards of academic objectivity, or

[65] Tenbruck, pp. 121, 124.

[66] Boorstin, *Genius of American Politics*, p. 182 (my emphasis); see the entire chapter "Our Cultural Hypochondria and How to Cure It" (pp. 161–86), which starts from the concept of American "givenness" (pp. 8 ff., 162 ff.) and an apology for manifest destiny, but proceeds to a rejection of the aggressive "crusading spirit" (pp. 185 ff.). It seems ironic that Boorstin, the maker of *images* and the champion of ideological autarchy, in the end felt haunted by the confusion and immobility of American image-thinking, which he came to consider as the symptom of a national alienation from reality. See his *The Image, or What Happened to the American Dream* (New York, 1961).

"neutrality." Says Stewart: "I must confess to a growing impatience with the traditional academic adoration of the objective, disinterested, neutral approach to all questions. . . . There is an uncomfortably close kinship, I fear, between neutrality and sterility." Behind these words there is the attempt, so characteristic of the fifties, to reconcile the more pragmatic position of American conservatism with the Christian orthodoxy represented by such writers as T. E. Hulme, T. S. Eliot, and Allen Tate. Stewart's work appears so significant because it takes up the orthodox perspective (which was associated with some of the leading representatives of the New Criticism) and proceeds to develop it, with some consistency, in the area of literary history. Stewart writes:

I have insisted upon certain tests of Christian orthodoxy—the chief test being a recognition of Original Sin—and I have tried to make it clear that while certain great writers meet these tests sufficiently to be called "orthodox," others—and among them, some of our most famous, influential, and "democratic" writers—have unmistakably strayed beyond the bounds of Christian orthodoxy. . . . It would be ironical indeed for the Christian standpoint if the unorthodox writers were regarded as more "American" or more "democratic" than the orthodox, and yet some of our most important historians have implied as much, and have led us to believe that our democratic culture can be defined best in terms of the ideas of such heterodox thinkers as Jefferson, Emerson, and Whitman.

Consequently, Stewart proposes "to reexamine the bases of our democratic assumptions, and especially to explore the needs of the present and future. For may it not very well be that certain writers, however important their contributions in the past, have lost in modern time much of their usefulness, and certain other writers, however disvalued by social historians in the past, are about to acquire a special, new usefulness?"[67]

[67] *American Literature and Christian Doctrine* (Baton Rouge, La., 1958), pp. viii f.

Here, the contradiction between past achievement and present function is quite conspicuous. The great writers in the democratic tradition, among them Emerson, Melville, and Whitman, have lost "much of their usefulness." There is a gap between the importance of "their contributions in the past" and their present function, just as there is a chasm between the past values and the modern revaluations of those writers who, "however disvalued" in the past, are said to acquire "a special, new usefulness" in the present. The reinterpretation is as drastic as it is consistent (and remarkably free from the complacency which, in this period, can be found in so many liberal historians).[68] Stewart takes up the cultural criticism of the Southern Agrarians, whom he follows in his deliberately "reactionary" position. Thus, in pointing to Allen Tate's *Reactionary Essays*, he does not hesitate to regret the fact that in North America the word *reactionary* still has a pejorative meaning ("so ingrained in America is the progressive idea").[69]

It is by challenging the admitted ingrainedness of the progressive idea that Stewart develops a revised view of American literary history. Jefferson for him now appears "a bit naive," the democratic idea of equality as a "great lie"— "Jefferson's 'great lie'" (in the sense of Robert Penn Warren's *Brother to Dragons*). Similarly, Thomas Paine is considered of no help in pointing the future, much like his fellow deist Benjamin Franklin.[70] And whereas Spiller in the *Literary History of the United States* was still able to consider Ralph Waldo Emerson the "spokesman for his time and country," even a "prophet" of the "American spirit," and to emphasize his "preeminence" and "eternal human verities," he appears now, like Walt Whitman, as an "archheretic" ("Emerson is the arch-heretic of American Literature, and Emersonism the greatest heresy").[71]

No further illustration is needed to reveal how this re-

---

[68]See ibid., pp. 57, 147. [69]Ibid., p. 128. [70]Ibid., pp. 40, 358, 387.
[71]Spiller, *Cycle of American Literature*, p. 57; Stewart, p. 55.

vision of American literary history culminates in an ideological affront against the greatest of its history-making figures and ideas. The postliberal historian is prepared, and even determined, to face the chasm between genesis and function, between the objective course of literary development and the subjective needs of its present reception. The area of concurrence between the past significance of the literature and the criteria of the critic's present meaning is reduced to a frightening degree. In terms of methodology, this provides a model diametrically opposed to that of older literary history: the object viewed and the subjective point of view of the critic cannot mutually enhance and support each other in their historical directions. There is a completely undisguised gulf between the writing and the reading of literature, between its genesis and previous functions (as transmitted by those liberal or Progressive "social historians in the past") and the revisionist postulate of its "special, new usefulness." Thus, *Wirkungsgeschichte*, the history of the impact of literature, is finally eliminated as a criterion of value. No correspondence and very little interconnection remain possible between the meaning of the literary work in the present and its former social and historical significance. The new tradition of orthodoxy has to be established not in terms of, but in opposition to, the actual complication of literature as a temporal process in history.

History as Myth: American Innocence Then and Now

The supersession of the New Criticism and the more recent developments in American literary history have already relegated Randall Stewart's antiliberal conceptions to the historical past. At the same time these developments have proved more clearly than ever before that there was, and still is, a deep and enduring dissatisfaction with literary history as both a discipline and a method. Perhaps the greatest dilemma is expressed in the resumed dichotomy between the formalist and the sociological modes of criticism and in the consequent difficulties involved in the attempt to overcome this dichotomy in such a way that the study of both aesthetic structure and social function (and origin) can form a new synthesis. But is it at all possible to achieve such a synthesis unless criticism becomes once more aware of its own social function and "historical vocation"?

It seems characteristic that the earliest and perhaps most important contribution pointing in such a direction, the work of F. O. Matthiessen, did not follow Parrington in his disregard of literary form ("with aesthetic judgments I have not been greatly concerned").[72] Rather, he charged Parrington with having used literature primarily as a means of documenting social history and the history of ideas. Against that, Matthiessen remarked that "you cannot 'use' a work of art unless you have comprehended its meaning": even the documentary or educational use of a work of art presupposes that its meaning and form are fully comprehended. Such comprehension confers on literature not only a representational quality but also a "quality of illumination" in the process of history, so that the nature of both representation and illumination has to be considered as a criterion of value. Again, this calls for critical discriminations and for critical standards that, from Matthiessen's point of view, include, rather than preclude, the social sense of responsibility by which the literary historian can answer affirmatively the question that results from Emerson's postulate in *The American Scholar:* "Are you using such gifts as you possess for or against the people?"[73]

While Matthiessen placed himself in the democratic tradition and sought in it "the challenge of our still undiminished resources," the majority of historical critics (and

---

[72] Parrington, *Main Currents in American Thought*, II, i.

[73] F. O. Matthiessen, *American Renaissance: Art and Expression in the Age of Emerson and Whitman* (New York, 1957), p. xvi.

even those who professed to be indebted to Matthiessen) did not follow him in this direction.[74] This was especially true of those who, in line with the counter-Progressive historians, developed a new interest in symbolic formulas of anthropology, psychology, and, of course, cultural history. Ever since Edmund Wilson in his sketch of the development of modern symbolism (*Axel's Castle*, 1931) pointed out the anticipation of a symbolic mode in Hawthorne, Melville, and Poe, American critics have attempted, not without justification, to understand the elements of symbolism in terms of a deeply rooted Calvinist legacy of metaphorical world-interpretation. However, it was not so much the literary and historical process of the transmutation of the Old Testament vision into a darkly sensuous mode of aesthetic perception that fascinated critics like Charles Feidelson or Philip Wheelwright. Rather, the symbolic element was taken as the expression of a nonrational stratum of experience on which the archetypal and the mythical endure. The complex passage of the historical world in a poetic work was put aside as superficial or used as an excuse for uncovering the archetypal symbol as the truly meaningful aesthetic mode and content. As such, the symbol became a "tool for liberation" from the limitations of the "scientific, rational age" and assumed a "redeeming, quasi-religious function."[75]

But such a critical procedure, usually based on theoretical suggestions provided by Ernst Cassirer and Susanne K. Langer, was problematic both as literary criticism and as literary history. As criticism it looked for the meaning of the work of art beneath or behind the concrete totality of plot, character, and verbal art, finding (as Ursula Brumm notes) "the meaning not within the work of art, in the deducible motivation of the action, but outside of it, in the original

[74] Ibid., p. xv.
[75] Ursula Brumm, "Der neue Symbolismus in Amerika," *Neue deutsche Hefte*, 5 (1958/59), 245.

meanings of the symbols used. The work of art became the text of a gigantic myth of mankind in which a few basic situations are portrayed in infinite variations."[76] As literary history such a procedure was equally questionable: the literature was not studied with respect to its functional relationship to the historical movement of American society, but was isolated from this movement. The actual transformation of the Calvinist legacy was covered up by an abstraction that inverted, rather than generalized, the temporal process in society. Artists like Hawthorne and Melville had reworked the legacy of Puritanism in the light of a humanistic and secular experience of reality; by artistically liberating the metaphoric potential of Old Testament myth, they had arrived at a modern consciousness of history. But the modern criticism of symbol and myth went exactly the opposite way: it led from the poetically suspended legacy of myth, not to the historical and aesthetic consciousness of the real world, but back to some new mode of mythological encoding.

However, the uses of the concept of myth must not be oversimplified. In American literary history and criticism, the concept draws on a wide variety of intellectual sources (among them Frazer, Malinowski, Jung, Cassirer, Lévi-Strauss). These are usually linked in so eclectic or pragmatic a fashion that one can find as many meanings of the term *myth* as there are critics.[77] On the more rational side there is the attempt to use literary symbols, topoi, and images of myth in order to define the unformulated, often unconscious or indeterminate ideas and attitudes by which literature can receive the impulse of a creative imagination. The idea was that the development of literature was to be more

[76] Ibid., p. 248.
[77] W. W. Douglas, "The Meaning of 'Myth' in Modern Criticism," *Modern Philology*, 50 (1952/53), 232. Like other critics, Harry Levin views the tendency to read myth into literature as part of a "reaction against the harsh pressures of history" ("Some Meanings of Myth," *Refractions: Essays in Comparative Literature* [London, 1966], p. 31).

specifically defined as the interior development of its forms
and conventions, as "semi-autonomous."[78] At this stage it
was still possible to apply the concept of myth to the poetic
structuring of such vast historical processes as the westward
movement, such as Henry Nash Smith's exploration of its
specifically literary forms in *Virgin Land: The American
West as Symbol and Myth* (1950).

But as the concept of myth was being incorporated into
the essentially historical enterprise of American Studies, the
methodological directions of literary history were increasingly affected. Since the referential function of literature was
not complemented with, but usually replaced by, its symbolic dimension, the concept of myth tended to be more and
more associated with nonrational and ahistorical manifestations of the human experience. As the intellectual commit-
ments of the liberal and Progressive historians to the present
relevance of the eighteenth-century heritage were being surrendered, the most basic elements in the dialectic of past
structure and present function, shared by such diverse historians as Tyler and Parrington, were uprooted or reversed.
Now the course and process of literary history no longer
seemed to confirm the values and results of a progressive
past. Inevitably, the area of concurrence between the object
of, and the *Subjekt* behind, the historical interpretation of
literature was drastically narrowed, and past writing and
present reading engaged in a problematic relationship. For
the values of myth (as a profoundly meaningful activity of
primitive man), although strangely at odds with the quite
different meanings and activities of American society, were
read as a timeless expression of an archetypal experience of
"modern man." What is more, the suppression of the
"mythical" habit of mind could now be deplored; the
Enlightenment was viewed as the deplorable center of those
"tremendous and destructive intellectual upheavals at the

[78] Leo Marx, "American Studies," pp. 80, 85.

end of the eighteenth century."[79] Thus, as some vague alternative to the "rational bias" of "modern man," the vital experience of myth seemed to point to a solution of the crisis in the relationship between past structure and present function, but a solution that involved a highly questionable historiography: both the received and the receiving modes of consciousness were defined (or so it was thought) beyond a historical frame of reference.[80]

Even though such extreme conclusions were certainly not the most widespread, still, the term *myth* had made its way into the language and logic of counter-Progressive criticism and helped promote the revision of American literary history. Small wonder, when it became "less an analytical than a polemical term, calling attention rather to a critic's mood or moral attitude than to observed facts in the work under discussion." Such an exclusive interest in myth, as one of its practitioners wrote, seemed "infallibly to lead to an exaggerated opinion of works which . . . premise the immanence of grace, of final harmony and reconciliation, in a world whose contraditions it seems no longer possible to bear."[81] It was one way of keeping history out of literary history and of defining the specific mode of literature not in reference to, but in isolation from, the most basic history-making activities of man.

In this direction, the recourse to Jungian and Freudian psychology has had similar effects, though again it may be said that depth psychology has occasionally been of real service to literary history, as when Leslie Fiedler interpreted Chingachgook as some "mythical" expression of the repressed guilt complexes of the expropriating whites who—like James Fenimore Cooper—were establishing themselves

[79] Richard Chase, *Quest for Myth* (Baton Rouge, La., 1949), p. 21. Although Chase himself practices the method of "pragmatic naturalism" (p. 89), he thinks it admissible to interpret Herder's ideas on the modern use of mythology as an anticipation of Nietzsche's conception of myth.

[80] See my earlier discussion of the New Criticism and myth criticism.

[81] Douglas, p. 237; Richard Chase, *The American Novel and Its Tradition* (New York, 1957), p. 245.

on land taken from the original inhabitants.[82] But an approach that can certainly illuminate individual motifs is doomed to failure if it is applied as a methodological formula to the historical process in its entirety: the psycho-mythological principle of interpretation has no sustained equivalent in the social process of history; it is as incongruous to it as anthropology is removed from modern history. As a consequence, the critic places himself so far outside of the actual historical dimension of literature that the postulated criteria of anthropology or Freudian psychology are defined and developed only with reference to the fictitious symbols of literature and not with reference to their actual correlations in history.[83]

The same can be said about a concept like American innocence. Again, it is true that critics like R. W. B. Lewis or Ihab Hassan utilize the concept to discuss the history of important literary themes and images. For instance, the myth of the American Adam, the natural man who, like Cooper's Leatherstocking, is on the brink of undreamed-of possibilities and untouched nature or, like Mark Twain's Huckleberry Finn, breaks away from an unnatural society only to clash, like Melville's Billy Budd, tragically with an opposing world, has indeed fruitfully been discussed. But the discussion, even when it involves the unresolved tensions between the American ideal and American reality, leaves the answer to some of the most essential questions open or even deliberately ambiguous. What, for instance, was exactly the contemporary meaning of the antithesis of "innocence" and "experience"? Writing in the fifties and early sixties, Lewis and Hassan must have been confronted with a more complex alternative than the obvious synthesis, "maturation." It is enough to ask this question to suggest that their stance was that of an ironic balance, some paradoxical linkage that, for all its complexity, was at bottom a quietist (not to say an apologetic) mode of reaction to a world and to activities in

---

[82] Fiedler, *Love and Death in the American Novel* (New York, 1960), p. 191.
[83] See Link, *Amerikanische Literaturgeschichtsschreibung*, p. 45.

this world that were neither ironic nor balanced nor, indeed, in the nature of a maturing synthesis. But if the political and social substance of American history (from Jamestown to the Gulf of Tonkin) cannot possibly be defined in terms of the antithesis of innocence and experience, the irony and the paradox were not in the making of history but in the mode of historiography. The relationship of past significance and present meaning itself was turned into an eighth type of ambiguity.

Perhaps the advocates of the image-symbol-myth approach would insist that they were deliberately foregoing all "extrinsic" abstractions in order to focus on the dialectic of the imaginative process itself. But when you consider images such as "Adam" or antithetical schemata such as "innocence and experience" or sensuous metaphors like the "machine in the garden," the mode of generalization is adequate neither to that of the poetic object of, nor to that of the rational activity behind, the historical interpretation of literature. It is certainly not a poetic mode of generalization (which would embrace both the universality and the particularity of the theme or image) but, rather, some pseudoarchetypal one. As such it can become almost as abstract and as troublesome as the typological antitheses of German *Geistesgeschichte*. This is the case, especially, when imaginative categories are intertwined with historical ones, as in the unfortunate distinction between the "innocent" *Party of Hope* and the Calvinist *Party of Memory*.[84] At this point, it is difficult to resist the impression that not only was the symbolic content of art overstrained, but history itself was turned into symbol and

---

[84] R. W. B. Lewis, *The American Adam: Innocence, Tragedy, and Tradition in the Nineteenth Century* (Chicago, 1955). But despite his emphasis on "the indestructible vitality of the Adamic vision of life" (p. 200), Lewis points to the crisis in the tradition of American literary history when he writes: "The illusion of freedom from the past led to a more real relation to the continuing tradition. . . . Without the illusion, we are conscious, no longer of tradition, but simply and coldly of the burden of history" (p. 9). The question that Lewis does not answer is, *Why* does the burden of history forestall a creative sense of tradition?

myth. Just as historians like Boorstin reduced the world of social and political struggle to a dimension of "experience" or "character," so the literary process was formulated in metaphorical and symbolic abstractions from society. It seems ironic that although these abstractions were supposed to promote a specifically literary approach to literature, they did not—in their abstractness—achieve a reintegration of history and literature. In fact, such an integration could not be attained by sacrificing history itself; it could not be achieved by an approach to literary history that conceived of culture not as social substance but as symbolic form.[85] While it was the declared intention of the formalist approach "to describe the work of art purely as a system of signs,"[86] it was the practical result of the critics of American "innocence" to view the literary past purely as a system of images, symbols, and myths. Although in both cases this involved a good deal of subtle interpretation and perceptiveness, neither formalism nor symbol criticism could point the way back toward literary history.

Since the sixties the preeminence of the image-symbol-myth approach has increasingly been questioned, but the contradictions and dichotomies of American literary history have not been automatically resolved. To be sure, there has developed a new interest in the theory of literary history and the philosophy of history, revealed by such newly founded journals as *New Literary History*, *History and Theory*, and *Clio*. But the hopes, so fervently held in the sixties, that post-Enlightenment developments, "like the whole of our past,

[85]For a perceptive critique, see G. C. LeRoy, "American Innocence Reconsidered," *Massachusetts Review*, 4 (1963), 638.

[86]Wellek and Warren, *Theory of Literature*, p. 264. This is a key statement that recurs in Wellek's essay "The Crisis of Comparative Literature." As such it corresponds with his formalist demand for an intrinsic, or "internal," history of literature. But see his *Concepts of Criticism* (New Haven, 1963), where the "new ideal" of an *internal history* has shrunk to "a new, *less external* literary history" (p. 6, my italics). This reflects Wellek's pluralistic position "that no other approach has been considered invalid"; thus, the "new ideal of literary history" envisioned by Wellek is never positively developed (*Theory of Literature*, p. 282).

will look different when we emerge from the cultural revolution through which we are now passing," must today appear a little premature. Yet despite setbacks and some disillusionment, the humanist tradition of historical inquiry seems more alive today than it was a decade ago. Here, the New Left reaction against the counter-Progressive consensus has been as violent as it was wholesome. The counter-Progressive reading of the past has lost its overwhelming appeal. In the words of a New Left historian, it was the awareness of the burning questions of the present out of which a new understanding of American history emerged: "For many, the rediscovery of poverty and racism, the commitment to civil rights for Negroes, the criticism of intervention in Cuba and Vietnam, shattered many of the assumptions of the fifties and compelled intellectuals to re-examine the American past."[87]

Thus, it was the need for a new look at the present that sparked a reconsideration of the past. As a radical activist put it: "The bureaucrats hold history as ended. As a result significant parts of the population both on the campus and off are dispossessed, and these dispossessed are not about to accept their ahistorical point of view."[88] At the same time, the more traditionally oriented humanism that in the fifties had retreated to defensive positions began to reassert itself. At its finest, contributions such as Walter Sutton's *Modern American Criticism* (1963) and the anthology *American Literature: Tradition and Innovation* (1969), edited by Walter Sutton, Harrison T. Meserole, and Brom Weber, showed signs of a new correlation between the democratic values of the culture of the past and a critical evaluation of present literature. Unfortunately, the humanist terms of such a correlation can become quite abstract and, some-

[87] May, "The Problem of the American Enlightenment," p. 214; *Towards a New Past*, ed. Bernstein, p. ix.

[88] Mario Savio, "An End to History," in *The New Radicals: A Report with Documents*, ed. Paul Jacobs and Saul Landau (New York, Vintage Books, 1966), p. 232.

times, vague if a critic like Leon Howard defines them as "a sort of intangible national quality." As he says in *Literature and the American Tradition,* "It is a belief in the creative power of the human spirit to endure and prevail and to exist in the meanest and queerest of individuals" which "budded beneath puritan orthodoxy" and reaches from the Declaration of Independence to the works of Faulkner and Hemingway.[89] However abstract in a historical sense such definitions of tradition must remain, they have countered "the current rejection of literary history either as guide to or knowledge of the present."[90] To say this is not to underrate the forces of the conservative and formalist reaction (which are still "entrenched in the sensitive, the powerful, areas of our academic, scholarly and journalistic life today").[91] Nor is it to close one's eyes to the deep contradictions among the New Left, which were recognized so early by Christopher Lasch in his book *The Agony of the American Left* (1969) and, more recently and so perceptively, in Peter Clecak's study *Radical Paradoxes: Dilemmas of the American Left: 1945–1970* (1973). And even though the New Left as a political movement has been in recent years seriously arrested, these contradictions continue in some of the left intellectual currents.

In a situation like this, pluralism and eclecticism are widespread; and despite the various advances toward literary history there remains, in the words of J. M. Cameron, a "deep dissatisfaction with the existing practice of literary historians." But the dissatisfaction also involves the questioning of previously accepted methodologies, and the questions that are being asked are far-reaching enough to affect the hitherto dominating types of criticism, even the work of the

---

[89] *Literature and the American Tradition,* 2d ed. (New York, 1970), p. 329.

[90] Ralph Cohen, "A Note on *New Literary History,*" *New Literary History,* 1 (1969/70), 6.

[91] The phrase is Maxwell Geismar's, in *Henry James and the Jacobites* (New York, 1962), p. 11.

leading myth critic. Referring *expressis verbis* to the student
unrest in the sixties, Northrop Frye develops the idea of an
"identity crisis" (to which I have referred above) in terms of
a critical confrontation between reality in America and
American "social mythology":

> Many feel that in America the democratic ideal was kidnapped at the be-
> ginning by a social movement which was really oligarchical, based on
> various forms of exploitation, including slavery and later racism, and
> hence exclusive, which built up a hysterically competitive economy on a
> thunderous cannonade of systematic lying, and finally began to spill over
> into imperialistic crusades like the Vietnam war. . . . The result is that
> many people, especially in the under-thirty age group, feel alienated
> from their own society, to the point of what is sometimes called an
> identity crisis.[92]

For Frye, the resulting question is how to redefine the
past so as to help revitalize the vision of an alternative
identity of North America. Such an identity he finds, not in
American reality, but in that traditional body of social attitudes and assumptions which he calls the "myth of concern." The question that he does not answer is, of course,
how to rediscover a great democratic heritage in history from
the point of view of a criticism that has committed itself to
the anatomy of literature as an archetypal system of pure
knowledge. How, it may be asked, is it possible to correlate
the *temporal* processes of past significance and present
meaning from the methodological position of a critic who
has maintained that "mythology and literature occupy the
same verbal space" and who has pleaded that one should
"conceive literature as an order of words, as a unified
imaginative system"?[93]

Frye's position here is illuminating in that it illustrates
the contradictions between the modes of myth criticism and

---

[92]Cameron, "Problems of Literary History," *New Literary History*, 1 (1969/
70), 9; Frye, *The Critical Path: An Essay on the Social Context of Literary
Criticism* (Bloomington, Ind., Midland Books, 1971), p. 138.

[93]*Fables of Identity: Studies in Poetic Mythology* (New York, 1963), p. 36.

the methodology of literary history. On the one hand, Frye is prepared to say that "for people on this continent at least, the cure for the identity crisis . . . is the recovery of their own revolutionary and democratic myth of concern. . . . Certainly there is a tremendous radical force in American culture . . . which could give a very different social slant to the American myth of concern."[94] The attempt made in this connection to draw "some curious parallels" between the recent radical movement of young intellectuals and Protestant sectarian activity in the nineteenth century may not convince. But Frye's aim is more ambitious and more comprehensive than such analogies betray. In reality, he undertakes the attempt, based on his entire work, at recovering a humanist and romantic tradition as a new perspective on literature and criticism. In this sense he challenges the rejection of the romantic tradition (in Eliot, Leavis, Ortega y Gasset) by drawing attention to what he calls the "revolutionary," "utopian," and "prophetic" elements in romanticism, which, he implies, are more meaningful today than the "absolute," neoclassical, and elitist standards of modernism.[95] Thus, the "social context" of literature from Blake to William Morris assumes a new and "immense significance." Morris, for example, is viewed "as a revolutionary artist trying to show how the arts could still recover something of their original social role."[96]

The irony of this position is that Frye the moralist appeals to the very standards that he theoretically rejected. For he did reject them when he claimed for criticism a mode of interpretation that was to be free from considerations of value and social function. Thus, he had dissociated "the

[94] *The Critical Path*, p. 139.
[95] *The Stubborn Structure: Essays on Criticism and Society* (London, 1970), pp. viii, 179, 200 ff.
[96] "The Critical Path: An Essay on the Social Context of Literary Criticism," *Daedalus*, 99 (Spring 1970), p. 303. The phrase is not in the book version; but see *The Stubborn Structure*, p. 58.

theorist of literature and the consumer of literature" and surrendered "the implicit moral standard to which ethical criticism always refers."[97] But how, it must be asked, can the revolutionary and prophetic elements in romanticism be evaluated and revitalized if those who wish to do so reject moral standards and dismiss the whole business of evaluation as incompatible with the true task of criticism? Again, the dilemma is that the past object of, and the present mode behind, the historical interpretation are not related in terms of the historical process. As a result, the historical dimension of a work's genesis and mimesis and the social and aesthetic standards of its impact and reception, *Entstehungsgeschichte* and *Wirkungsgeschichte*, do not enter into a fully functional and functioning connection.

The neoromantic position of myth criticism points beyond modernism, but it has failed in working out a new historical vocation for criticism. Frye's advocacy of the romantic tradition cannot revive the revolutionary and prophetic functions of literature in the present. This is not to say that the democratic tradition in Jefferson, Lincoln, Thoreau, and Whitman was not, and cannot now be, of great inspiration for a progressive historical consciousness of the present. Rather, it cannot through critical definitions be made the source of a living culture. The crisis in the correlation of past significance and present meaning reaches deeper, right into the center of the contradiction between the past function of romantic literature and the present mode of its reception. A modern correlation of the aesthetic and the social is hindered by the very fact that the social function of past literature and the ahistorical orientation of myth criticism still cannot engage in a mutually illuminating relationship. The critical consciousness, once it is dissociated from the historical consciousness, has lost its unifying

[97] *Anatomy of Criticism: Four Essays* (Princeton, 1957), p. 20.

potential: it has relinquished the ability to integrate history and criticism in such a way that the social and the aesthetic dimensions of literature are comprehended as indivisible and themselves attain a correlation from their function in the social process of living.[98]

[98] Since the appearance of a first version of this essay in German (1965), the literature touching on various aspects of the problem in hand has grown to an even more formidable degree. But of the several studies of central interest to my discussion, I would like to mention at least Richard E. Ruland, *The Rediscovery of American Literature: Premises of Critical Taste, 1900–1940* (Cambridge, 1967), Wesley Morris, *Toward a New Historicism* (Princeton, 1972), and Bruce Kuklick, "Myth and Symbol in American Studies," *American Quarterly*, 24 (October 1972).

IV
Structuralism and Literary History

WHEN Ferdinand de Saussure developed a synchronic mode of linguistic studies (to complement, rather than supersede, the diachronic approach), it was hard to predict that from it would emerge a crucial challenge to the traditional methods of historical philology as well as a profound reaction against the historical orientation of the social sciences. The historical tradition in romantic and positivist philology had, by and large, reflected the needs and possibilities of a social consciousness which preceded both the decline of liberal bourgeois society and the crisis in the relations between science and ideology. Out of this crisis (which was also one of individualism and laissez-faire) emerged the most searching criticism and the most valuable contributions of the new philology: the standards and criteria of individual speech (parole) were complemented by the idea of a collective system of linguistic symbols (langue), and the empiricism of the *Junggrammatiker* was replaced by a more abstract pattern of linguistic analysis characterized by a stronger tendency to differentiate between the psychological, physiological, and material components of language. Along these lines there seemed to be some hope to bridge the widening rifts between the methods of science, the study of language, and the directions of ideology. But the crisis in the relations between the natural and the social sciences was postponed and its ideological implications circumvented by a new methodology which disregarded the temporal dimension ("ce grand obstacle à toute rationalité")[1] and which culminated in that triple abstraction from

[1] Viggo Brøndal, "Linguistique structurale," *Acta Linguistica*, 1 (1939), 7.

the "external linguistic" reality: an abstraction from (1) both the speakers and the contexts or situations of speaking, from (2) the subject matter or object of discourse, and finally from (3) the history of language.

Today there is no need to defend the evolutionary theories of the romantic school and the traditions of philological positivism in order to criticize this abstraction from the social, ideological, and historical contexts of language. No matter how fruitful de Saussure's idea about language as a system of signs and no matter how stimulating the thesis that linguistics could become "le patron général de toute sémiologie," the new approach was to reflect and to further the tensions that had developed between the methods of scholarship and the world of history. In an age of war and revolution and growing international class divisions there was established the idea of a *système* which, ultimately, helped to resist or to belittle a sense of change and history by conceiving, from the beginning, of an "organisme linguistique interne" to be distinct from, and opposed to, "des phénomènes linguistiques externes."[2]

[2] Ferdinand de Saussure, *Cours de linguistique générale*, ed. Charles Bally and Albert Sechehaye, 5th ed. (Paris: Payot, 1955), pp. 101, 42. Theoretically de Saussure comprehended language as "à la fois un système établi et une évolution; à chaque moment, il est une institution actuelle et un produit du passé" (p. 24). However: "Les altérations ne se faisant jamais sur le bloc du système, mais sur l'un ou l'autre de ses éléments, ne peuvent être étudiées qu'en dehor de celui-ci" (p. 124). While de Saussure's concept of an "organisme linguistique interne" was rigorously and perhaps more consistently treated by Brøndal and Hjelmslev as some "objet autonome" ("Linguistique structurale," p. 39), that is, as "a self-sufficient totality, a structure *sui generis*" (Louis Hjelmslev, *Prolegomena to a Theory of Language*, trans. F. J. Whitfield [Baltimore, 1953], p. 2), the "phénomènes linguistiques externes" were more carefully considered in the Prague circle as a constitutive element of change in language: "l'étude d'une langue exige que l'on tienne rigoureusement compte de la variété des fonctions linguistiques et de leurs mode de réalisation dans le cas considéré. . . . C'est d'après ces fonctions et ces modes que changent et la structure phonique et la structure grammaticale et la composition lexicale de la langue" ("Thèses," *Travaux du Cercle Linguistique de Prague*, 1 [1929], 14). The extralinguistic concept of function was more strongly emphasized in the retrospect discussion ("K diskussii po voprosam strukturalizma," *Voprosy yazykoznaniya*, 6, No. 3 [1957], 44–52), but "du point de vue de la fonction poétique" ("Thèses," p. 17), "la va-

But against the widening chasm between the concept of
le système and the idea of history (which is so characteristic
of Saussurean structuralism and its development and continuation in the work of Louis Hjelmslev and Leonard
Bloomfield), a number of French critics and theoreticians
have made a point of departure which—in a way different
from, and hardly cognizant of, related attempts emanating
from the Prague circle—claims to challenge or at least to
modify the ahistorical orientation of structuralism. By applying the principles of structural linguistics to various social
studies or, conversely, by the attempt to introduce
considerations of history and society into structural analysis,
the work of authors like Roland Barthes, Lucien Goldmann,
Lucien Sebag, and, above all, Claude Lévi-Strauss, has posed
a number of methodological questions. In some of these the
theory and, partly, the practice of literary history is directly
or implicitly involved. What is more, a new "Méthode
structuraliste génétique en histoire de la littérature," as first
developed by the late Lucien Goldmann, has advanced
claims that amount to nothing more and nothing less than a
"bouleversement radical" postulating "just as much a
radical overthrow of customary thinking . . . as was the case
with the formation of the positive natural sciences" in its
time: "L'analyse structuraliste-génétique en *histoire de la
litérature* n'est que l'application à ce domaine particulier

---

leur autonome du signe" was stressed: "il faut étudier la langue poétique en elle-
même" ("Thèses," p. 21). So even though the *langage poétique* was considered
historically, as a "forme de la parole, c'est-à-dire d'un acte createur individuel"
(p. 18), what mattered was "la caractérisation immanente de l'évolution de la
langue poétique." If, "dans les études d'histoire littéraire," this had hitherto
played "un rôle subordonné" (p. 21), it was close to similar trends in Russian formalism. But by accepting and, partly, incorporating elements of historical
criticism in the thirties, the Prague approach opened possibilities and allowed for
developments out of which were to emerge the remarkable contributions of Jan
Mukařovský and Felix Vodička (which point beyond the Russian formalist concepts of *literaturnost*' and structural "evolution," but which are only now, and
still only partially, becoming accessible in translation).

d'une méthode *générale* que nous pensons être la seule valable en sciences humaines." So structuralism claims to bring about a radical conversion of literary history, "analogous to that breakthrough which made the transition from royal chronicles to real history possible." Ultimately, this program envisages "a revival of historical research" which, according to A.-J. Greimas, will mark "le passage de la philosophie de l'histoire à la science de l'histoire."[3]

The extraordinary, if not extravagant, nature of these claims invites some critical questions as to the methodological assumptions of the structural genetic approach. What specifically are the theoretical and practical foundations on which, in the French tradition, the principles of structural linguistics are applied to the historical study of literature and society? The following notes will raise these questions in a critical survey of some of the more influential positions in the work of Roland Barthes and Lucien Goldmann and discuss some of the more general assumptions on structure and society by Claude Lévi-Strauss, and from there proceed to reconsider some of the possibilities and problems of a contribution of structuralism to the theory and method of literary history.[4]

---

[3] Lucien Goldmann, "La Méthode structuraliste génétique en histoire de la litterature," *Pour une sociologie du roman* (Paris: Gallimard, 1964), p. 221; ibid., p. 11; A.-J. Greimas, "Structure et histoire," *Les Temps modernes*, 22 (1966), 826.

[4] By "structuralism" I here understand the seminal work of Ferdinand de Saussure and that of his more immediate followers and its impact on French literary critics like Roland Barthes or sociologists like Claude Lévi-Strauss. This essay does not consider recent developments in structural linguistics, such as its growing concern with problems of syntax and semantics, its remarkable achievements in the creation of generative models, or its bold metatheoretical approach to grammar. Nor can these notes do full justice to the most recent work of authors such as Julia Kristeva, or even mention the attempt, by linguists and critics such as Manfred Bierwisch, to apply the principles of transformational grammar to the study of literary theory and poetics (see, e.g., *Mathematik und Dichtkunst*, ed. Helmut Kreuzer [Munich: Nymphenburger Verlagshandlung, 1965], pp. 49–65; or *Literaturwissenschaft und Linguistik: Ergebnisse und Perspektiven*, ed. Jens Ihwe [Frankfurt a.M.: Athenaum-Verlag, 1971]).

The Criticism of Function as Structure

One of the first manifestations of a structuralist rejection of the traditional principles of academic literary history in France can be found in the well-known controversy Nouvelle Critique versus Critique Universitaire. Roland Barthes, in his repeated attacks on *Lansonisme*, provides a number of polemical suggestions for a new approach to the history of literature. He proceeds from the postulate that what is needed is something more than a history of art: the awareness of the relationship between art and history. According to Barthes, the traditional academic literary history, embodied in France by the work of Gustave Lanson, does not limit itself to demanding the application of objective standards but "il implique des convictions générales sur l'homme, l'histoire, la littérature, les rapports de l'auteur et de l'œuvre."[5] Its particular form of ideology (which it carries "dans le bagage du scientisme") is expressed in a determinism and a so-called objectivity that never examines its own assumptions. Thus, the absence of any methodological self-consciousness conceals a conception of art that seems to be historical but in reality stands in the way of history:

Car refuser de s'interroger sur l'être de la littérature, c'est du même coup accréditer l'idée que cet être est éternel, ou si l'on préfère, naturel, bref que la littérature *va de soi*. Et pourtant, qu'est-ce que la littérature? Pourquoi écrit-on? Racine écrivait-il pour les mêmes raisons que Proust? Ne pas se poser ces questions, c'est aussi y répondre, car c'est adopter l'idée traditionnelle du sens commun (qui n'est pas forcément le sens historique), à savoir que l'écrivain écrit tout simplement pour *s'exprimer*, et que l'être de la littérature est dans la "traduction" de la sensibilité et des passions.[6]

The academic historian of literature (says Barthes) grants prime importance to sources and biographies and expends a great deal of effort studying a petty detail but will

---

[5] Roland Barthes, *Essais critiques* (Paris: Édition du seuil, 1964), p. 253.
[6] Ibid., p. 247.

"withdraw without a fight to a purely magical conception of the work when it comes to the essential": he stops as soon as he approaches *l'histoire véritable*. This is his verdict on the French academic tradition of literary history: "Voici une histoire de la littérature (n'importe laquelle: on n'établit pas un palmarès, on réfléchit sur un statut); elle n'a d'histoire que le nom: c'est une suite de monographies, dont chacune, à peu de chose près, enclôt un auteur et l'étudie pour lui-même; l'histoire n'est ici que succession d'hommes seuls; bref ce n'est pas une histoire, c'est une chronique."[7]

This is a challenging indictment which makes some sense even though its exaggeration may seem to oversimplify matters. But what, then, is the methodological alternative? Instead of a history of literature conceived from a biographical, chronological, or aesthetic point of view, Barthes proposes "une histoire . . . de la fonction littéraire." The important thing to examine is not the single work in regard to the author but the "rapport entre *tout* l'auteur et *toute* l'œuvre, *un rapport des rapports,* une correspondance homologique, et non analogique."[8] In the case of French classicism this involves the sociological composition of the audience and the function of the theater for them ("distraction? dream? identification? alienation? snobbism?"). Thus, the feeling of an entire epoch is involved; in other words, exactly that which "dans l'auteur, n'est pas l'auteur lui-même." What matters is not biographical evidence but the functional study of "techniques, rules, rituals, and collective mentality." Barthes concludes: "C'est donc au niveau des fonctions littéraires [production, communication, consommation] que l'histoire peut seulement se placer, et non au niveau des individus qui les ont exercées. Autrement dit, l'histoire littéraire n'est possible que si elle se fait sociologique, si elle s'intéresse aux activités et aux institutions, non aux individus."[9]

[7] Roland Barthes, *Sur Racine* (Paris: Édition du seuil, 1963), p. 148.
[8] Ibid., p. 150; *Essais critiques,* p. 250.   [9] *Sur Racine,* pp. 152, 156.

But what is the nature of these "functions"? If they are to be defined in terms of the sociological foundations of literature, the history of, say, the social mode of seventeenth-century drama would then constitute the backbone of that chapter in French literary history. However, would the sociological approach to function, then, not have to be accommodated to the structuralist study of the literary equivalent of what de Saussure called the "organisme linguistique interne"? For Barthes, the concept of a function which is rooted in society and the idea of *le système* as a functional whole of structures make up a problematic relationship. On the one hand, he is concerned with function in the context of "production, communication, consommation"; on the other, he proposes an "analyse immanente" of the text from a purely aesthetic viewpoint "dans un domaine purement intérieur à l'œuvre." For Barthes, such *analyse immanente* involves an approach "qui s'installe *dans* l'œuvre" and "qui tient l'œuvre pour un système de fonctions."[10]

The structuralist concept of a "système de fonctions" raises a number of questions, in particular, its relationship to social function as a changing phenomenon. And his resort to *conscience paradigmatique* (for which Barthes pleads) does not resolve the difficulty. The paradigmatic (like the syntagmatic) consciousness is seen to embrace the relation between each aesthetic sign and a specific stock of other (existing or preceding) signs. It implies the existence of an ordered stock, or "memory," of forms for each sign "from which it differentiates itself on the basis of the slightest variation which is necessary in order to effect a change in meaning." Undoubtedly, such a structural relationship can be of great interest and some consequence; but how, in literary history, would it come to terms with an *ensemble* of works or genres in a historical process of change, decay, and creation? For Barthes, the *conscience paradigmatique* has a formal relationship to the consciousness of history. Its emphasis is not

[10] *Essais critiques*, pp. 250, 251.

placed on the relationship of the *signifié* and the *signifiant* (nor does it consider this relationship as subjected to historical change) but mainly on the way in which the latter is paradigmatically or syntactically related to an autonomous stock of other signs. In this sense, Barthes with some consistency calls the paradigmatic consciousness "une imagination formelle." It is this "imagination formelle (ou paradigmatique)" which, by being exclusively concerned with the variation of recurring elements, views only the formal side of the *signifié*, only its "demonstrative role"—in other words, the sign, not its referent. This is why it tends to "deplete" the *signifié:* "Naturellement, en ne retenant du signifié que son rôle démonstratif (il désigne le signifiant et permet de repérer les termes de l'opposition), la conscience paradigmatique tend à le vider." But this depletion of the *signifié* is a depletion of both historical substance and historical function.[11]

[11] Ibid., pp. 211, 209. Barthes (*Le Dégre zéro de l'ecriture suivi des éléments de sémiologie* [Paris: Éditions du seuil, 1953], pp. 111 f.) does use terms like *substance* or *contenu* when he says: "Le plan des signifiants constitute le *plan d'expression* et celui des signifiés le *plan de contenu* . . . chaque plan comporte en effet . . . deux *strates:* la *forme* et la *substance:* . . . La *forme*, c'est ce qui peut être décrit exhaustivement, simplement et avec cohérence (critères épistémologiques) par la linguistique, sans recourir à aucune prémise extralinguistique; la *substance*, c'est l'ensemble des aspects des phénomènes linguistiques qui ne peuvent être décrits sans recourir à des prémisses extralinguistiques." However, this distinction, which is also taken up in his *Système de la mode* (Paris: Édition du seuil, 1967), pp. 79 f., does not contradict the depletion of the *signifié* which I have criticized. It so obviously follows the *linguistique immanente*, as when Louis Hjelmslev defines "substance" as "nonlinguistic stuff," mere matter, on which "form" impresses itself (*Prolegomena to a Theory of Language*, p. 49) and says about the equally autonomous concepts of "expression" and "content": "Their functional definition provides no justification for calling one, and not the other, of these entities *expression*, or one, and not the other, *content*" (*Prolegomena*, pp. 37 f.). Barthes, like other French structuralists, is obviously much indebted to the Danish *glossématiste* and his basic idea "that linguistics describes the relational pattern of language without knowing what the relata are" ("Structural Analysis of Language," *Studia Linguistica*, 1 [1947], 75). But how can such an "imagination formelle" be applied to the study of literature, when linguists themselves have warned against the dangers of formalism? See, e.g., L. L. Hammerich, "Les glossématistes danois et leurs méthodes," *Acta Philologica Scandinavica*, 21 (1950–51), 1 ff., 87 ff.; or the excellent survey by Klaus Hansen, "Wege und Ziele des Strukturalismus," *Zeitschrift für Anglistik und Amerikanistik*, 6 (1958), 341 ff.

Here the contradiction between the sociological concept of function and the concept of function "dans un
domaine purement intérieur a l'œuvre" seems obvious. It
remains unsolvable as long as the structural "système de
fonctions" obscures the full semantic dimension of the sign
and underestimates the connection (which is a changing one)
between sign and reference and, again, the more highly complex relations between sign and referent. When Barthes
defines structuralism as the transition from a symbolic consciousness to a paradigmatic consciousness, then, in his view
of literary history, he drives out the referential and mimetic
functions of literature and its social correlative which (especially in the tradition of realism) is a *functional* moment of
great *structural* consequence.

Thus Barthes's vision of "une critique des fonctions et
des significations," when it hopes to inspire a methodological
reorientation of history, raises more questions than it can
answer. To begin with, is not the social *function* of literature
already an essential factor in the formation of the *structural*
relationship between *signifié* and *signifiant?* Using a fruitful
observation as a starting point (that is, that a sign is not determined by its *signifié*), the structuralist casts aside not only
any consideration of the art work as the *signifié* of a
signifiant, but, even more emphatically, any conception of
the work of art as a product. Thus, he treats the art work,
"non comme l'effet d'une cause, mais comme le signifiant
d'un signifié." Consequently, the terms that are now
considered superfluous ("like source, genesis, mimesis, etc.")
are discarded together with the conception of the work as
"product," and the literary work is totally subsumed under
the concept of the sign: "l'œuvre serait le signe. . . ."[12]

The deplorable antithesis between literature as
"product" and literature as "sign" (or structure) reproduces
the antinomy between history and *le système* on a new level.

---

[12]*Sur Racine*, p. 158.

There remains no such room, then, for a historical view of aesthetic structures which, through the interplay of their paradigmatic and referential functions, are both sign and meaning, image and *agens*, in a changing world of which *le système* is itself a functional part. Instead, the work of art is viewed as the *signifiant* of a *signifié:* but is not, in contrast to everyday language, the artistic *signifiant* structured in such a way that the function of its parts cannot be fully comprehended without considering its relationship to a semantic dimension of value, that is, the achieved content? And does not an element of history affect the paradigmatic and syntactic functions of the sign itself so that, in literary history, it pervades the specifically aesthetic relationships between the *signifiant* and the *signifié?*

As these questions suggest, *la critique des fonctions et des significations*, even when it is seriously concerned with the sociological aspects of literature, fails to integrate aesthetics and history. Eventually, there emerges that unacceptable alternative which Barthes, in the title of one of his most important essays, calls "La littérature ou l'histoire"—literature *or* history. If, as he there suggests, the literary work is considered as "document" and if it is traced back to its "institutional" context, then the history of literature has indeed surrendered the hope to be anything more than a sociology of literature. It has abandoned the claim to conceive of literature itself as a historical phenomenon. The renunciation of *literary* history seems a high price which Barthes, however, is perfectly prepared to pay when he says that "ramenée nécessairement dans ses limites institutionelles, l'histoire de la littérature sera de l'histoire tout court."[13]

It is, perhaps, true that the institutional and sociological reduction of the object of literary history provides a more congenial (and limited) frame of reference for the *analyse immanente*. But even if this is so, the linguistic origins of the

[13] Ibid., p. 156.

method of structural analysis present a burden that is all the heavier for being only partially adapted to the quite different world of literature. For the literary critic as historian the relationship between the *signifié* and the *signifiant* assumes a *functional* quality (which admittedly does not exist in the normal linguistic sign). While in the history of languages a *signifié*, which (in English) is expressed by the *signifiant* "the flower blooms," takes on the most various linguistic forms, in the history of art the same meaning, or *signifié*, cannot quite so arbitrarily be related to a *signifiant*: the latter, by its more intense and symbolic association with the meaning itself, assumes (like alliterative or rhythmical expression in poetry) a pictorial, mimetic, musical, or technical quality which serves as a constituent factor in the (lyrical, musical, or pictorial) realization of the artistic *signifié*. And the artistic *signifié*, or reference, although much less directly related to a referent in the world of history, is part of a semantic dimension that is interrelated with the creative or receptive *Subjekt* and his social *Praxis*.

To abstract from that and to ignore the interrelatedness of verbal form and social meaning is not helpful. It neglects the peculiar potency of the artistic sign which—in contrast to the linguistic sign proper—cannot be grasped without recourse to the social mode of both its genesis and its effect upon an audience or reader. To refuse to view the work of art as a biographical, individual, or social "product," as well as a "producer" of personality in history and society, is to impoverish irretrievably its relatedness (however tenuous or indirect) to the historical process.

This does not mean that Barthes, in his attack on subjective and individualistic assumptions and pseudoscientific aspirations of the traditional type of literary history, is not at least partly justified. But his reaction to bourgeois individualism and the crisis in the relations of science and ideology leads not to a more complex view of the historical process of literature but to a formalization of some of its aesthetic and sociological ingredients. For Barthes, the basic fact that a social and artistic *subjectivity* can help constitute the *objective* substance of the historical process (in society or literature) seems incomprehensible. For him, as for other structuralists, only that is valid "which in the author is not the author." The work of art is not a product: creation is not considered a historical category (nor, for that matter, is reception seen as a creative form of experience). The acts of a poet, the making of a work, are not historical activities. Small wonder, then, that the most philosophical-minded of all the French structuralists, Michel Foucault, rejects humanism as the heritage "which has burdened us most" and which "it is high time to get rid of." But to oppose humanism is to oppose a theory in which the dialectical relationship of literature and society and the interaction of creation and reception provide the basis for *literature becoming history*. Roland Barthes's is a desperate attempt to attain to the objectivity of literary history by annihilating poetic subjectivity. In this, he does not go quite so far as Foucault, but for him, too, *amputer la littérature de l'individu* seems essential.[14] "De nos jours on ne peut plus penser que dans le vide de l'homme disparu."[15] These are Foucault's words, but they might have been Barthes's. It is this attempt to systematize history at the expense of its creators that, finally, accounts for the strange coupling of sociology and *analyse immanente* which, here, for all their contradictions, find their joint functional (and ideological) raison d'être.

The Structure of Genesis

In his book *Sur Racine*, Roland Barthes cites Lucien Goldmann and remarks that he more than anyone else has worked out the theory of what one might call "criticism of

[14]Ibid.
[15]Michel Foucault, *Les mots et les choses* (Paris: Gallimard, 1966), p. 353.

signification" as applied to a historical *signifié*. Following in the tradition of Kant, Hegel, Marx, and Lukács, Goldmann uses the dialectical concept of totality as an element of the analysis of historically "meaningful structures": "des structures significatives globales . . . à la fois pratiques, théoriques et affectives."[16] In his works on Racine and Pascal as well as in his introduction to *Pour une sociologie du roman*, he rejects the unhistorical type of structural analysis whose development he interprets as representing an apologetic outcome of the newer sociology, which accommodates itself more and more to the "inhuman and anticultural system of organized capitalism." To Marxist critics Goldmann up to the late sixties appeared to be "the most talented and interesting" representative of the historical mode of structural analysis, and it was possible, in 1969, to greet his contribution as that of "one of the fathers of literary structuralism."[17]

Goldmann's opposition to formalism and unhistorical analysis certainly goes beyond the more eclectic position of Roland Barthes and is based on more coherent theoretical principles. Among these, there are some concepts of historical materialism which Goldmann, in his introduction to *Sciences humaines et philosophie,* applies to a critical analysis of structuralism: the supersession of the "capitalism of crisis" (at the time of both world wars, the great economic crises, mass unemployment, and fascism) by the so-called organized capitalism of the postwar period corresponds, according to Goldmann, to the "transition from a philosophical, historical, humanist sociology to the unhistorical sociological thinking of today." This would parallel the replacement of a philosophy that was directed either toward

---

[16] Lucien Goldmann, *Le Dieu caché: Etude sur la vision tragique dans les "Pensées" de Pascal et dans le théâtre de Racine* (Paris: Gallimard, 1955), p. 7.

[17] Rita Schober, *Im Banne der Sprache: Strukturalismus in der Nouvelle Critique, speziell bei Roland Barthes* (Halle: Mitteldeutscher Verlag, 1968), pp. 20, 24; Günter Schiwy, *Der französische Strukturalismus: Mode—Methode—Ideologie* (Reinbek b. Hamburg: Rowohlt Taschenbuch Verlag, 1969), p. 14.

anxiety and death, or history, by a belief in cognitive and rationalistic standards which, however, abandon the "humanistic and individualistic values" that characterized the rationalism of the Enlightenment. The basic mistake of unhistorical structuralist analysis (according to Goldmann) is in its failing to recognize the extent to which the structures of social behavior fulfill a function within an encompassing social organization. To direct research only toward the most general thought patterns which one can find in all social forms and which are scarcely affected by history is to ignore the problem of change and to favor an apologist "functionalism" which shows interest only in the conserving feature of each institution and in the specific behavior of a given society.[18]

Goldmann is able to offset the weaknesses of such formalist and ahistorical analysis by justifying the "interrelationship of structure and function" and thereby stressing the changeability, the continual formation and deformation, of structures. By using concepts like "sujet de l'action," "réponse significative," or "object," and "meaningful structure," in cultural and literary history, he lays claim to setting up theoretical standards for the structuralist genetic method. As in the opening section of his study "La Méthode structuraliste génétique en histoire de la littérature," where he develops some of these "principes fondamentaux," he says: "Le structuralisme génétique part de l'hypothèse que tout comportement humain est un essai de donner une *réponse significative* à une situation particulière et tend par cela même à créer un équilibre entre le sujet de l'action et l'objet sur lequel elle porte, le monde ambiant."[19]

At the center here is the idea of a "balance" between man and society which, in a different context, is defined as a "balance between the intellectual structures of the subject

[18]See Goldmann's introduction to the second edition of his *Sciences humaines et philosophie* (Paris: Gonthier, 1966).
[19]Lucien Goldmann, *Pour une sociologie du roman*, p. 221.

and his surroundings." Evidently this concept of *équilibre* is
to provide some theoretical basis on which judgments on
both subjective and objective phenomena can structurally be
related in terms of "une rélation du même type." Contrary
to the traditional French history of literature, which seeks to
understand literature in relation to its author and which,
consequently, does not illuminate relationships "of the same
type," the sociological study of great works "parvient plus
facilement à dégager des liens *nécessaires* en les rattachant à
des unités collectives dont la structuration est beaucoup plus
facile à mettre en lumière." It is the relations between the
artistic work and the social group from which it emanates,
then, that are taken to reproduce that "balance between the
intellectual structures of the subject and his surroundings."
According to Goldmann these relations "sont du même
ordre que les relations entre les éléments de l'œuvre et son
ensemble."[20]

This theoretical point of departure, for all the stimulating suggestions that it makes, leaves a number of questions unanswered. It is true that in the analysis of social
classes and groups we are confronted with simpler and more
coherent structures than in the study of an artistic sensibility,
whose background is composed of multiple factors (ancestry,
education, profession, talent, psychology, and the like), the
effects of which can hardly be systematized. But can this
basic fact (which makes the concept of social class indispensable to an understanding of historical phenomena) be
reconciled with Goldmann's idea of "balance" or "tendency
towards balance"? The concept of *équilibre* or *tendence à
l'équilibration* may perhaps more adequately reflect subconscious or psychological phenomena; but if we transpose it to
social processes, the possibility (and, indeed, the content) of
such "balance" would depend upon the state of those economic, social, and political activities which, primarily, relate

[20] Ibid., pp. 224, 225.

to one another in regard to the reality that is constituted by them. This reality is continually moved and changed by social struggle and man's effort to appropriate his natural environment. The attempt to conceive of economic, political, social, and aesthetic activities in terms of an *équilibre* may tend to lose sight of this; it certainly leads to a quantification of constantly changing processes which, one suspects, is stressed for the sake of their structural analysis.

Notwithstanding the helpful emphasis on the deformation of old structures and the formation of new ones, this frame of reference still has something static or mechanical to it: subject and object, literature and reality, are reduced to a homological pattern in which the *changing functional relations* of art and society are either ignored or conceived as fixed correspondences of supposedly the same type. In other words, structural relationships of a homological nature are derived from the postulated balance between the intellectual structures of the subject and his environment, which, at the same time, are applied to the aesthetic formation of the work, or, in Goldmann's words, to "les relations entre les éléments de l'œuvre et son ensemble." Thereby social relations are viewed as structural correspondences of aesthetic elements: as the work stands in relationship to a "social group" (as its creator), so the single aesthetic structural element, Goldmann argues, stands in relationship to the whole work of art ("son ensemble"). This suggests a view of the interplay of function and structure that may illuminate certain works at a certain time, but it remains unsatisfactory as soon as it attempts to equate *changing* social relationships with the *unchanging* structures of the art work.

Some of the more problematic assumptions emerge when, in *Pour une sociologie du roman*, Goldmann elaborates the statement that the literary form should originate from the economic life, so that the relationship between the "forme littéraire" and the "réalité économique" is a direct and primary one that remains basically unaffected by the ideological expression of the collective consciousness of the social group or class within which the work of literature has originated. Since he rejects the idea of "une relation entre les ouvrages littéraires le plus importants et la conscience collective," the rise of the art of the novel is seen to reflect the growth and structure of trade (rather than the ideological and social constellations of economic activities as reflected in morality, science, or the weltanschauung). What matters is the homology between two structures, that of the form of the novel and that of economic exchange in liberal bourgeois society: "ainsi les deux structures, celle d'un important genre romanesque et celle de l'échange, s'avèrent-elles rigoureusement homologues au point qu'on pourrait parler d'une seule et même structure qui se manifesterait sur deux plans différents."[21]

It seems difficult to accept the structural rigor of such *histoire homologue*, for more than one reason. To begin with, the homological correspondence between the literary structure of the novel and the economic structure of "exchange in liberal society" can provide no solution for that paramount problem of method, in literary history, of the unity (and the contradiction) of genesis and value. Evidently, the concept of *histoire homologue* rests on the assumption that structural relationships "of the same type" exist within economic and aesthetic processes—an assumption which entirely disregards the fact (of basic importance to any literary history) that the novel of the nineteenth century possesses a capacity for survival and a quality of truth and value which the "homological structures" of contemporary economic life have not enjoyed.

Nor is this difficulty met by Goldmann's consideration of "coherent and meaningful structures." To use the criterion of "coherence" involves highly general (not to say

[21] Ibid., pp. 27, 26.

abstract) standards, by which the historical content and quality of the relations between the literary work and *le groupe créateur* cannot adequately be defined, let alone evaluated. The standards of evaluation, according to which a work is judged mediocre or important, are said to correspond to the degree to which the work achieves that ideological "coherence" which "is not produced by the group" but is only conceived by the work itself in regard to its "constitutive components." The poetic structure of the imaginary world, which is seen to be more coherent than the ideological structures of the social consciousness, would correspond nonetheless to that structure toward which the "totality of the group strives for."[22] And, *entre autres*, the greater this correspondence, the more "important" the work as an art work!

Although this mode of evaluation may do some justice to certain periods in literary history, it is unsatisfactory as a theoretical generalization. How, for instance, are we to evaluate that tradition of critical realism that Goldmann has described as "une forme de resistance" against the rising bourgeoisie? Would not the achievement of the critical realists be defined by the degree to which they rejected (rather than perfected) any coherent patterns in the ideology of the class which created the structure of trade as an economic activity? Is not their work or, say, that of the Jacobean and metaphysical poets, rather a factor of dissolution, instead of coherence, in the prevailing ideology? On the other hand, if the pattern of coherence is to be sought, not between the ruling classes and the novelist, but between the artist and a group of dissident intellectuals, the assumed "homological" relationship between *forme littéraire* and *réalité économique* would appear to be even more problematic and, in no way, a "homologie."

It seems difficult not to be struck by the vagueness with

[22] Ibid., pp. 226 f.

which such genetic-structural concepts like *tendance à l'équilibration* or *cohérence* are applied. On the one hand, there is a very emphatic insistence on the possibility of "une homologie rigoureuse entre les structures de la vie économique et une certaine manifestation littéraire," to which the whole idea of "cette transposition directe de la vie économique dans la vie littéraire" corresponds. On the other hand, there is the almost opposite concern with *les valeurs authentique* of the novel: "cettes valeurs sont spécifiques à chaque roman et différentes d'une roman à l'autre." Between them there is the structuralist refusal to consider the art work in correlation to the social consciousness of which it is both a reflection and an agent.[23] This refusal must finally be seen against two perspectives between which there is itself an ideological connection: one is that of one particular kind of modern art and literature (such as the *nouveau roman*) which is believed, and believes itself, to be independent of any social type of consciousness. Obviously it is the experience of this art form that provides Goldmann with an important (though perhaps unconscious) frame of reference, as when he remarks: "la création poétique moderne et la peinture contemporaine sont des formes authentiques de création culturelle sans qu'on puisse les rattacher à la conscience—même possible—d'un groupe social particulier."[24]

Similarly (and this is the second aspect) the methodological refusal to consider consciousness as an element of genesis and effect reflects the perspective of structuralism (so close to that of the *nouveau roman*); particularly, the structuralist endeavor to establish that *homologie rigoureuse* between economic and aesthetic processes. This is not to say that there cannot be some highly important analogous and, perhaps, causal relations between, for instance, the principles of commercial exchange and the structure of a novel—

---

[23] Ibid., pp. 16, 28.		[24] Ibid., p. 29.

relations the genetic structural approach succeeds in illuminating quite brilliantly. But with all its rewarding insights it cannot provide a methodological position from which the most basic problem of method in literary history, the relationship of past values and present evaluations, can be seen historically, in terms of both the unity and the contradiction of genesis and impact, *Entstehungsgeschichte* and *Wirkungsgeschichte*.[25]

Anthropology as History

The ethnologist and sociologist Claude Lévi-Strauss has contributed more than anyone toward applying the principles of modern linguistics to nonlinguistic subjects. It was his work that first made possible the insertion of historical concepts into structuralist thinking. Without taking literary history as his point of departure, Lévi-Strauss has interpreted not only language (in the strict sense of the word) but also the most various social, cultural, and mythological expressions as messages or utterances, that is, as signs in a system of man's social communication and existence. Going far beyond the traditional ties between philology and ethnology, he has found, in the application of the principles of structural linguistics, not only a number of significant insights but (in his own words) a methodological *révélation*. According to Lévi-Strauss, structural linguistics "ne peut manquer de jouer, vis-à-vis des sciences sociales, le même rôle rénovateur que la physique nucléaire, par exemple, a joué pour l'ensemble des sciences exactes." The renovation of philology was possible since Trubetskoi and Jakobson had attacked the "atomistic" and "individualistic" methods of positivism—a positivism in which, as Lévi-Strauss felt, an ethnology oriented to both the study of customs and com-

[25] For some suggestions toward developing these concepts, see below, pp. 184–87.

parative methods produced equal amounts of anarchy and discontinuity: "une débauche de discontinuité."[26]

Challenging the methodological assumptions of traditional ethnological research, Lévi-Strauss attempts to shed light on the kinship relationships of primitive tribes and peoples by comprehending (as is done with phonemes) the designations of kinship as elements of meaning within a system of relationships. He seeks to understand the primitive kinship relationships, rules of marriage, incest prohibitions, and the like by means of models in which the possible systems of kinship are coordinated through the use of transformational rules. In this manner the foundation for very different rules of marriage is seen as the socialization of a biological process, as "l'integration des familles biologiques au sein du groupe social." According to this theory, the ultimate function of exogamy and of incest prohibition is not based on blood ties but fulfills a social purpose: "d'établir, entre les hommes, un lieu sans lequel ils ne pourraient s'élever au-dessus d'une organisation biologique pour atteindre une organisation sociale."[27] By connecting a system of blood relationships with a social system of alliances, Lévi-Strauss could explain very different customs and practices, widespread geographically, by tracing them back to certain forms of reciprocity in the structures of primitive exchange.

Thus, to apply structural principles to studies in a *sociologie primitive* proved fruitful insofar as this subject matter presented relatively stable units whose change and development take place over long periods of time—a fact that makes them particularly accessible to synchronic study. As with the relatively limited quantities of the phonological systems, such social groups of prehistoric origin can actually be studied in terms of certain rules and regularities contained in a "formalization type." (As Lévi-Strauss noted: "il n'y a

---

[26]"L'Analyse structurale en linguistique et en anthropologie," *Word*, 1 (1945), 35.

[27]*Les Structures élémentaires de la parenté*, new ed. (Paris: Mouton, 1967), p. 565.

que trois structures élémentaires de parentés possibles; ces trois structures se construisent à l'aide de deux formes d'échange."[28] This challenge to purely empirical descriptions of ethnic customs seemed to justify the claim that the methods of structural linguistics can draw studies in the social sciences closer to the exact criteria of the natural sciences. Fulfilling this claim, Lévi-Strauss's *Structures élémentaires de la parenté* (1949) represented the first meaningful application of structuralist methods to ethnology as a social science.

But with all the noteworthy achievements of this experiment, one question remained unanswered from the very beginning: the question about the aims and limits of transposing linguistic categories to social phenomena. To be sure, Lévi-Strauss has frequently (beginning in 1945) emphasized "la différence très profonde qui existe entre le tableau des phonèmes d'une langue et le tableau des termes de parenté d'une société."[29] However, this has not hindered him from seeing the kinship relations themselves as language, that is, as information or message. It is true that both language and exogamy possess positive functions in the formation of society, and in this limited functional sense incest might be considered as some *abus du langage.* The linguistic version of the ethnological state of affairs might even be plausible where the attempt is made to view the kinship designations themselves, including the rules of marriage, "comme une sorte de langage, c'est-a-dire un ensemble d'opérations destinées à assurer, entre les individus et les groupes, un certain type de communication." But the use of linguistic categories becomes problematical where the rules of marriage and the systems of kinship are no longer seen as a mode of social communication or where the concept of social communication fails to relate to a sender or receiver. This is the case when Lévi-Strauss raises (and affirms) the question as to whether these kinship systems as well as "divers aspects de la

---

[28] Ibid.   [29] "L'Analyse structurale," p. 39.

vie sociale . . . ne consistent pas en phénomènes dont la nature rejoint celle même du langage."[30] This question seems crucial: it provides the theoretical basis for the structuralist approach, in terms of language, to myth and religion as well as to "every meaningful unity or synthesis, be it of a verbal or a visual kind." Indeed, as Barthes is quick to deduce, "the objects themselves are capable of becoming statements if they signify something."[31]

This assumption (which informs the most general and widespread application of linguistic principles to the study of social objects) wants a good deal of reconsideration. To begin with, this goes beyond the original suggestion of de Saussure, who, in passing, first considered "tout moyen d'expression reçu dans une société" (for example, signs of courtesy) as subject matter for semiology, although language always remained for him "le plus complexe et le plus répandu des systèmes d'expression." From a different angle, the students of semiotics have defined the nature of the sign more comprehensively by turning it into an object of epistemological analysis. In this sense Charles S. Peirce distinguished "three trichotomies," according to which a sign must function simultaneously in its quality (or existence), in its object-relations, and as a subject for interpretation. Developing these ideas, Max Bense has ascribed to its object-relation a "function of realization," to its relation to an interpretant a "function of coding," and to its quality of "medium" (*Mittel*) a function of communication. It is this last aspect which the study of the problems of communication, inspired by Peirce as well as Charles W. Morris, has stressed by employing the term *sign* (almost like *signal*) for every impulse used for the purpose of communication.[32] Even more

---

[30] *Anthropologie structurale* (Paris: Plon, 1958), pp. 69, 71.

[31] Roland Barthes, *Mythologies* (Paris: Édition du seuil, 1957), p. 216.

[32] De Saussure, *Cours de linguistique générale*, pp. 100 f.; Peirce, "Logic as Semiotic: The Theory of Signs," *Philosophical Writings of Peirce*, ed. Justus Buchler (New York, 1964), p. 101 (see also C. W. Morris, *Signs, Language, and Behavior* [New York, 1946], p. 59); Bense, *Semiotik* (Baden-Baden: Agis-Verlag, 1957), pp. 9–17, 59, and *Einführung in die informationstheoretische Ästhetik* (Reinbek b. Hamburg: Rowohlt Taschenbuch Verlag, 1969), pp. 10 f., 92, 113;

deliberately, and quite consistently, the Marxist theory of knowledge views the sign as a "means of exchanging, storing, and processing information," thereby making a distinction between the sign proper and the activity of the "carrier," "for a physical carrier is necessary to transmit a sign from a sign-producer to a sign-receiver."[33] In this context (which is emphatically one of communication) the nonlinguistic sign may well be considered as a means of exchanging and storing information: the verbal sign and the nonverbal sign, then, can both be fitted into a general definition which views the communicative function of the sign as its main characteristic, thereby recognizing that the process of communication is the basis for its investigation. Consequently, the distinction made between the characteristic (natural) sign and the proper (artificial) sign can only underline the fundamental point "that the sign must be analyzed in the context of the process of communication, and that, therefore, an object or a phenomenon can only be a sign within the framework of this process."[34]

This excursion into some philosophical definitions of the sign may perhaps help to circumscribe some of the boundaries within which ethnological and social facts can be fruitfully treated as part of a system of signs. This alone should make us pause to consider if the "great development" of the "Saussurean conception on behalf of anthropology" (as well as its application to the study of diverse phenomena, including fashion) can be considered as a methodological model from which it is safe to generalize.[35] As a French critic

---

and see Colin Cherry, *On Human Communication: A Review, a Survey, and a Criticism*, 2d ed. (Cambridge, Mass., 1966).

[33]*Philosophisches Wörterbuch*, ed. Georg Klaus and Manfred Buhr (Leipzig: Bibliographisches Institut, 1969), II, 978; Georg Klaus, *Spezielle Erkenntnistheorie* (Berlin: Deutscher Verlag der Wissenschaften, 1966), p. 33; see also Ehrhard Albrecht, *Sprache und Erkenntnis* (Berlin: Deutscher Verlag der Wissenschaften, 1967), p. 270.

[34]See Adam Schaff, *Einführung in die Semantik*, trans. Liselotte and Alois Hermann (Berlin: Deutscher Verlag der Wissenschaften, 1966), p. 148.

[35]See Barthes, *Le Degré zéro*, p. 98; *Système de la mode*, especially the "Introduction: Méthode," pp. 13–66.

put it: "le modèle linguistique est-il le modèle fondamental des sciences humaines?"[36] This is not the place to discuss the full extent of what Julia Kristeva has called "la problematique du signe";[37] but would not a more functional definition of the sign (as in the context of communication) rule out a good many of the structuralist presuppositions in the analysis of primitive social activity? The kinship systems and rules of marriage may be viewed in the light of social communication, but there is more to them than that. To suggest the limitations of the structuralist approach, one would only have to ask questions about the content of a given rule or "sign" and examine the specific social function of this content. Lévi-Strauss circumvents these questions by reducing social activity to an act of communication. Starting from kinship *designations*, he ends with kinship *relations*. The result is an unstable and sometimes ambivalent equation between the *vocabulary* of kinship and the *practice* of kinship, as when the purpose of exogamy is treated as some function of language. In "this human system of communication which forms the rules of marriage and the vocabulary of kinship," the concept of "communication" is increasingly abstracted from any concrete social content or process. But even where this is not the case, there are some startling consequences, such as when women are viewed as elements in a system of signs: "qu'est-ce que cela signifié, sinon que les femmes elles-mêmes sont traitées comme des signes. . . ." Because the rules of marriage and the systems of kinship represent "un ensemble d'opérations" which secure a certain type of communication, they are viewed as *une sorte de langage*—a language whose elements consist not of phonemes, morphemes, or phrases but of daughters, sisters, and mothers. "One can justifiably be amazed," writes Lévi-Strauss, "that women are accorded the role of elements in a

---

[36] Jean-Marie Anzias et al., *Structuralisme et marxisme* (Paris: U.G.T., 1970), pp. 85 ff.

[37] See "L'Expansion de la sémiotique," *Recherches pour une sémanalyse*, collection "Tel Quel" (Paris, 1969), pp. 43–59.

system of signs."[38] But is it not equally amazing to see how readily the linguistic element in communication is here equated with the function of women in primitive society? The resulting formalization deserves our attention because it helps to illuminate a characteristic tendency in the application of structuralist principles to social phenomena. The various aspects of social life, including the members of society (who actually are the "producers" of signs), are *themselves* understood as signs and treated as part of a language. Here, as elsewhere, the structuralist is preoccupied with *le système:* he is concerned with langue at the expense of the social function and process of human speech (in questions, answers, dialogues, and the like) as related to the most varied forms of human activity. Consequently, the essential difference between language as a *system of signs* and language (*discours*) as an *instrument of communication* is blurred when the instrument and those who wield it are exclusively treated as "signs." This entirely ignores the fact, as pointed out by Emile Benveniste, that it is not the sign (the phoneme, morpheme, or lexeme) but the sentence which constitutes the basic unit of language *as an instrument of communication.* Now the sentence does not correspond to the structure but to the event, not to the structural system but to the activity, which can change structure. "C'est dans le discours, actualisé en phrases, que la langue se forme et se configure." The sentence involves meaning, value, volition, process; it refers to that external linguistic reality which *le discours* relates to in the process of communication. "La phrase, création indéfinie, variété sans limite, est la vie même du langage en action."[39] And this *langage en action* points beyond langue as a system of signs and precedes it: *nihil est in lingua quod non prius fuerit in oratione.* The social system originates in, and changes as a result of, social activity (even

---

[38] Lévi-Strauss, *Les Structures élémentaires*, p. 565; *Anthropologie structurale*, p. 70.

[39] Emile Benveniste, *Problèmes de linguistique générale* (Paris: Gallimard, 1966), pp. 131, 129.

though the system, once it is set up, exerts a powerful influence on the kind of activity that develops within it).

If, therefore, the ethnological (or any nonlinguistic) state of affairs is to be illuminated by linguistic categories, social relationships must be seen not only as a system of signs abstracted from time but as a temporally changeable organization of activities. If the kinship *designations* correspond to the structural sign, then the actual kinship *relations* would correspond to the temporal sentence as *langage en action*. Now, just as the sentence presupposes a context of verbal action (and, consequently, the activities of human beings in history), so primitive social *relations* cannot be conceived as signs or reduced to the system of langue precisely because, in the last resort, they derive, not simply from tribal exchange or communication, but from the more basic needs of primitive living (to which the various forms of exchange are themselves related). But so long as "la société dans son ensemble" is viewed "en fonction d'une théorie de la communication,"[40] it can only be seen as a system of langue, not as *discours;* as a coordination of signs, not as the production of values—that is, as historical activity.

It is true that primitive societies, being prehistoric, have forms of organization vitally different from the modern type of society which produces literature as a historical activity. For them, the communicative act (such as the exchange of women) certainly is an even more basic fact of living when it secures "la prise du social sur le biologique, du culturel sur le naturel."[41] But it seems possible to agree with the emphasis on the social function of exogamy (in contrast to the biological) without having to sanction the way in which the process of communication is made into an absolute. There are still the more elementary facts of life: that people have to eat, drink, and—when necessary—clothe themselves; that they can secure these basic needs only *en ensemble*, that is,

[40]Lévi-Strauss, *Anthropologie structurale*, p. 95.
[41]Lévi-Strauss, *Les Structures élémentaires*, p. 549.

by forming a group or society. To be aware of these is not to minimize the momentous importance of the various forms of social communication; but it does make it possible to view communicative processes as part of a larger whole that is constituted by the sum total of all social activities. Again, it is true that economic processes in the primitive community are remarkably static so that, as Friedrich Engels noted, "auf dieser Stufe die Art der Produktion weniger entscheidend ist."[42] But does this justify the treatment of economic and social activities exclusively, or mainly, from the point of view of communication?

It is from assumptions like these that, in the end, a highly questionable conception of nonlinguistic exchange processes follows: they become "des systèmes symboliques, sous-jacents à la fois au langage et aux rapports que l'homme entretient avec le monde." Ultimately, the nature of the "systems of kinship" ("because they are systems consisting of symbols") is understood as symbolic. So Lévi-Strauss arrives at the conclusion that we are dealing with symbolism in both sociological and linguistic studies. This is what the inflation of the sign is finally about: "le monde du symbolisme est infiniment divers par son contenu, mais toujours limité par ses lois."[43] *Le système*, once it is attached to a mode of symbolization, will encompass the most diverse content and yet allow the application of structural principles. The object of analysis (such as kinship or primitive custom) is reduced to a system that remains "closed"; for the structural analysis confines itself to a pattern formalized by a logic of symbols (which is finally rooted in the unconscious)[44] without conceiving its object as a *system in motion*, that is, in relation to historical criteria or other systems. This, in the words of Julia Kristeva, never transcends "les limitations du symbolism": "Par conséquant, toute tentative de *symboli-*

---

[42]Engels to Marx, 8 Dec. 1882, Marx and Engels, *Werke* (Dietz Verlag), XXXV, 125.
[43]*Anthropologie structurale*, pp. 363, 62, 110.   [44]See ibid., p. 225.

sation des pratiques sémiotiques d'une société post-syncrétique est une réduction de ces pratiques, une élimination de leurs dimensions non symboliques."[45]

This logic of symbols is finally faced with a hermeneutic gap between the changing meaning of history and the formalized order of *le système signifiant*. As one of Lévi-Strauss's most brilliant pupils has remarked: "Un hiatus existe bien qui sépare l'existence profane dans toute la variété de ses manifestations et ce que recouvre le système signifiant qui l'ordonne." Between the two there is no interchange because *le système signifiant* provides the preconceived pattern of a logic of symbols according to which the structural meaning of human thought and social action is defined. The world of history and society (what else is "l'existence profane"?) is already ordered in advance. *Praxis* as a potent mode of social activity in history is reduced so as to work within the prearranged frame that some autonomous *schème logique* has provided: "Cette mise en système est le propre de l'intellect; elle définit le passage de la nature à la culture, les cadres à l'intérieur desquels se développe toute praxis humaine."[46] But if this is so, the passage from nature to culture reflects, not a process of tremendous change and struggle, but, primarily, the unconscious logic of the human spirit as expressed, for example, by such *oppositions* as "le frais et le pourri," "le sec et l'humide," or "le vide et le plain," which *Le Cru et le cuit* has elaborated as part of that "mythe de la mythologie"[47] which it itself is. But

[45] *Recherches pour une sémanalyse*, p. 47.

[46] Lucien Sebag, *Marxisme et structuralisme* (Paris: Payot, 1964), pp. 180, 184.

[47] Claude Lévi-Strauss, *Le Cru et le cuit*, "Mythologiques," I (Paris: Plon, 1964), 20. Ultimately, the brilliant ethnologist's method itself reflects a nostalgic attitude toward the timeless world of myth "par lequel une société qui se livre à l'histoire croit pouvoir remplacer l'ordre logico-naturel qu'elle a abandonné, à moins qu'elle-même n'ait été abandonnée par lui" (*L'Origin des manières de table*, "Mythologiques," III [Paris, 1968], 106). I have attempted a critique of Lévi-Strauss's approach to myth ("Literaturwissenschaft und Mythologie," in my *Literaturgeschichte und Mythologie*, pp. 410–27), which I do not repeat here.

if, ultimately, the logic of symbols of the object (be it primitive custom, or myth, or literature) determines the method of its investigation, so that the study of mythology is turned into a modern version of *mythologique*, then history has, once and for all, ceased to be meaningful either as a mode of the object or as an element in the methodology of the *Subjekt*, that is, the historian himself. There remains the widening gulf between the symbolic classifications of structure and the disorder of history. Says Lévi-Strauss:

Il y a donc une sorte d'antipathie foncière entre l'histoire et les systèmes de classification. Cela explique peut-être ce qu'on serait tenté d' appeler le "vide totémique," puisque, même à l'état de vestiges, tout ce qui pourrait évoquer le totémisme semble remarquablement absent des grandes civilisations d'Europe et d'Asie. La raison n'est-elle pas que celles-ci ont choisi de s'expliquer à elles-mêmes par l'histoire, et que cette entreprise est incompatible avec celle qui classe les choses et les êtres (naturels et sociaux) au moyen de groupes finis?[48]

But to go back beyond the *vide totémique* is, finally, to go back on all objects and methods of historiography. It is to reject both the results and the modes of history, including the history of literature, which is itself a historical product and an agent of historical consciousness.

Literary History as a System in Motion: Some Counterproposals

At this point, to ask the question whether Saussurean structuralism, as developed by Lévi-Strauss, can make a contribution to literary history is to realize that such a contribution, if it is to be valid, will have to bridge the gap between the historical process ("dans toute la variété de ses manifestations") and *le système signifiant*. But any attempt to overcome this dichotomy involves a methodological position according to which the history of literature can be seen as both creation and signification in its genetic as well as

[48]Claude Lévi-Strauss, *La Pensée sauvage* (Paris: Plon, 1962), pp. 307 f.

its communicative processes. What is wanted is a historical-dialectical correlation of both origins and effect in terms of the unity (and the tension) of past significance and present meaning—a correlation that would have to conceive of the history of literature synchronically as well as diachronically, as a history of both langue and *discours*, structure and *Praxis*.

For that to elaborate some methodological foundations seems a formidable task which, among other things, would call for what Julia Kristeva has termed a "théorie scientifique des systèmes signifiants dans l'histoire et de l'histoire comme système signifiant."[49] The following notes cannot, of course, claim anything of the kind. What they attempt to do is in the nature of some prolegomena that are based on the assumption (illustrated, it is hoped, in the preceding section) that the contradiction between the positions of the foremost French structuralist and that of the most radical form of historical consciousness allows of no facile synthesis. It does not seem helpful to gloss over the differences between the methods of structuralism and those of Marxism; they are not the same, and to confuse them would be to give in to the "confusion of levels" and the eclecticism philosophers from the most divergent positions have warned against—for instance, Lucien Sebag or Georg Klaus.[50]

But this is not to say that the study of literary history cannot be enriched by consulting the methods and results of structural linguistics, semiotics, cybernetics, or information theory. On the contrary, every school of literary history, including the Marxist, would be ill advised if it did not carefully weigh the possibilities and perspectives of the new sciences. At the same time, to consider aspects of their application is not to argue that the traditional methods of historical study become obsolete or superfluous. Rather, this might help to view the history of literature less exclusively

---

[49] *Recherches pour une sémanalyse*, p. 22.
[50] Georg Klaus, "Kybernetik und ideologischer Klassenkampf," *Einheit*, 25 (1970), 1180 ff.; Sebag, *Marxisme et structuralisme*, p. 142.

from a *literary* angle by stimulating a more interdisciplinary perspective not only in the histories of language and literature but even more so in the changing context in which literature finds itself together with, and as a consequence of, the development of new artistic media, materials, and techniques. In a situation like this, the history of literature would do well not to follow a narrowly philological orientation but relate its own problems of history and value to some broader aspects of the development of the other arts. Each of these has a "language" of its own which, being historical, undergoes changes and which, being an aesthetic phenomenon, might be considered within a comparative framework as part of a more general history of the language of art. For that, the most comprehensive and most practicable concepts, it is suggested, would have to be derived from an area where the interplay of social function and aesthetic structure allows some generalizations that include, but also transcend, the specific problems of literature as a verbal art form.[51]

[51] Here I do not consider the structural analysis of the verbal art of literature which, from the point of view of the aims and methods of literary history, is not of primary interest in the present context. However, there is a rapidly growing literature on the subject with some impressive contributions, like Jean Cohen's *Structure du langage poétique* (Paris: Flammarion, 1966), or J. M. Lotman's most recent *Analis poeticheskogo teksta: struktura stikhi* (Leningrad, 1972)—a good deal of it indebted to Roman Jakobson's interpretations of poetic texts, from his early analysis, undertaken together with Claude Lévi-Strauss, of "Les chats de Charles Baudelaire" (*L'Homme*, 2 [1962], 5–21) to the study, written together with Lawrence G. Jones, *Shakespeare's Verbal Art in* Th'expence of Spirit (The Hague, 1970). What these attempt to do is almost invariably to analyze poetic language in terms of what Lotman (pp. 6, 119) calls its "vnutrennaja struktura," that is, the internal structure according to which the literary text is taken as a self-contained whole ("poetichesky tekst, vziaty kak otdel'noye, uzhe zakonchennoye i vnutrenne samostoyatel'noye tseloye"). But almost never, except by Julia Kristeva ("Le Mot, le dialogue et le roman," *Recherches pour une sémanalyse*, pp. 164–68), is the text considered "comme activité social"; rather, the emphasis is on the formal analysis of the destructuring and restructuring of poetic language, and the demonstration of correspondences (agreements or oppositions) at the phonological, lexical, syntactic, and, more rarely, semantic levels.

Reading these newest versions of *explication des textes* one is tempted (in the words, though not in the sense, of I. A. Richards) to think "of these new revelations of order as a powerful helping hand offered to us in this time of

If literature, in the unity of its lexical, syntactical, and semantic functions, is to be comprehended in terms of its historical and cultural contexts, then a specifically aesthetic (and not simply verbal or linguistic) equivalent must be found for the structural concept of *le système signifiant.* Such an equivalent does not lie in the linguistic material of literature but, rather, in the total interplay of all the structural elements peculiar to literature as an art form. But such a totality of structural signs, if it is to be viewed historically, can never be seen as autonomous or as constituting a closed system; on the contrary, the formalist (threefold) abstraction from the social, thematic, and historical contexts must be overcome in order to integrate the symbolic logic of aesthetic wholes functionally, semantically, and temporally into a vision of literature as history. For this, no *analyse immanente* will ever do. It is precisely the pragmatic and the semantic aspects of the aesthetic system of structures which refer beyond *le système.* They do not simply reflect it; they help constitute it as social action and ideological meaning. In other words, the process of literature, when seen in terms of both its creation and reception, is functionally, significantly, and historically part of the social activity of its creators and recipients. And it is this activity, or *Praxis,* which, in the last resort, helps to constitute and change *le système signifiant* in the language of literature.

The language of literature, therefore, if it is to be treated historically, must be conceived on two levels (which, of course, interact): the one is that of the concrete work of literature, the poem, novel, or drama, where the aesthetic

---

frightened and bewildered disaffection" ("Jakobson's Shakespeare: The Subliminal Structures of a Sonnet," *TLS,* 28 May 1970, p. 589). This gives away some unconscious ideology; but if structuralist exegesis goes beyond the apologetic functions of formalism it may still be a helpful way of *describing* poetically organized verbal structures. However, what this type of exegesis cannot do is to provide an understanding of literature either as systematic history or as a historical system.

character of language would be in the nature of parole, or (to use E. D. Hirsch's pregnant definition) "a particular, selective actualization from langue."[52] The individual work of literature is, somewhat like the phrase, both the result and the cause of activity, social and individual. To adapt Emil Benveniste's definition of the *phrase* to a literary context, one might say that the individual work, "création indéfinie, variété sans limite, est la vie même de la littérature en action."[53] In others words, the history of literature, if considered as a changing system of creative possibilities, is permanently reconstituted from within by the social and aesthetic activity of its creators and recipients: the whole system of the literary langue (its available conventions and perspectives, its stock of thematic or verbal devices) is constantly changed and renewed through the *Praxis* of the creation and the reception of new literary works.

On the other hand, a systematic history of literature would be unlikely to take the concrete work as a point of departure. There must be a vision of the whole of the literature of a nation, an age, or a society. The true historical sense, as T. S. Eliot noted long ago, induces an awareness that literature "has a simultaneous existence and composes a simultaneous order."[54] This may not be (as Eliot thought) an "ideal order," but it reflects the present availability of past works in terms of their changing modes of reception. The availability is, of course, only a relative one (exposed, as it is, to the pressures of taste and ideology), but it does allow of a kind of simultaneousness in the perception and recreation of the language of literature in history. In this, both the literary historian and the creative writer are confronted with more than an actualization or even a segment of the language of literature: what they have

---

[52] E. D. Hirsch, Jr., "Objective Interpretation," *PMLA*, 75 (1960), 473 f.

[53] *Problèmes de linguistique générale*, p. 129.

[54] *Selected Essays: 1917–1932* (London, 1932), p. 20. But see my critique of Eliot's concept of tradition, above, chap. 2.

at their disposal is, more or less, an equivalent of langue, the total stock of literary kinds, conventions, and devices.

But this distinction between the literary equivalents of langue and parole must not conceal the fact that there is also some interrelationship between them—an interrelation that points to a crucial problem of all literary history. At the level of his most elementary decisions, the literary historian does not even have a choice: were he to view only the individual work (or a succession of works) as parole, no historical-systematic generalizations, such as about genre and society, would be possible. Similarly, a preoccupation with langue would tend to neglect the great works themselves and reduce the constitutive quality of their contributions to the growth of a literature. For this reason systematic or typo-logical statements (about theme, genre, composition, style) seem helpful insofar as they generalize the infinite variety of individual works; and, conversely, valid statements about the individual work and its position in literary history are possible only in full consciousness of all (past *and* future) literary achievements of the age, class, nation, or genre. In very much oversimplified terms: a statement in literary his-tory will be the more historical, the more *langue* is particu-larized in terms of the individual work (as creation or event), and it will be the more systematic or typological, the more *parole* is generalized in terms of all the forms and meanings of the language of literature.

This dialectic of langue and parole seems quite incom-patible with any understanding of artistic structure as op-posed to, or excluding, consciousness. Structural form, in the individual work and, *consequently*, in the whole of literature, is not (as Roland Barthes has it) "un domaine purement intérieur à l'œuvre." As seen from a dialectical point of view, *le système signifiant* is not a closed system of formal structures; for its actualization on the level of the in-dividual work involves a relationship between *signifiant* and *signifié* which is unlike that in ordinary language, because in both artistic creation and effect *le signifiant* assumes the status not only of a sign but of an action. *Although* it is part of a system of signs, it *yet* serves as an instrument of expression and reception.

It is this twofold connection of the language of literature that seems essential: on the one hand, it may be understood in relation to the available stock, or the total system, of formal and linguistic devices; on the other hand, in relation to the experience, the consciousness, and *Praxis* of its sender and receiver. Once this connection is seen as an *inter*connection, the literary activity of the sender and receiver, like some *langage en action*, can be understood to draw on and, at the same time, to constitute and change, the available stock of signs. Given that this interconnection is established, the system of formal devices may be abstracted from the *langage en action*, even though their quality, the extent of their availability, and the degree of their usefulness are all of a historical nature and coordinated with a certain level of social, intellectual, and stylistic developments.

The important thing is that these aesthetic signs, or devices, as well as some of the works of art which use them, are not, in Hegel's sense of the word, *aufgehoben* ("suspended") in the course of literary history. The elements of drama (dialogue, monologue, conflict, epilogue), poetry (rhythm, meter, verse), and narrative fiction (first-person narration, third-person narration, omniscient point of view) are similar to the signs of a language in that the historical conditions of their genesis do not limit the possibility of their use to the period of their origin. This is one of the reasons why a literary technique can be transplanted. It is true that in certain cases the context of the transplantation (like the history of origins) can provide a very powerful clue in deciphering the current uses and meanings of the technique. Yet it must be said that very important forms and techniques, such as the monologue in drama, alliteration in poetry, first-person narration in the novel, still fulfill functions today that no longer reflect the social context of their origins. Their quality is determined, among other things, by their structural relation to other devices, that is, by their being part of the same langue in which their own specific place is defined syntagmatically, by the existence of dialogue, prose, third-person narration, and so on, as part of a larger *système signifiant*. Abstracted from a concrete work, that is, beyond their function as parole, these devices do not constitute a meaning; they are signs which attain semantic functions only in relation to an achieved content, and pragmatic functions only in relation to some creative or receptive activity.

Any attempt to integrate these functions and to face the full weight of the contradiction between historical movement and paradigmatic order cannot simply rely on models borrowed from either linguistics or sociology.[55] For one thing, it cannot simply transfer the sociological, epistemological, or linguistic definitions to the literary sign. To specify the aesthetic quality of its relations, one would have to make a number of distinctions. The first distinction would be that, as opposed to the sign in ordinary language, the aesthetic sign serves in *specifically* pragmatic functions. It is differently and certainly more profoundly related to the creative faculties of the people who produce and receive it; for in literature as *langage en action* the three basic pragmatic functions of ordinary language—which serves (1) as symbol, or representation and description, (2) as symptom, or expression and evaluation, (3) as signal, or rhetoric and communication—are all quite changed. In literature the representative or descriptive function, which becomes entirely indirect and fictive, is radically contaminated by expression and evaluation so that the content of the aesthetic "signal" is primarily determined neither by (1) nor (2) but by

[55]This is where I would disagree with Hayden White's perceptive summary ("Literary History: The Point of It All," *New Literary History*, 2 [1970–71], 174 f.) in which he suggests "the possibility of a virtual language of literary history, with a lexical, a grammatical, and a syntactical dimension."

a new kind of unity between them which the correlating art of rhetoric itself helps to achieve. Consequently, and this is the second distinction, the semantic function of the sign in aesthetic discourse is more highly complex and of a more polysemantic dimension, because the referential relationship to the world of objects is (without being entirely canceled out) subjected to creative forms of both expression and rhetoric. It is only after these two basic specifications have been observed that, thirdly, the most valuable of the structuralist propositions can be considered. The aesthetic sign is more flexibly and, again, more creatively related to the existence of other signs, syntactically in connection with the concrete work of art, as well as paradigmatically in a general connection with the historically available stock of literary devices. But to consider seriously the syntactic and paradigmatic context of the literary sign is to realize that this context, far from being purely formal, can assume evaluative and semantic functions: it is by considering the syntactic relationships of the literary sign that its full significance within the semantic pattern of the work of art will emerge.

These still very rough (and highly generalized) distinctions might be illustrated in connection with the semiotic triplet. Although the triplet with its generally accepted differentiation between the sign (S), the object (O), and the reference (R) may be helpful for a definition of the language of literature, the relationship, in literature, of both (R) and (S) to (O) is fundamentally different and extremely complex. Here it must suffice to say that both reference and sign—in their very different ways—engage in a relationship to an object or situation (Ogden and Richards's *referent*) which, being imaginary, enjoys a metaphorical, rather than actual, status. At the same time this relationship is subjected to a process of rhetoric and evaluation which tends to stress the tension (rather than the congruity) between reference and object. It is in this sense that concepts like denotation (defining the relationship between signs and referents) or connotation (stressing the relationship between signs and references) have been widely used to specify the qualities of poetic language.[56]

This is not the place to go into the theory of the sign as an aesthetic phenomenon, but some idea of its specific quality is required if the language of literature is to be seen in a historical perspective. At this point an illustration can perhaps serve to suggest that the specifically aesthetic connection between reference and sign presents, in the history of literature, a historical relationship by which *le système signifiant*, far from being an autonomous logical structure, is in constant interplay with the changing semantic function of *le signifié*.

The history of the novel, in particular the art of narrative perspective, is a case in point. If perspective in the novel may be defined as the total interplay of consciousness and technique, then a correlation seems necessary between (1) the basic attitudes and values of the author, as embodied in, say, a proletarian, catholic, liberal position or in a critical, ironic, detached, committed attitude toward his subject matter and (2) the strategy of presentation—the imaginary point of view (first person, first-person observer, third person), the use of scene or summary, and so on. Now the two different connections of point of view may be said to constitute a *système signifié* as associated with (1), and a *système signifiant*, as associated with (2). In a novel like *Robinson Crusoe* this involves the unity but also some tensions between the historical meaning of the author's statement about the world (that is, his Protestant point of view) and the first-person narrative medium. So if narrative perspective in *Robinson Crusoe* is to embrace consciousness and technique, (1) the achieved author-narrator's standpoint (which is not

[56]See, e.g., B. C. Heyl, *New Bearings in Esthetics and Art Criticism: A Study in Semantics and Evaluation* (New Haven, 1943), p. 6; and the more prominent work of Susanne K. Langer, Charles W. Morris, or that of critics like Philip Wheelwright which, however, is in considerable disagreement with my own argument.

identical with his individual consciousness or intention) and (2) the technical point of view of the narrative must be seen to be correlated as reference and sign, or conception and presentation.[57] The important point is that the particular fiction of Robinson Crusoe's technical point of view, which yields the *signifiant* (and the typological aspect of the narrative), is not independent of the author's historical point of view, which, on the other hand, it helps to embody and even to constitute. In the literary history of the novel, then, the semantic and the paradigmatic aspects can be separated only by abstraction. They achieve their historical and typological significance only to the extent that out of the interrelationship of *le système signifié* and *le système signifiant* the language of the novel is seen at the crossing-points of narrative fiction and narrative conscience, structure and history.

Now although this highly schematic illustration may perhaps be said to point beyond the antinomy between the structural *analyse immanente* and the sociological concern with function, it still cannot (in its oversimplified way) suggest the changing historical quality of the relations between reference and sign. In order to view these relations historically and to establish their changing connections in terms of both the unity and the contradiction of creation and reception, one must make an important distinction. While (in semiotic terms) the *sign* as the materialized result of creative activity has more of an objective quality, the *reference*, resulting from both creative and receptive processes, involves a higher degree of subjectivity and change. In terms of linguistic analysis: the *signifiant* (that is, the first-person convention, Crusoe's fictitious point of view) is the more permanent and stable entity, the issue of a particular creation in literary history, more or less recorded and to be verified in

[57]This is based on my approach to point of view in fiction, as outlined in "Erzählerstandpunkt und *point of view*," *Zeitschrift für Anglistik und Amerikanistik*, 10 (1962), 369–416, and "Erzählsituation und Romantypus," *Sinn und Form*, 18 (1966), 109–33. For some practical interpretations see chapter 6 and the two articles referred to therein in n. 25.

the text of the novel. The *signifié*, on the other hand, is more radically involved in that historical process of literature, which stretches from the action of the author to the reaction of his first audience and, again, from the receptive activity of the first reader to that of the last reader. In this process of *Wirkungsgeschichte*, the reference of the work (which reflects a changing indirect relationship of sign and referent) itself changes. This historicity of the reference, that is, the considerable changes in the meaning of *Robinson Crusoe*, or *Hamlet*, over the centuries, is associated with the permanent attempt at recreating and reproducing a meaningful correlation of *signifiant, signifié*, and referent. The sign is made to *refer* to an imaginary object, and it is the permanently renewed search for this *reference* that may be seen to reflect the never-ending need for interpretation and reinterpretation.

Now the object, or referent, to which the work of art (indirectly) refers is, as has been pointed out, quite unlike the referent in ordinary language. It is certainly not the concrete object to which, for example, the verbal signs [teibl], [tish], [tabl] refer; rather, it is the object of the metaphorical reference of the standards and values of the imaginative world of the art work to the experience of the real world of history. In terms of the unity of literary genesis and reception, this referent to which the sign indirectly refers becomes exceedingly complex because, in the historical process of literature, it is being sought on more than one level. First on the genetic plane, the time of composition, as when a great work like *Hamlet* is viewed as an image of the Elizabethan world; such reference of the work to its own time points to its *past significance*. But second, the total meaning of a work of art cannot simply be deduced from its historical setting; it also comprehends the deliberate or unconscious, but in many ways inevitable, reference of the work to the time of its effect. According to this, a figure like Hamlet or Robinson Crusoe would be viewed as *present meaning*—a modern symbol and an ever-present problem. In literary history, however, both past and present references constantly interact; for the literary historian who is confronted with this interaction of *Entstehungsgeschichte* and *Wirkungsgeschichte*, the question is not *whether* to accept both worlds as points of reference but rather *how* to relate them so as to have as much as possible of the past significance and as much as possible of the present meaning merged into a new unity. And it is this permanently renewed *reference* of the *sign* to an ever-changing connection of *referents*, past and present, that constitutes the meaning of literary history and makes the integration of historiography and evaluation so paramount and so difficult a task for the literary historian.

However, this dialectic of literary history rests on the presupposition that aesthetic structure is seen as a correlative of the social function in the historical activity of the creative and receptive *Subjekt* (and not that activity as a function or reflection of the logic of symbols of *le système*). This, it is hoped, makes it possible to avoid both the autonomous fallacy of Roland Barthes's *analyse immanente* (and the dissociation of structure from the context of social *Praxis* and human values) and the determinist fallacy of Lucien Goldmann's *histoire homologue* with its equation of economic and literary structures (and the dissociation of historical objects from their present aesthetic experience). From a dialectical point of view these reservations seem crucial. They once more underline the fact that, in literary history, the method of historical materialism and the method of structuralism are not the same. At the same time, one can grant that linguistic or semiotic concepts, if properly specified, possess a certain usefulness in the clarification of old problems and the opening of new problems and perspectives on the relationship of texts and contexts in literary history.

V

Metaphor and Historical Criticism: Shakespeare's Imagery Revisited

AMONG the various symptoms of change and crisis in British and American criticism, the study of the verbal and symbolic patterns of imagery, especially in the work of Shakespeare, has been affected more radically than perhaps any other area in literary scholarship. If the 1971 World Shakespeare Congress may still be regarded as a reliable register of the current trends and directions in criticism, the prominence of imagery studies, so conspicuous in the fifties and early sixties, has receded considerably. Imagery criticism was relegated to the rank of a special session, where it had to accommodate itself with subjects such as Shakespeare's sources and analogues or conceptions of love and lust in Shakespearean and Elizabethan drama. What is more, the dislodgment from its previous position of preeminence was hardly noticed, and the obvious questions as to the way the study of imagery was affected by new critical emphases (such as that on the theater) either were not raised or did not appear worthy of serious consideration. This alone (though there are many more symptoms) would seem to make it safe to say that the criticism that looked for metaphor and symbol in "the pattern below the level of 'plot' and 'character'" may still be widely practiced, but as a creative force in scholarship it has had its day.[1] Once in the forefront

---

[1]The phrase is T. S. Eliot's, in his Introduction to G. Wilson Knight, *The Wheel of Fire*, rev. ed. (London, 1949), p. xviii. Among recent critics of Shakespeare, Kenneth Muir ("Shakespeare's Imagery—Then and Now," *Shakespeare Survey 18* [1965], 54) was one of the first to notice "that in recent years the study of imagery has fallen into disfavour."

The literature on metaphor is, of course, vast; see, e.g., Warren A. Shibles, *Metaphor: An Annotated Bibliography and History* (Whitewater, Wis., 1971), whose actual bibliography (pp. 23–318), although somewhat uncritical and not really exhaustive, adumbrates the dimension of the subject. The excellent survey

of the revulsion from the nineteenth-century romantic tradition, this criticism itself has now become part of the history of criticism, and its aims and methods can more nearly be seen in perspective, including the perspective of the traditions of the neoclassical and romantic criticism it claimed to have refuted so conclusively.

But this claim must now be seriously questioned; for as soon as a wider perspective on structure and society is brought to bear on the problem, some of the critical assumptions characteristic of the Enlightenment or romanticism, particularly those of the correlation of life and literature, no longer seem so absolutely out of date. It is true that the neoclassical and, to some extent, the romantic approach to metaphor contained an element of crudity (such as the idea of metaphor as ornament) that should not be minimized; and it is of course equally true that the dialectical perspective sought for cannot be borrowed from the past. All the same, a more balanced reassessment of these traditional approaches to metaphor can be quite useful in questioning the different assumptions of the purely verbal and symbolic modes of interpretation as against a more consistently historical view of the interaction of idea and form as a constitutive factor in the structure and function of imagery.

In this respect a good deal of the uneasiness that for some years has been voiced about some of the main directions of mid-twentieth-century English and American criticism seems relevant. For instance, as a point of departure, there developed a new readiness to diagnose the "modernistic over-ingenuity" of the school of Knight, with its confusions "between literal and metaphorical meanings" or, more generally and more recently, to point out the dissociations of the common experience of the plays and the

---

by Terence Hawkes, *Metaphor* (London, 1972), which I have seen after the present chapter was written and revised, contains a useful "Select Bibliography" (pp. 92–98). For more recent trends in criticism of metaphor, see the *Forschungsbericht* by H. A. Pausch, "Die Metapher," *Wirkendes Wort*, 24 (1974), I, 56–69.

symbolic and thematic abstractions of scholarship (its "reductiveness").[2] For if these have been attacked as disturbing symptoms of a criticism in trouble, then surely the study of metaphor and the approach to verbal and symbolic patterns is involved. To characterize the nature of the involvement is to draw attention to a seeming paradox: it was precisely the criticism that initiated a most detached scrutiny of the concrete texture of the play, of all its verbal parallels and patterns, its ironies and similes, and, of course, its images and image clusters, which ended up in the most vague abstractions, symbolic and thematic. The underlying contradiction (which, quite often, involved the strange contrast between the brilliance of the critical performance and the tenuousness of the generalized "theme") is not sufficiently accounted for by an indictment of "this vocabulary of explicating, elaborating, questioning, defining and so on." Nor can it be countered by the charge that these critics "have been betrayed by a bias toward what can be set out in rational argument."[3] If rationality, as Nietzsche sensed so passionately and so painfully, is part of the burden of historical consciousness, then these critics can be shown to have relied too little on it, rather than too much. And it may be suggested that their abstractions, far from being too rational, are not quite adequate as generalizations; as one scholar-critic pertinently remarked, they are so many ways of "imposing our preferred reductive terms arbitrarily on poems," especially "such familiar and all-embracing dichotomies as life and death . . ., good and evil, love and hate, harmony and strife, order and disorder. . . ."[4]

But, again, the ultimate fallacy is not in "the cult of the 'concrete'" or in the "monism" of any critical language but

[2] John Holloway, *The Story of the Night* (London, 1961), p. 5; Norman Rabkin, "Meaning and Shakespeare," *Shakespeare 1971*, Proceedings of the World Shakespeare Congress, ed. Clifford Leech and J. M. R. Margeson (Toronto, 1972), p. 99.

[3] Holloway, p. 3; Rabkin, "Meaning and Shakespeare," p. 99.

[4] R. S. Crane, *The Languages of Criticism and the Structure of Poetry* (Toronto, 1953), p. 123.

in the absence of a methodology by which the structure of a past text and the abstractions of the present consciousness can be meaningfully related as some form of *historical activity*. This is not to say that those who embrace these critical positions would wish to see themselves free from any commitment in the present world with its problems, but their perhaps unconscious bias usually amounts to some form of conservative weltanschauung (the more effective when the impulse is still felt to be radical), by which "a selective use of the past against an unruly present" is made.[5] Since the selection is probably even more unconscious than the bias on which it is based, the subtle structure of the past art work and the symbolic abstraction of the modern critic, the roles in society fulfilled by the work and the functions of its present interpretation, and the way these roles and functions are irreconcilable and yet linked to the common world of history—these are never fully made conscious.

The approach to the plays as dramatic poems, with the emphasis on theme and structure most completely expressed in symbol and imagery, reduces the whole question of function to a structural problem. If it is asked at all, it is thought of as an autonomous category by which, say, the relationship of texture to structure, part to whole, is considered, but never the relationship of the whole work of art, or any of its parts, to the society which it both reflects and helps to constitute. The attention is directed to what the text signifies or means, never to what it did, or does, to the spectator or the reader. It is the bias of a *Darstellungsästhetik*, an aesthetic of representation and signification, never a *Wirkungsästhetik*, one of function and reception.

At this point, the recent emphasis on the theatrical quality and context of Shakespeare's plays seems a genuine

---

[5] Raymond Williams, in a review of L. C. Knights's *Further Explorations*, cited by Arnold Kettle, "Some Tendencies in Shakespearian Criticism," *Shakespeare Jahrbuch*, 102 (Weimar, 1966), 28.

advance. The readiness to view Shakespeare as a man of the theater, like the recent interest in the Elizabethan stage, is, as T. J. B. Spencer noted, "not merely an archaeological one." If it were possible "to consider the play as a dynamic interaction between artist and audience," then indeed the concept of function would have to be defined beyond the confines of an autonomous and ahistorical conception of structure. For that some of the historical revisions, such as the rejection of a self-contained "multiple stage" and the new light on the open nature of the Elizabethan platform, are certainly significant, not only in that they should lead ideally to better modern productions, but in that they reflect a new awareness of the possibilities of the role of the theater in society.[6] Such awareness, it is hoped, contradicts the traditional view of the theater's social function as "the preservation of great works of literature." Or it may help to challenge the traditional habit to push the plays in a literary direction and to use them for a *Bildungsbürgertum*, "and thus to *reduce* them to the level of a mindless, social pseudo-event which, like many another such, serves merely to comfort and confirm where it ought to disturb and revitalize."[7]

But even though one would not wish to minimize the potential critical significance of the recent interest in the Elizabethen stage, it has as yet produced few clarifications of any theoretical or methodological consequence. In particular, it has not presented us with a viable alternative to the literary and formal modes of analysis. From a methodological point of view, it has not come to terms with the process of interaction between the theatrical and poetic dimensions in Shakespeare's work. Although there is a rapidly

---

[6]Spencer, "Shakespeare: The Elizabethan Theatre-Poet," in *The Elizabethan Theatre*, ed. David Galloway (Toronto, 1969), p. 1; Rabkin, "Meaning and Shakespeare," p. 102. I have considered at some length the social, structural, and verbal context of these revisions in my *Shakespeare und die Tradition des Volkstheaters* (Berlin: Henschelverlag, 1967).

[7]Terence Hawkes, "Postscript: Theatre against Shakespeare?" in *The Elizabethan Theatre*, pp. 123, 126.

growing literature on the subject, the results are not such that they have established the extent to which the metaphoric quality of dramatic speech is itself an agent in, and a reflection of, the social mode of the theater. Thus, while the ahistorical and nontheatrical modes of Shakespeare criticism have come to be distrusted, a more satisfying and comprehensive approach to Shakespeare's verbal art has been slow to take their place. At this juncture, to plead for a new kind of psychological aesthetic of the drama or to suggest that a critic adopt the perspective and experience of the actor will raise many more questions than it can solve. As a recent survey put it, rather disarmingly: "Criticism based on a strong sense of the play as something that is incomplete until it is performed seems likely to grow in importance, but it is a difficult area of discussion."[8]

Today any new approach to Shakespeare's imagery is confronted with this failure to achieve a new synthesis. That is only one reason why (somewhat self-consciously) the present approach has to attempt to define its own frame of reference in terms of a larger and more comprehensive view of the subject. What is needed is a dialectical synthesis of history and criticism by which both the past significance and the present meaning of Shakespeare's theater can, among other things, be defined through the quality of his dramatic poetry, and vice versa. It is only when Elizabethan society, theater, and language are viewed as interrelated that the structure of dramatic imagery (like that of wordplay, verse, or prose) can be seen as fully functional, that is, as part of a larger (and not only literary) whole. To achieve an understanding of metaphor as an element in the total function of, and response to, Shakespearean drama demands an approach

[8]Stanley Wells, "Shakespeare Criticism since Bradley," in *A New Companion to Shakespeare Studies,* ed. Kenneth Muir and S. Schoenbaum (Cambridge, 1971), p. 261. The most telling titles characteristic of the present phase of uncertainty, transition, and (one hopes) new synthesis are supplied by industrious dissertations; see, e.g., A. S. Hilliard, "Shakespeare's Botanical Imagery: Its Meaning to the Elizabethan Audience and Its Dramatic Function in the Plays," Tennessee 1965.

by which, ultimately, metaphorical speech can be comprehended as both a process and a vision of history: as part of the history of the society the Elizabethan theater both reflected and helped to constitute. It is true that such a concept of function cannot easily (and, in very many cases, hardly, if at all) be traced in terms of its poetic and linguistic manifestations; but as a matter of principle it is of great consequence, and the wider frame of reference it provides will help to induce a correspondingly complex analysis of structure. Ultimately, the increased awareness of the social and theatrical functions of Shakespeare's plays need not preclude, but should in fact stimulate, a more theoretical view and a more practical criticism of the verbal arts of drama.

The most pressing task, then, is to develop some such theoretical and aesthetic perspective, not independently of, but in close contact with, the requirements of a new historical consciousness of the literary process.[9] But how, in this particular case, to strengthen the links between theory and history? How to link the theory of metaphor and the mode of historical criticism? This essay attempts, however tentatively and experimentally, to comprehend a theory of metaphor in the actual process of its application to, and conception in, the work of a great dramatist. Naturally, this cannot be done without a reconsideration of some of the basic tenets in the history of the criticism of Shakespeare's imagery. Such a reconsideration would wish to have recourse to any genuine insight by which a historical and practicable theory of metaphor can profit; but primarily it will involve a critique of formalist concepts and some suggestions toward a new approach to imagery.

Accordingly, and in terms of the larger function of structure stipulated here, metaphor is viewed as neither an

---

[9]To point out that this is the postulate and the position of many of my colleagues at the Zentralinstitut für Literaturgeschichte, Berlin, DDR, gives me a welcome opportunity to acknowledge the unfailing inspiration that I have drawn from discussions and conversations with scholars like Werner Mittenzwei, Manfred Naumann, Hans Kaufmann, Werner Bahner, Dieter Schlenstedt, and others.

autonomous aspect of poetry (as the New Critics argued) nor (as some of their predecessors believed) an ornamental one. Rather, it forms the very core and center of that creative and receptive activity by which, through poetry, man as a social being imaginatively comprehends his relation to time and space and, above all, to the world around him. The essence of metaphor is to connect; to interrelate and to associate the physical world and the world of ideas, the concrete and the abstract, but also the general and the particular, the social and the individual. It is because the metaphoric process itself involves these interrelations that the study of metaphor in its turn must not lose sight of the dialectic that is involved. Poetic metaphor in general and in Shakespearean drama in particular points to the most vital and intense links by which the world of experience and its poetic evaluation, the sense of the real world and the illusion of the play-world, are correlated and thus transmuted into art. The process of their correlation, which is at the heart of metaphor, involves both the unity and the contradiction of mimetic and expressive functions. This potent merging of representational and nonrepresentational modes of perception stimulates the powers of apprehension and releases an energizing experience whose quality can be defined by the degree to which the poet's objectivity and subjectivity, the audience's sense of reality and the faculties of their imagination, are made one in the verbal expression of their interaction.

This approach to metaphor (though of course much oversimplified here) may perhaps help prepare and, indeed, anticipate a theoretical position that, it is hoped, can provide an opening through which a perspective on history can illuminate the discussion of imagery. For, in the first place, the world of history and society does not exist outside the work itself; it is not like a frame that may be detached from the picture or a background that may be deleted or ignored. Rather, it provides a historical dimension that, in the case of Shakespeare, is inseparable from the quality of his greatness. If Ben Jonson's epitaph may serve once more to convey some basic truth about his rival's work, the phrase "Soule of the Age," itself a metaphor, can be taken to point to the width and the depth of Shakespeare's range of reference that he realized, at least in part, through the quality and structure of his metaphorical language. This phrase draws attention to the creative process by which both the dramatist's reference to his "Age," the world as it objectively is, and his "Soule," his subjective capacity for experiencing and comprehending this world, are metaphorically joined in a verbal expression of their unity. It was out of this union that the universalizing energy of his own metaphorical transmutations actually thrived upon the profound awareness with which the dramatist responded to the form and pressure of his age.

Mimesis and Expression in Neoclassical and Romantic Imagery Criticism

This is not the place to attempt anything like a survey of the history of the study of metaphor in Shakespeare's drama, but perhaps it will be helpful to draw attention to some aspects in the social background and the changing methodology of the earlier study of Shakespeare's imagery. To begin with, let us consider the well-known fact that imagery criticism is of curiously recent origin and that the metaphorical quality of Shakespeare's language has—with the exception of Walter Whiter's *Specimen of a Commentary on Shakespeare* (1794)—been either ignored or even, in the seventeenth and eighteenth centuries, somewhat deprecated. Of course we have the remark of Dryden, who was prepared to appreciate Shakespeare's metaphors as an expression of passion in human nature, although he was not prepared to accept too many of them too often: "to use 'em at every word, to say nothing without a metaphor, a simile, an image, or description, is I doubt to smell a little too strongly of the buskin." And we have the important statement of Pope in the Preface to this edition of Shakespeare (1725) that "all his metaphors [are] appropriated, and remarkably drawn from the true nature and inherent qualities of each subject." Still, the predominant attitude was one of caution and reserve or a mixture of suspicion and respect in the face of what Dr. Johnson called Shakespeare's "idle conceit," so that some of the so-called metaphorical passages were considered (in the words of Pope) as "unnecessary" excursions, and of course they suffered considerably from various emendations and alterations, as when (to give one notorious example) Steevens changed the pregnant metaphor "Glamis hath murder'd sleep" (*Macbeth* II.22.41) into the nonmetaphorical direct reference "Glamis hath murder'd a sleeper."[10]

But perhaps we should be wary of treating these things condescendingly. At any rate, it seems wrong to dismiss them as the reflection of an immature sensibility too blunt or too ignorant to be aware of the meaning of Shakespeare's verbal artistry. It is probably nearer the truth to say (but even this is to oversimplify) that the neoclassical approach to Shakespeare was based on a different view of the total function of drama in which verbal art was, though not unimportant, yet "last to be considered." As Dryden put it: "Now the words are the colouring of the work, which, in the order of nature, is last to be considered. The design, the disposition, the manners, and the thoughts, are all before it: where any of those are wanting or imperfect, so much wants or is imperfect in the imitation of human life, which is in the very definition of a poem." In the drama such imitation of human life was thought to be best achieved in the portrayal of the actions of men, so that Rymer in *The Tragedies of the Last Age Consider'd* could sum up his consideration by

---

[10]John Dryden, Preface to *Troilus and Cressida*, in *Of Dramatic Poesy and Other Critical Essays*, ed. George Watson (London, 1962), I, 257; Alexander Pope, Preface to *The Works of Shakespear* (1725), in *Eighteenth Century Essays on Shakespeare*, ed. D. Nichol Smith, 2d ed. (Oxford, 1963), p. 49; the Steevens emendation is cited by Wolfgang Clemen, *The Development of Shakespeare's Imagery* (London, 1951), p. 13.

stating, "I have chiefly consider'd the *Fable* or *Plot*, which all conclude to be the *Soul* of a *Tragedy*."[11]

For this there was of course the authority of Aristotelian poetics, but nonetheless the priority given to plot rather than to "the colouring of the poem" reflected the historical position of the poet in a society in which it seemed most meaningful for drama to explore the individual and the social angles of human relationships in both their contradiction and their unity. To a considerable degree, the dramatists, the public, and the critics were agreed in this; for it seemed possible, as Pope said in the closing lines of his *Essay on Man*, to believe "That true Self-love and Social are the same." Even the obvious contradictions and tensions in the postrevolutionary settlement of the early eighteenth century seemed a necessary element in the social balance of power. In the words of Pope:

> Know, all enjoy that pow'r which suits them best . . .
> 'Till jarring int'rests of themselves create
> Th'according music of a well-mix'd State.
> Such is the World's great harmony. . . .[12]

This points to the historical and social context in which the dramatic plot, not the verbal texture, could be considered as the major critical term of reference and in which the plot itself could be considered as a dramatic image of human relationships in society, no matter how stylized or idealized or abstracted from actual life it happened to be.

Even after the advent of romantic criticism in the second part of the eighteenth century, when the standards of mimesis were more and more surrendered to those of the imagination, the balance was in favor not of the verbal texture but of the human and social context of poetic ex-

[11]John Dryden, Preface to *Fables Ancient and Modern*, in *Of Dramatic Poesy*, ed. Watson, II, 275; Thomas Rymer, *Tragedies of the Last Age Consider'd*, in *Critical Essays of the Seventeenth Century*, ed. J. E. Spingarn (London, 1908), II, 183.

[12]Alexander Pope, *An Essay on Man*, III, 80, 293–95, Twickenham Ed., vol. III, pt. i, ed. Maynard Mack (London, 1950).

pression and effect. As the enlightened and optimistic idea of "the World's great harmony" was confronted with the actual practice of "self-love" in the course of the Industrial Revolution, and as—in connection with this—the philosophy of Bacon and Locke turned out to coarsen (in Blake's vision) into a "Mechanical philosophy" which (as he said about Bacon) had "no notion of anything but Mammon,"[13] the entire frame of critical reference began to shift. Again, this is not the place to examine (and certainly not to defend) a set of critical assumptions that finally resulted in the well-known irresponsibilities of romantic impressionism and psychological speculation about character. But when all is said and done, there remains an overriding context in which the whole as well as the parts of drama, including metaphorical expression, could potentially at least be discussed within a more or less coherent frame of reference. If imagination was (as Blake said) "the Divine Vision" which "alone makes a Poet"; or if imagination (as Wordsworth wrote)

> Is but another name for absolute power
> And clearest insight, amplitude of mind,
> And Reason in her most exalted mood,[14]

then indeed it seemed legitimate both to express and to experience these creative faculties, if necessary (as Hazlitt said of Wordsworth) "in the busy solitude of [one's] own heart."[15]

But before imagination triumphed at the height of the romantic period, it was possible, throughout the latter half of the eighteenth and well into the nineteenth century, to maintain the compromise position that was first taken by Addison, who did not wish to abandon mimetic criteria but

[13]*Complete Writings of William Blake*, ed. Geoffrey Keynes (London, 1947), p. 403.
[14]William Wordsworth, *The Prelude*, ed. Ernest de Selincourt and Helen Darbishire, 2d ed. (Oxford, 1959), XIV, 189–92.
[15]Cited by John Jones, *The Egotistical Sublime: A History of Wordsworth's Imagination* (London, 1954), p. 29.

sought to reconcile them with the new delights of the imagination. In a passage that is remarkable because it points to the consequences of all this for the theory and interpretation of metaphor, Addison says: "For though whatever is New or Uncommon is apt to delight the Imagination, the chief Design of an Allusion . . . should be always borrowed from what is more known and common, than the passages, which are to be explained. . . . A noble Metaphor . . . casts a kind of Glory round it . . . and, that they may please the Imagination, the Likeness ought to be very exact, or very agreeable, as we love to see a Picture where the Resemblance is just."[16] To identify resemblance with emotion, or the element of exact likeness with the agreeable effect on the audience, may have pointed the way to the nineteenth-century aesthetics of the novel and the picture-frame stage; but as a contribution to the theory of metaphor or poetic allusion, it could emphasize only one aspect of imagery, which was linked with the effect of verisimilitude in the representation of great and almost lifelike characters. The poetic creation of a "Likeness" was admired, but at the same time creation was perhaps even more highly valued as the poetic expression of the personality of the great genius himself. The characters were the true "children of his art," as a late Victorian critic put it, the most diverse and direct expression of all his moral and intellectual qualities. "The plot," wrote Coleridge, "interests us on account of the characters, not *vice versa*"; its "calamities and catastrophe," said Bradley, "follow inevitably from the deeds of men, and . . . the main source of these deeds is character."[17]

To sum up this short excursion into the history of the study of Shakespeare, one can say that in seventeenth- and early eighteenth-century criticism, metaphor was considered important insofar as (in the cited words of Pope) it was

---

[16] *The Spectator*, ed. G. G. Smith (rpt.; London, 1957), III, 305.

[17] Walter Raleigh, *Shakespeare* (London, 1907), p. 7; *Coleridge's Shakespearean Criticism*, ed. T. M. Raysor (London, 1930), I, 226; A. C. Bradley, *Shakespearean Tragedy* (London, 1918), p. 13.

"drawn from the true nature and inherent qualities of each subject." Metaphor was mainly seen and evaluated in relation to the criteria of mimesis and the representational requirements of the action or plot. In the criticism of the romantic period metaphor was increasingly seen in relation to the poet's self-expression, which was largely taken to be achieved in the creation of character as well as in relation to the effect on the reader, so that the poet's (as well as the reader's) main inspiration was the sympathetic overflow of powerful feelings from the heart of the poetic creation, which was the genius himself.

Both the neoclassical and the romantic approaches to Shakespeare imposed obvious limitations on the study of all kinds of imagery. We may even blame these critics for indifference, or lack of curiosity, but again we should be in no hurry to describe their view of metaphor (which was, after all, implicitly functional) as merely ornamental. I submit that these critics related metaphor to some basic mimetic or expressive function of drama, and however superficial or underdeveloped their concepts and theories of metaphor were, in this they were on somewhat safer grounds than a good many modern critics of imagery who, in their concern with patterns of imagery, lose sight of the work of art as a whole. A dialectical theory of metaphor will find little inspiration in eighteenth- and nineteenth-century approaches to poetic drama, but it will again endeavor to be informed by a thorough awareness of the social functions of literature, among which representation and expression cannot easily be dismissed.

The Spatial "Pattern" of Modernism

It is in this regard that the modernist approach to Shakespeare's imagery, which developed in the late twenties and thirties and culminated in the era of the New Criticism, is most vulnerable. A good deal of this criticism is already part of the history of Shakespeare criticism, but the present perspective of change and transition does not minimize—rather, it enhances—the role this criticism has played in effecting the revulsion in Shakespeare criticism away from the nineteenth-century romantic tradition. If this revulsion had to be summed up in one formula or one phrase, I would again quote Eliot's reference with regard to imagery (in his Preface to Knight's *Wheel of Fire*), to that "search for the pattern below the level of 'plot' and 'character.'" Here we have not simply a reaction against the impressionism of the late romantics (although it is that too) but, above all, the first sustained apology for an approach to Shakespeare's meaning according to which that meaning is sought outside both the mimetic and the expressive functions of drama. It is an approach to Shakespeare's drama in which the imagery, the patterns of metaphor and symbol, are seen as part, not of a structure comprehending plot and character, but of what Knight calls "the spatial content of the play." If plot imitates or represents the sequence and interdependence of the actions of men in society and if character expresses the experience and emotions of personality, then certainly the critical search for the autonomous and timeless status of literature (inspired by so much modern art and literature) had to go beyond plot and character. It had to dispense with "the more easily extractable element of 'plot' and 'character'" in order to define "the figure in the carpet of the canon as a whole."[18] But these formulas, more negative than positive and more impressionistic than conceptual, which circumscribe the direction of so many modern studies in Shakespeare's imagery, have—ever since they were devised—left many questions unanswered. They not only failed to integrate the study of metaphor into a larger theory

[18]L. C. Knights, *Some Shakespearean Themes and an Approach to Hamlet* (Harmondsworth, Penguin Books, 1966), p. 14. My repetition is intentional: the terminology here, as elsewhere (pp. 17 f.), is Eliot's, and to leave no doubt about that, he is quoted (in a motto) in favor of an "interpretation of the pattern in Shakespeare's carpet" (see n. 1, this chapter).

of the functions of drama, but they also seemed to insinuate that the true imaginative secret of Shakespeare's drama was somehow not quite compatible with such rather blunt categories as plot or character or with the theatrical conventions of the Elizabethan stage.[19] What is more, by the assertion that "pattern" was somehow *below* the level of these categories, or *behind* them, plot and character were relegated to some surface status. They were a mere "crust," almost like an irksome kind of packing that had to be unwrapped as quickly as possible in order to reveal the true core of poetic significance: here was "that structure of meaning" which seemed "especially closely connected with recurring and inter-related imagery" and which was no longer regarded as of temporal but of spatial dimensions, as best illustrated by a metaphorical terminology like "carpet" or "pattern."[20]

This summary, of course, oversimplifies the direction of the work of critics such as Wilson Knight, L. C. Knights, Derek Traversi, Cleanth Brooks, Robert B. Heilman, and, partly of course, F. R. Leavis; and it does not even take into account the quite different methods of scholars such as Caroline Spurgeon or Wolfgang Clemen. To be sure, there is a distinction to be made between the proclaimed theory and the achieved critical practice of these critics. At their best, they are successfully involved in seeing pattern and detail as one, and in any case their thematic abstractions do not invalidate a good deal of very perceptive close reading. Still, when the difference between theory and practice is allowed for, the spatial aesthetic is nothing external that can be ignored or, somehow, dissociated from the interpretation itself. The language of pattern and the spatial approach do affect both the method and the result of these critics' work,

[19] It has to be noted that when *Some Shakespearean Themes* first appeared (1959), L. C. Knights was already anxious "not to promote an orthodoxy" (p. 14), and he protested that the "larger pattern that lies behind the plot and the characters" cannot be discussed "apart from the living tissue of which it forms a part" (p. 17).

[20] Ibid., p. 18.

and they must be taken seriously as reflecting a position of some historical and theoretical significance. For it was in the context of this position that the interpretation of imagery in poetic drama became a dominating element in the methodological reassessment of Shakespearean studies that occurred in the thirties, forties, and fifties.

The conception of recurring metaphor as the essential core of some kind of symbolic meaning formed the nucleus of an attempt by critics, which is powerful even today, to focus upon a new mode of unity in the interpretation of Shakespearean, or poetic drama. Most of these critics—and this was their starting point—had a lively sense of the futility and the naturalism of a good deal of late romantic character study. They showed a sense of crisis, largely justified, and a deep discontent with both the methods of positivism and the mere record of critical emotion. As Wilson Knight wrote in *The Shakespearian Tempest:* "We have failed to focus correctly the Shakespearian unity. Thus there being no common starting-point for our inquiry, indeed no purely objective element at all in our subject matter . . . we have become involved in mere emotionalism, individualism, and anarchy." It was all very well to plead for a new kind of "objective basis of an imaginative understanding," and certainly the effort to search for the "imaginative solidities of Shakespeare" was as timely as it was necessary. But if the result was—in Wilson Knight's own words—"a mystic understanding" in which, as he said, "we should follow our dramatic intuitions," then this answer caused new and grave problems that could not provide a convincing or satisfying approach to the theoretical and practical criticism of metaphor in the work of Shakespeare.[21]

As already noted, the attempt to define the unity of Shakespearean drama in some metaphorical pattern or atmosphere corresponds with a good deal in modern poetry and the criticism of it. Modern poets have again and again

[21]G. Wilson Knight, *The Shakespearian Tempest* (London, 1953), p. 3.

stressed metaphor as the life-principle of poetry. As C. Day Lewis noted in his perceptive study *The Poetic Image*, "Novelty, audacity, fertility of image are the strong-point, the presiding demon, of contemporary verse—and, like all demons, apt to get out of hand."[22] It is true that this modern critical and practical emphasis on metaphor has some important romantic origins; yet it was T. E. Hulme who, in his reaction against the liberal romantic tradition, was the first in England to celebrate the image as "the very essence of an intuitive language," compared with which "subject doesn't matter." His position was to find an echo in Ezra Pound's understanding of the image as giving "that sense of sudden liberation; that sense of freedom from time limits and space limits." And the metaphor that was thought of as providing a freedom from time limits was a modernist one, very much in line with related attempts in contemporary art and literature. When, for instance, Joseph Frank analyzed the tendency toward "spatial form" in modern literature, he opposed it to the naturalistic (or realistic) depth perspective, which gives objects a "time-value because it connects them with the real world in which events occur." In contrast to this depth perspective (which, I believe, was certainly Shakespeare's), Pound, Eliot, and Joyce are claimed to introduce a new perspective that is no longer temporal but spatial: "When depth disappears and objects are presented in one plane, their simultaneous apprehension as part of a timeless unity is obviously made easier."[23] Joseph Frank summed up

[22]Cecil Day Lewis, *The Poetic Image* (London, 1948), p. 17. Since these words were written, there have, of course, been various attempts to deny the image its central position, or even to make "war on metaphor," bring "death to the image" (Nicanor Parra, *Poemas y Antipoemas*). The most impressive anti-metaphoric platform is probably that of the post-Nerudian, revolutionary school in Latin America (Cesar Vallejo, Octavia Paz, Gonzalo Roja, Ernesto Cardenal, and others). See Carlos Rincón, "Metamorphosen einer Entdeckung: Probleme der Literatur Lateinamerikas," *Sinn und Form*, 25 (1973), 494–530, esp. 509. I have commented on this in "Welt und Ich in der Metapher," *Sinn und Form*, 26 (1974), 181–93.

[23]T. E. Hulme, *Speculations: Essays on Humanism and the Philosophy of Art*, ed. Herbert Read (London, 1924), pp. 135, 137; *Literary Essays of Ezra*

this tendency in these words:

The objective historical imagination . . . is transformed by these writers into the mythical imagination for which historical time does not exist—the imagination that sees the actions and events of a particular time merely as the bodying forth of eternal prototypes. These prototypes are created by transmuting the time-world of history into the timeless world of myth. And it is this timeless world of myth, forming the common content of modern literature, which finds its appropriate aesthetic expression in spatial form. . . .[24]

This points to some of the ideological needs and premises from which the two-dimensional approach to the figures in the carpet and the pattern made its "selective use of the past against an unruly present." The work of the modernist writers that Frank hoped "to apprehend . . . spatially, in a moment of time, rather than as a sequence" was historically close to the group of early modern poets who called themselves Imagists and whose practice and theory of poetry reflected new and problematic social bearings. The unconscious ideology of their position corresponded to a significant change in their relationship to society, which is well summed up by Vivian de Sola Pinto:

The Imagists were the first true "modernist" group in the sense that they no longer attempted to communicate with a general public of poetry lovers which had ceased to exist, but concentrated on searching for a means of expressing the modern consciousness for their own satisfaction and that of their friends. . . . The poets had to recognize that they were living in a new age of barbarism and vulgarity where the arts could only survive in small islands of culture, which was no longer the possession of a securely established social class but which had to be fashioned anew by a self-chosen *élite* that managed to escape the spiritual degradation of a commercialized world.[25]

Pound, ed. with an Introduction by T. S. Eliot (London, 1954), p. 4; Joseph Frank, "Spatial Form in Modern Literature" (1945), quotations from the revised version in *Criticism: The Foundations of Modern Literary Judgment,* ed. Mark Schorer et al. (New York, 1948), p. 32.

[24]Frank, "Spatial Form," p. 392. I have developed this argument further in *New Criticism und die Entwicklung bürgerlicher Literaturwissenschaft,* rev. ed. (Munich, 1974).

[25]*Crisis in English Poetry: 1880–1940* (London, 1951), pp. 151.

One way to escape the degradation of a commercialized world was to relinquish, much more radically than the romantics had done, not only the mimetic function of literature, but also the romantic principle of expression, and to achieve, even outside the mimetic *and* affective dimensions of poetry, some spatial or symbolic correlative of poetic awareness and craftsmanship. It is in this context that the "historical imagination" could be "transformed . . . into the mythical imagination," by which the actions and events of the world of history were reduced by both the modernist poets and the critics to the universal, not to say abstract, contraries and dichotomies of a symbolic structure. The resulting prototypes (such as life themes and death themes, good and evil) were seen to be eternal or autonomous, that is, outside the pale of social and, even, literary history. The ensuing crisis in the relation of metaphor and reality was hardly noticed; but the new function of figurative language involved so extreme a revulsion from its traditional uses and definitions that it was reflected only by the most radical and, as it were, paradoxical advocates of modernist poetics. Most representative is perhaps José Ortega y Gasset when he said that metaphor "obliterates or annihilates an object" because it corresponds to an elementary instinctive need of man "to shun certain realities." It is owing to the metaphorical process, therefore, that we possess "the possibility to get away from things." Thus, while in previous centuries metaphor embraced some aspect of reality, the aim today is "to get rid of any extra-poetic, that is real subject-matter and poetically to realize metaphor as the *res poetica* itself."[26]

This, of course, is a statement that does not reflect the whole of Ortega's view of metaphor, but it points to one

[26]*Obras Completas* (Madrid: Revista de Occidente, 1962), III, 373: "La metáfora escamotea un objeto enmascarándolo con otro, y no tendría sentido si no viéramos bajo ella un *instinto* que induce al hombre a evitar realidades. . . . Sólo la metáfora nos facilita la evasión. . . ." "Ahora, al revés, se procura eliminar el sostén extrapoético o real y se trata de realizar la metáfora, hacer de ella la res poética (p. 375)."

basic aspect of the modernist conception of figurative language. From a somewhat different position, this aspect has
been explored by Frank Kermode, who suggests in *Romantic
Image* that the modern artist's devotion to the image
reflects the isolation of the poet in society who believes
himself to be "differentiated from other men." Kermode
goes on to say that these "two beliefs in the Image as a
radiant truth out of space and time, and in the necessary
isolation or estrangement of men who perceive it, are
inextricably associated" and that there is an "interdependence" between such assumptions. But the picture is
more complex than Kermode in his suggestive book is inclined to believe. For there is, notwithstanding the continuity (which is very much stressed), an element of discontinuity between the romantic and the modernist practice and
theory of metaphor: it is, more than anything else, the
modernist concept of autonomy that is absent in the
romantic tradition, as when Shelley, to take the most distinguished example, says that metaphor "marks the before
unapprehended relations of things and perpetuates their apprehension." While it is evidently misleading to ignore such
fundamental points of difference between the modernist and
romantic conceptions of metaphor, it seems equally unjustified to set up too rigid a barrier between the two, as
when it is claimed, for instance by Cleanth Brooks in
Modern Poetry and the Tradition, that the romantic conception of metaphor is one that considers figurative language
as mere illustration or ornament, while "the modernists
stand opposed to both the neoclassic and Romantic poets on
the issue of metaphor."[27]

But the real problem posed by these widely diverging
positions on the history and value of the romantic image is
one of methodology and literary history. As such it involves

[27] Kermode, *Romantic Image* (New York, 1957), pp. vii, 2; Shelley, *A De-
fence of Poetry*, in *English Critical Essays: Nineteenth Century*, ed. Edmund D.
Jones (Oxford, 1947), p. 705; Cleanth Brooks, *Modern Poetry and the Tradition*
(London, 1948), p. 22, but see the entire first chapter, "Metaphor and
Tradition."

an awareness, which seems essential to any reconsideration of the problem, of the changing interrelations between the poetic structure and its function, but also between the contemporary theories of metaphor and the changing social mode of poetry. It is in the absence of such methodological awareness that those two quite irreconcilable judgments were put forward which, between themselves, hinder, rather than promote, a reintegration of the study of metaphor into a coherent and systematic approach to the history of English literature. With Frank Kermode the late romantic tradition of metaphor is admired for its structural, but deplored for its functional, aspects: the element of critical evaluation and, indeed, appreciation does not really come to terms with the historical critique of the social function of the late romantic image and its context of "isolation and estrangement." Hence, the literary critic is really fascinated by a structural development which the same author as historian at least implicitly disapproves of. On the other hand, Cleanth Brooks, precisely because he ignores the social context of romantic metaphor, cannot adequately approach its poetic achievement: he finds it unacceptable and disapproves of its links with nineteenth-century affective and mimetic criteria of the function of poetry, which, in judging them by his own intrinsic frame of aesthetic reference, he in some cases misunderstands as a call for "ornament" and "illustration." As an alternative, it simply will not do to claim "the essentially functional character of all metaphor" for metaphysical and modern poetry, and to reject "the Romantic and neo-classical account of the functions of figurative language" without pausing to consider the contradictions (which need not preclude some potential unity) *between* the mimetic and the nonmimetic dimensions of function that are here alluded to.[28] To plead for the unity

---

[28] *Modern Poetry and the Tradition*, p. 26. It seems curious that in the face of so rigorous a rejection of "the prevailing conception of poetry" as one "still primarily defined for us by the achievement of the Romantic poets" (p. viii) Brooks, after praising the metaphysical poets for their revelation of "the essentially func-

of idea and form as a methodological category seems perfectly justified; but as soon as this pleading tends to obscure the potential contradiction that (in the work of art) such unity contains, it runs the risk of an inversion of ends and means.[29] The danger is that the achieved content can be reduced to some autonomous status according to which the concept of function has ceased to convey anything but the arrangement of verbal and symbolic order. Thus, the mimetic and affective dimensions that are behind some, though not all, of the (admittedly superficial) concepts of "illustration" and "ornament" are written off, and a potential perspective on society is closed. The metaphoric mode is cut off from the process of literature as history and from that larger function by which the structure of figurative language serves as both an agent and a reflection of the poet's work in society.

Image and Society: Some Links
of Vehicle and Consciousness

Since the New Criticism has lost its former position of influence and preeminence, the symbolic and thematic approach to metaphor is not so much superseded as submerged

---

tional character" of metaphor, proceeds to use Keats to illustrate "the fundamental function of figurative language" (p. 27). Here, the literary theory of metaphor and the literary history of poetry seem to engage in a highly characteristic contradiction.

[29] William J. Rooney ("'The Canonization'—The Language of Paradox Reconsidered," *ELH*, 23 [1956], 46) pointed to another problematic use of the word *function* when he noted a comparable inversion in the method of Cleanth Brooks: "It is one thing to say that a poem is *made of paradoxical meanings* and quite another thing to conclude that the poem functions to convey a paradox." I owe this reference to Jackson J. Cope's illuminating study *The Metaphoric Structure of Paradise Lost* (Baltimore, 1964), p. 9, which, "in contradistinction to the ways of the New Criticism," uses the term *metaphor* "with an eye to the function rather than to the nature of metaphor"—a usage which corresponds to the assumption "that *Paradise Lost* can best be understood as a poem in which certain repeated metaphors mimetically express the epic theme with an unprecedented tenacity" (pp. 4, 6).

in a growing number of theories and interpretations. The difficulties in the way of a methodological clarification, to which R. A. Foakes referred in his highly perceptive "Suggestions for a New Approach to Shakespeare's Imagery," have, therefore, increased rather than diminished: for in the sixties as well as in the fifties, the majority of the critics of imagery "seem either to have taken over another's method . . . or to have criticised and adopted another's method of approach, without considering the attitudes upon which it was based."[30] It is thus difficult to generalize, especially when the concept of metaphor (or image) is so extended as to blur the core of its definition as a verbal figure of pictorial structure.

In approaching Shakespeare's imagery, I suggest, it is equally unhelpful either to classify, and to treat separately, metaphor, simile, metonymy, synecdoche, and personification or to widen the scope of the concept of image to cover "direct and literal description" or "the representation of any sense experience." For practical and theoretical reasons, I prefer to use the term *image* as a more synthetic term for figurative language, covering both metaphor and simile and related figures, without, however, blurring the specific meaning of *metaphor*, which, according to Aristotle's definition (*Poetics*, XXI, 1457b) involves "the sense of transference, the process of transferring a word from one object of reference to another." This definition, even though it comprises synecdoche and metonymy, is still both precise and flexible enough to be extended in the sense that I. A. Richards suggested, so as "to cover all cases . . . where we compound different uses of the word into one, and speak of something as though it were another," which includes, "as metaphoric, those processes in which we perceive or think or feel about one thing in terms of another." It is this basic core of meaning that differentiates metaphor from simile, but yet provides the justification to comprise the various figures of

---

[30] *Shakespeare Survey* 5 (1952), p. 81.

speech involving some transference or likening under the term *image*.[31]

But the criticism with which I am concerned has departed from the linguistic and figurative criteria of image and metaphor, in two rather problematic directions. The first tendency to which I have alluded would extend the meaning of the term *image* to cover the most various elements of drama, not only figurative language but also direct statement and reference—in short, any form of "the conveying of meaning through appeal to the various senses." In this sense S. L. Bethell has undertaken to "widen the scope of the term 'image' to cover any reference in word or phrase to a distinct object or class of objects, whether used figuratively or directly." Similarly, M. C. Bradbrook, who has done so much to show us the poetry in Shakespeare's theater, has argued that "dramatic characters are only another, though the most complex, form of image," while M. M. Charney has asked us "to extend our concept of 'image' beyond the mere words of the play to the actual performance in the theater. Costume, stage properties, gestures, grouping, and the theater itself all provide us with significant images." This tendency was anticipated by Una Ellis-Fermor's plea for "extending it [the term] to include the frontiers of symbolism, description, or even, it may be, the setting itself." As

[31]Cleanth Brooks and Robert B. Heilman, *Understanding Drama* (New York, 1945), Appendix B, p. 49; Cleanth Brooks and Robert Penn Warren, *Understanding Fiction* (New York, 1943), p. 605; W. Bedek Stanford, *Greek Metaphor: Studies in Theory and Practice* (Oxford, 1936), pp. 9 f.; Richards, *The Philosophy of Rhetoric* (New York, 1936), p. 116. S. J. Brown differentiates the various rhetorical figures and is still somewhat reluctant to venture "to range them under the general term 'Imagery'" (*The World of Imagery* [London, 1927], p. 1). But after Middleton Murry the word *image* is widely "used to cover both metaphor and simile" (*Countries of the Mind: Essays in Literary Criticism*, 2d ser. [London, 1931], p. 4). See especially Caroline Spurgeon's careful distinctions in *Shakespeare's Imagery and What It Tells Us* (Cambridge, 1935), p. 5, and "Shakespeare's Iterative Imagery," in *Aspects of Shakespeare*, British Academy Lectures, ed. J. W. Mackail (Oxford, 1933), p. 256. See also Clemen, *Development of Shakespeare's Imagery*, p. 7; E. A. Armstrong, *Shakespeare's Imagination: A Study of the Psychology of Association and Inspiration* (London, 1946), p. 9.

long as there is behind this widening of the concept a concern for the specific quality of imagery in drama, the motivation at least may be applauded. But if figurative speech
can serve to deepen "the imaginative significance of a play"
and to help "drama to overcome the limitations inherent in
its brevity" and if costume, stage properties, and the
representation of characters can perform the same service,
why should these, simply because they share the same capacity (in this respect) with figurative language, be called
imagery?[32] Apart from the fact that such terminology is unnecessarily confusing, it seems a curious reflection of a climate of critical opinion in which the literary terms
themselves were used almost as a concession to the prevailing modes of criticism, so that the word *image* was in
danger of becoming an incantatory gesture. From the point
of view of the New Critics, however, the blurring of the
difference between literal discourse (or "the representation
of any sense experience") and figurative speech must have
provided a welcome opportunity to justify the spatial or symbolic approach to metaphor and to its "freedom from time
limits" as against the dramatic revelation of the progressive
dialectic of action and character in motion, as a sequence of
events in time.

The second tendency is, in this respect, even more consistent and theoretically more sophisticated: at the bottom
of it there is the claim, made by critics like Wilson Knight,
L. C. Knights, and Robert B. Heilman, that the play itself
must be seen as a metaphor. This is usually based on the
assumption that Shakespearean drama weaves a web with
threads of language or imagery so that—as Heilman says
about *King Lear*—"in its fullness the structure can be set

---

[32] Brooks and Heilman, p. 49; Bethell, "Shakespeare's Imagery: The Dia-
bolic Images in *Othello*," *Shakespeare Survey* 5 (1952), p. 62; Bradbrook, "Dramatic Rôle as Social Image: A Study of *The Taming of the Shrew*," *Shakespeare-
Jahrbuch*, 94 (1958), 132; M. M. Charney, "The Dramatic Use of Imagery in
Shakespeare's *Coriolanus*," *ELH*, 23 (1956), 183; Una Ellis-Fermor, *The Frontiers of Drama* (London, Paperback ed., 1964), pp. 78, 77.

forth only by means of the pattern of imagery."[33] So if the full structure of the play is metaphoric, why not consider the play itself as "an expanded metaphor," as "that large metaphor which is the play itself"?[34] To phrase the question like this may oversimplify the direction and the complexity of these critics' arguments. (A critic of the stature of L. C. Knights would presumably wish here to make a distinction, which is largely justified, between the nature of simile or analogy, and that of the metaphoric process: while the former link "the unknown to the known . . ., closing the problematic entity into a familiar pattern," the metaphoric process "shatters the ground on which we had settled down in order to widen our view beyond any limit of a special practical use.")[35] For Knights, therefore, the metaphoric process, thus defined, constitutes "the central drive of all literary creation (the making of a living image of experience that goes beyond the immediate representation.")[36] Still, the underlying tendency is there, according to which, again, the difference between literal and metaphorical meanings is lost. Whatever elements of a larger realism the historical imagination might probe are surrendered for the eternal prototypes of a symbolism verging on myth.

This bias, which turns the problems of terminology into questions of principle, is of much greater consequence when it comes to theoretical definitions of the nature and structure of image and metaphor. Here, again, modernist conceptions are so widely held and so much taken for granted that I feel compelled first to question some of their problematic aspects and to make their bias, as it were, appear as a bias, before alternative suggestions can be offered. As a point of departure,

[33] Robert B. Heilman, *This Great Stage: Image and Structure in* King Lear (Baton Rouge, La., 1948), p. 32.

[34] Knight, *Wheel of Fire*, p. 15; Heilman, p. 12.

[35] Martin Foss, *Symbol and Metaphor in Human Experience* (Princeton, 1959), p. 56, cited by L. C. Knights, "*King Lear* as Metaphor," in *Myth and Symbol: Critical Approaches and Applications*, ed. Bernice Slote (Lincoln, Neb., 1963), p. 24

[36] Knights, "*King Lear* as Metaphor," p. 25.

we may consider the essential difference between modernist and metaphysical (or Elizabethan) theory and practice. This is an important point that was made by Rosemond Tuve:

The earlier author's subject was different, however similar his stuff; his subject was still "his meaning," not "himself-seeing-it." One finds the choice of images made upon different grounds, and their structural function differently affecting their nature. . . . The measure of the difference is the strict logical coherence of Donne's images. This does not mean that the images are not sensuously vivid; only that they are not primarily so. Each is chosen and presented as a "significant" part of an ordered pattern. . . .[37]

It was precisely these criteria, the priority of the subject and its meaning together with the resultant coherence of the images, that modernist poets and critics were not interested in. Hulme's remark, "Subject doesn't matter," sums up their position neatly. Similarly, T. S. Eliot in his seminal review of Grierson's anthology *Metaphysical Lyrics and Poems of the Seventeenth Century* made a point of stressing quite different aspects. For him, "the sudden contrast of associations" and "this telescoping of images and multiplied associations" seemed particularly meaningful; and he generalized his perspective by saying that "we find, instead of the mere explication of the content of a comparison, a development by rapid association of thought. . . ."[38]

Such statements more than anything else reflect the practice and perspective of early modernist poetry, where so many metaphors draw on discordant materials, sometimes in the way of "a mere putting together of two things to see what will happen." Accordingly, modern critical theory, like that of I. A. Richards, even when it disapproves of "the crude 'clash them together—no matter what' view of metaphor," does emphasize the element of disparity. Its criteria for evaluation are based on the degree and the moment of disparity, so that tension, not fusion, is approved of. In the

[37] *Elizabethan and Metaphysical Imagery: Renaissance Poetic and Twentieth-Century Critics* (Chicago, 1947), pp. 43 f.
[38] *Selected Essays: 1917–1932* (London, 1932), p. 268.

words of Richards: "As the two things put together are more remote, the tension created is, of course, greater. . . . Talk about the identification or fusion that a metaphor effects is nearly always misleading and pernicious."[39]

Accordingly, and with some consistency, the pictorial vehicle of the metaphor is emphasized. Perhaps it can be said that it is this conception of the vehicle as almost autonomous which, directly or indirectly, is connected with the spatial and, ironically, the abstract mode of many modern studies of Shakespeare's imagery. To question this connection, we may remind ourselves that its assumptions certainly do not underlie Shakespeare's imagery nor, for that matter, do they reflect Elizabethan theory, as recorded by contemporary opinion. For instance, Ben Jonson's view of metaphor can be seen as directly opposed to the idea of autonomy and the related emphasis on disparity, as when he says in *Timber, or Discoveries:* "Quintilian warnes us that in no kind of Translation or Metaphore, or Allegory, wee make a turn from what wee began. As, if wee fetch the originall of our Metaphore from sea and billowes, we end not in flames and ashes: It is a most fowle inconsequence." This of course takes its cue from classical precepts, and it is certainly not based on an observation of Shakespeare's practice. Still, it has more implications for the study of Shakespeare's imagery than is commonly believed. For this there is a good deal of evidence provided by E. A. Armstrong's study of the "peculiar associative processes" of Shakespeare's imagination; for once the mechanism of metaphorical association is examined more closely, it becomes clear that "so far as the linkages [between metaphors] are concerned the outstanding fact is that none of them was found to be arbitrary or irrational."[40]

This would confirm a tradition of critical theory and poetic practice of which Dr. Johnson is perhaps the most outspoken representative, as when he says: "The force of

---

[39] Richards, pp. 123, 126, 125, 127.
[40] Jonson, *Timber*, in *Critical Essays of the Seventeenth Century*, ed. Spingarn, I, 40; Armstrong, *Shakespeare's Imagination*, p. 92.

metaphors is lost, when the mind, by the mention of particulars, is turned more upon the original than the secondary sense, more upon that from which the illustration is drawn than that to which it is applied."[41] This is exactly the opposite of the modern habit, so influential in imagery studies, of stressing the nature of that with which the comparison is made. In other words, Johnson stresses the tenor, the main notion of the metaphor, its underlying idea or principal subject, while modern imagery critics emphasize the vehicle, the pictorial material, which is not in itself identical with the actual subject of dramatic discourse. To quote Dr. Johnson here is helpful, not because he is an infallible guide to Shakespeare's practice, but because he points to a complementary perspective on metaphor that is most relevant when we come to consider how functional in a historical sense, and how much part of a larger movement of literary history, Shakespeare's metaphors can be.

At this point, two or three examples from Shakespeare can perhaps best illustrate the problem in hand. Let us take from *Richard II* the words of the gardener: "When our *sea-walled* garden, the whole land, / Is full of weeds; her fairest flowers chok'd up . . ." (III.iv.43–44). Or, from *As You Like It*, Jaques's speech:

> give me leave
> To speak my mind, and I will through and through
> Cleanse *the foul body of th'infected world*,
> If they will patiently receive my medicine.
>
> [II.vii.58–61]

Or, from *1 Henry IV*, the King's own words spoken to Harry: "Such as is bent on *sun-like majesty* / When it shines seldom in admiring eyes . . ." (III.ii.79–80; my emphasis).[42]

These are images in the sense that they involve some form of verbal transference or likening which affects our

---

[41] Samuel Johnson, *Lives of the English Poets*, ed. G. Birkbeck Hill (Oxford, 1905), I, 45.

[42] The text is that of *Complete Works of William Shakespeare*, ed. Peter Alexander (London, 1951).

understanding or perception of one thing in terms of, or in reference to, another. If we consult those scholarly studies which, as noted above, accept this definition, we are yet confronted with a number of questions arising out of the relationship that the two basic notions (involved in the process of transference or likening) are seen to engage in. Caroline Spurgeon who, even before Wolfgang Clemen, first demonstrated the immense range of Shakespeare's imagery, classifies these images under (1) gardening, (2) sickness and medicine, and (3) celestial bodies. She is concerned with finding out about the various areas of experience Shakespeare was acquainted with, for in the imagery (or so she believed) the poetry revealed "to us the man himself."[43] By thus collecting and classifying all the various images, she charted, as Wolfgang Clemen acknowledged, "a second world" within Shakespeare's universe,[44] an almost autonomous world that (in Johnson's words) was based "upon that from which the illustration is drawn" rather "than that to which it is applied." With the possible exception of the recent renaissance of studies in imagery as a (presumably biographical) criterion of authenticity, subsequent critics tended to reject any consideration of Shakespeare's imagery as "the touchstone" of his personality, but they usually accepted the purely pictorial "second world" as their point of reference.[45] So, at any rate, did Cleanth Brooks when he discussed the clothing images in *Macbeth,* or Wilson Knight when he conceived the notion of Shakespeare's tempests or the pictorial element of the sea, or the imagery of death, and

[43] *Shakespeare's Imagery and What It Tells Us,* p. 11.

[44] *Development of Shakespeare's Imagery,* p. 9.

[45] See the articles in *Shakespeare Quarterly* by Karl P. Wentersdorf, "Imagery as a Test of Authorship," 6 (1955), 381–86; "Imagery as a Criterion of Authenticity: A Reconsideration of the Problem," 23 (1972), 231–59; and C. H. Hobday, "Why the Sweets Melted: A Study of Shakespeare's Imagery," 16 (1965), 3–18. But generally the hazards involved in classifying imagery as a criterion of style have come to be more generally recognized; see, for instance, E. B. Partridge, *The Broken Compass* (London, 1958), pp. 19–36. Here L. H. Hornstein's skepticism as to "the assumption that imagery . . . always has a direct basis in physical experience" seems still very pertinent ("Analysis of Imagery: A Critique of Literary Method," *PMLA,* 57 [1942], 639).

so on. Wolfgang Clemen, it is true, developed a more consistently contextual approach, which was based on "the fundamental fact that the image is rooted in the totality of the play." Although from this position Clemen could very profitably inquire into "the relationship of the images to their occasion" (How is the metaphor related to the different characters, or "to the train of thought"?) and although he, much like Una Ellis-Fermor, recognized and appreciated the particular functions of imagery in drama, his use of the concept of function still remained essentially limited to the aesthetic sphere.[46] That, perhaps, was the reason why he accepted, or at least failed to question, some of the prevalent assumptions, as when he said that Caroline Spurgeon classified the images "according to their *content*" while his own study attempted to "investigate the *form* of the images and their relation to the context."[47]

But these assumptions (as well as the terms used to convey them) pose a number of questions. For instance, what is the "content" (or, as Spurgeon says, the "subject-matter") of "our sea-walled garden" or "sun-like majesty"? Is it gardening or the nation, celestial bodies or the head of state? Or perhaps a synthesis of both? These questions have—with the exception of scholars such as R. A. Foakes or Rosemond Tuve—troubled few critics of imagery, and it is probably safe to say that the majority of them have not been concerned with such theoretical considerations. Foakes attempted to remedy the situation by suggesting that it is not enough to study the metaphorical material because "the underlying idea," or what he called "the object-matter of the image," is very often "dramatically more important" and that therefore "a new definition of imagery, one derived from drama, is needed."[48]

These are very helpful suggestions, as far as they go.

---

[46]Clemen, pp. 4, 3. But Clemen also viewed imagery as a dramatic means used "to prepare in the mind of the audience a whole net of expectations, intuitions and conjectures" (p. 6).

[47]Ibid., p. 9.

[48]Tuve, pp. 422–23; Foakes, pp. 82, 85.

They certainly indicate an awareness—and critically so—of the general tendency, so obvious in modern poetry and criticism, to abstract the vehicle, or the pictorial element, from the underlying idea, or tenor. But this abstraction has all too often led critics to consider metaphors, similes, or the representation of any sense experience as purely symbolic—that is, apart from their representational, expressive, and dramatic meanings which, in the rich concreteness of each play, point beyond that almost timeless "second world" that can so easily be reduced to a spatial pattern of eternal prototypes. There is some reason to suppose that the mode of symbolic abstraction (which is one source of the much discussed "reductiveness" of modern Shakespeare criticism) has a good deal to do with the related tendency to stress the moment of disparity rather than the unity, the tension rather than the comprehension of the metaphoric process. By unity I do not mean to imply that it is possible to fuse, say, the concept of majesty with the sensory experience of the sun or one's knowledge of the problems of the world with the sense of a human body stricken with ill-health. I do think, however, that the full force and meaning of a metaphor is achieved only if and when an element that is *not* pictorial (such as the king or the world) is related as intensely as possible to a pictorial notion. The sun, an infected body, or a garden are by themselves natural or physical objects; their verbal expressions are primarily independent of any poetic or evaluative function: this they assume only through the association of the interrelated idea or object which alone, in the historical context of the work of art, defines the nature of the fusion and diffusion of the metaphorical imagination.

To explore the nature of this metaphorical process of association and comprehension a little further, let me suggest that an interpretation of these images might—from a theoretical point of view—distinguish two functions. On the one hand, the images serve a referential, or even representational, function that makes us imaginatively aware of some more abstract or remote idea or situation by substituting, or drawing upon, some more immediate sensuous and concrete object or quality. Thus, a highly complex situation is referred to when Hamlet says, "There is something *rotten* in the state of Denmark" (I.iv.90), or "The time is *out of joint*" (I.v.188), or when he refers to "*a sea* of troubles" (III.i.59; my emphasis). On the other hand, the metaphoric process involves an expressive, or evaluating, function. The pictorial vehicle—the sea, the sun, the body—is substituted for a more complex object, not to reflect it as it is but to evaluate it, to enhance it or to reduce it, to praise it or denounce it, to make it more subtle or more vivid; in short, to fit it into the perspective in which it is imaginatively perceived and experienced.

While the *referential* function of metaphor is more objective, the *expressive*, or *evaluative*, function involves a more subjective activity. The former refers to an object or a situation which, within the play-world or even outside it, actually exists: Here, it is the Danish court to which Hamlet returns, the nation that is actually an island and thus sheltered by the sea, the corruption and disease in a society which is out of order, and so on. While the more objective nature of these metaphorical references links the images with the subject matter or plot or the theme of the play, the more subjective function of evaluation associates the image with either the character's or the dramatist's *vision* of these objects. But in practice these two functions cannot be so schematically differentiated. In the metaphoric process itself the referential and the expressive functions, objectivity and subjectivity, constantly interact. In fact the poetic and dramatic effect of a metaphor thrives on this interaction, by which reality and vision, knowledge and feeling, and, on a different plane, the abstract and the concrete, the social and the individual, become indivisible. And it is this interaction which achieves that characteristic blend of congruity and incongruity that is at the heart of the metaphoric mode of perception.

If this definition of function (although still an

oversimplification) can be accepted, certain theoretical and practical conclusions follow. Once the sterile dualism of the extrinsic and the intrinsic is overcome, the notion of metaphor as some mere vehicle within a symbolic or spatial pattern or as some autonomous entity outside time and space can be rejected in favor of a more dialectical and historical approach. This calls for a more complex view of the relationship of tenor and vehicle in its correlative and comprehensive dimensions: It is the *Ablenkung,* or link, between the two that is marked by the degree of both congruity and incongruity which, in the creative and perceptual process, constitutes the energy with which the referential and evaluative functions interact as a poetic form of social activity in history. Such emphasis on the comprehensive function of the link between tenor and vehicle (as the creative and receptive result of their correlation and "comparison") will help overcome that facile impressionism or symbolism which results from a preoccupation with the pictorial element; but it will also reject that eighteenth-century view of metaphor as ornamental which results from a preoccupation with the tenor, or the underlying idea that the vehicle is merely taken to "illustrate."

The former fallacy, with which we are mainly concerned, seems unavoidable if, say, an image like "sea-walled garden" is formally interpreted as part of a purely pictorial web of the threads of figurative language. But this impoverishes the meaning of the image, for from the point of view of historical criticism the metaphor must appear highly suggestive both in its reference and in its evaluation: there is behind it the Tudor idea of a modern nation as a cultivated, ordered, and productive unit, which is self-contained: "this little world," "this earth, this realm, this England" surrounded by "the silver sea, / Which serves it in the office of a wall" (*Richard II* II.i.45 ff.; cf. *3 Henry VI* IV.i.43 f.). Being "water-walled," England is "hedg'd in with the main" (*King John* II.i.26 f.); her island boundaries are conceived of as a protective as well a unifying factor, in a way which would have been unthinkable in the fourteenth or early fifteenth centuries. Even when the metaphor "sea-walled" is used in medieval literature, as "sæ-weal" in *Beowulf* (l. 1924), it does not refer to the sea as a protective element but implies the opposite meaning, denoting the coast which, as it were, surrounds the sea, not the land. There are many related metaphors that confirm this notion, such as "holm," which, in Bornholm, refers to a hill rising out of, but not protected by, the waves of the sea. There are similar expressions such as "hron-rād," or "gar-sec," which all view the sea as an open element but never realize its function as a sheltering wall.

To refer to *Beowulf* may appear at first sight as a somewhat farfetched excursion into literary history. But perhaps it can serve as a paradigm of the historical function of metaphor, as revealed by a consideration of the changing correlation between vehicle and tenor. In this process of correlation, to stress the tenor helps to realize that the ideological and historical context is not something outside the peculiar process of the metaphorical imagination. To understand the relationship between text and context as historical, it is clearly not enough solely to emphasize its tradition, or continuity, as Ernst R. Curtius did in tracing certain topoi (metaphors such as the book, or those taken from the theater, the human body, or food) as some form of "historische Metaphorik der Weltliteratur." As Hans Blumenberg has demonstrated, such metaphorical concepts, especially those taken from the language of philosophy, involve change as well as continuity as soon as they are approached in terms of their unformulated assumptions, or some "Substruktur des Denkens."[49] If there is genuine ground for comparison between metaphors of critical or

---

[49] Curtius, *Europäische Literatur und lateinisches Mittelalter*, 6th ed. (Bern, 1967), p. 138; Blumenberg, "Paradigmen zu einer Metaphorologie," *Archiv für Begriffsgeschichte*, 6 (1960), 11: "Auch absolute Metaphern haben daher Geschichte. Sie haben Geschichte in einem radikaleren Sinne als Begriffe, denn der historische Wandel einer Metapher bringt die Metakinetik geschichtlicher Sinnhorizonte und Sichtweisen selbst zum Vorschein, innerhalb derer Begriffe ihre Modifikationen erfahren." The methodological problem of the approach to such *Substrukturen* or unformulated assumptions has been raised very perceptively by C. B. Macpherson in the introduction to *The Political Theory of Possessive Individualism* (Oxford, 1962).

philosophical discourse and those of poetry, the tertium quid is historical and ideological, "for in both provinces the recourse to metaphor, although directed to different ends, is perhaps equally functional."[50] But to elucidate such functions, the concept of tradition as some immanent synthesis of influence and self-renewal is even more inadequate than the method of *Geistesgeschichte*, with its unhelpful abstraction from the history of society. As a detailed and, indeed, definitive study of one central metaphor has shown, the history of "speculum," mirror, or looking glass, cannot, even in its elements of continuity, be accounted for by literary influences; it at least equally reflects the nature and use of the object as a product of social history.[51] Conversely, the interaction between the metaphorical vehicle (the mirror) and the changing structure of the underlying *Weltsicht*, or ideology (concepts of analogy, *imitatio*, and moral assumptions), marks the historical content of the link between the two. But as soon as the underlying ideology changes more rapidly, as in the late sixteenth century, the image of the mirror becomes increasingly replaced by that of anatomy: "in einer Hinsicht war die Anatomiemetapher Ausdruck einer veränderten Weltsicht, für die der Spiegel nicht länger das angemessene Modell sein konnte."[52] As a metaphor, anatomy was so much more expressive of, and referential to, new social relations in a rapidly changing world where the structure of the mental activity of the individual became more analytical and critical.

It is true that such common and antithetical metaphors as "mirror" and "lamp" or figurative topoi like "book" or "stage," or even Shakespearean images like "sea-walled garden" or "sun-like majesty" are, with their submerged analogies and ideologies, more suggestive in a historical way

---

[50]M. H. Abrams, *The Mirror and the Lamp: Romantic Theory and the Critical Tradition* (New York, 1953), p. vi.

[51]Herbert Grabes, *Speculum, Mirror und Looking-glass* (Tübingen: Niemeyer, 1973), p. 12.

[52]Ibid., p. 242; see also the chapter "Die Metapher als Weltauslegung," pp. 240–43.

than many others. But if metaphor can achieve some historical and social content at all by virtue of its referential and expressive functions, then it is precisely the consideration of these functions that helps go beyond the assumption of autonomy by integrating the study of imagery into a historical understanding of the whole of the work of art. Such an awareness of mimetic and expressive functions would correlate the imagery to plot and character without minimizing the specific contribution that it can make to the development of atmosphere or certain themes or motifs of the play.

This procedure, finally, would avoid the element of reductiveness in Shakespeare criticism, to which I have previously referred. It is true that in talking about the danger of "reducing" Shakespeare's plays, we must not forget that it is the task of the critic to abstract and to generalize. But the tendency, in Dr. Johnson's words, to turn the mind "more upon that from which the illustration is drawn than that to which it is applied" has indeed led to an unnecessary amount of abstraction and vagueness. When, for instance, Wilson Knight writes about Shakespeare's "hate theme" or says that "the Shakespearian evil is a vision of naked spirit, which appears as a bottomless chasm of 'nothing,'" or when R. B. Heilman, after all his close reading of *King Lear*, says that the play is about "the problem of understanding" and "about the ways of looking at and assessing the world of human experience," or when Cleanth Brooks says about the "naked babe" metaphor in *Macbeth* that it represents "essential humanity, humanity stripped down to the naked thing itself" and that Shakespeare uses the same image "for the unpredictable future that he uses for human compassion"—then indeed the plays are reduced to a level of abstraction that is not helpful.[53] And this is not a tendency that expired with the demise of the New Criticism. "The theme of *Othello*," we can read in a recent study of its

[53] Knight, *Wheel of Fire*, p. 264; Heilman, p. 134; Brooks, "The Naked Babe and the Cloak of Manliness," *The Well Wrought Urn: Studies in the Structure of Poetry*, (New York, Harvest Books, 1959), p. 46.

"patterns," "is the relationship between human behavior and human motivation, between words and thoughts, actions and purposes." Such a reading seems all the more disturbing since the author is well aware of recent changes in critical directions and of the danger "that the symbolic approach may oversimplify the issues of the play. Carried over into actual production, the identification of Iago with Evil, Desdemona with Good, and Othello with Good Overthrown can rob *Othello* of its vitality and plausibility."[54]

At first sight, it may seem paradoxical that the most subtle and thoroughgoing studies of the verbal and pictorial texture of the plays can end up in vast and rather vague generalizations that might equally well be applied to many plays, Elizabethan and modern, yes, and to novels and poems, good and bad. But if my critique of what I have called the autonomous fallacy is at all justified, then this method of abstracting the metaphorical vehicle from its referential and expressive functions and (ultimately) its social and historical context is bound to reduce not only these functions but also the structure and meaning of Shakespeare's metaphors. Because these critics and their followers tend to isolate the sensuous element from which the illustration is drawn, they feel compelled to compensate by a symbolic mode of generalization that must remain vague because it does not draw upon the total social and aesthetic meaning and experience of drama. But this meaning is finally inseparable from the concrete theatrical and imaginative activity that released the universalizing force of the poetic transmutation of the real world, material, ideological and psychological, in which Shakespeare lived.

Toward the Historical Context of Shakespeare's Imagery

To work out the comprehensive functions of figurative language as part of this activity is one way of overcoming the

    [54]Ralph Berry, "Pattern in *Othello*," *Shakespeare Quarterly*, 23 (1972), 17, 3.

formalism and the methodological inadequacy of some of the most influential of imagery studies in Shakespeare. For that, a good deal of empirical work, historical and analytical, remains to be done, without which the dramatic uses of imagery cannot be seen in their social and theatrical context. But, again, this context is not like a frame that can be detached from the verbal picture. Rather, the imagery is indissolubly linked with a poetic and theatrical medium of communication that draws on the resources of the English language at a certain, very specific, stage of its development. And the language in its turn was part of a culture that combined a vast range of reference, social and natural, with a unique capacity for epiphora: a freedom to "transpose" and to experiment, an unparalleled liberty of transference and association.

This freedom is inseparable from the conditions in society where (as the historians tell us) there was an unprecedented "mobility of social classes" amounting to a "babylonian confusion of classes," which was a matter of some consequence not only in the theater, its organization and audience, but also for its dramatic and verbal art.[55] This was seen most clearly when (in the 1580s) the theatrical gallimaufry was about to be complete by a humanist who (like Lyly) was in close contact with the court:

At our exercises, Souldiers call for Tragedies, their object is bloud: Courtiers for Commedies, their subject is love: Countriemen for Pastoralles, Shepheards are their Saintes. Trafficke and travell hath woven the nature of all Nations into ours, and made this land like Arras, full of devise. . . . Time hath confounded our mindes, our mindes the matter; but all commeth to this passe, that what heretofore has been served in several dishes for a feaste, is now minced in a charger for a Gallimaufrey. If wee present a mingle-mangle, our fault is to be excused, because the whole worlde is become an Hodge-podge.[56]

It is the social and theatrical "mingle-mangle" and the

[55] A. L. Rowse, *The England of Elizabeth: The Structure of Society* (London, 1950), p. 243; J. B. Black, *The Reign of Elizabeth: 1558–1603* (Oxford, 1949), p. 226.
[56] *Complete Works of John Lyly*, ed. R. W. Bond (Oxford, 1902), III, 115.

related principle of "complementarity" which, I suggest, can be shown to inform the very range and richness of Shakespeare's figurative language.[57] Just as the plays themselves, their themes, characters, and compositions thrived on the dramatic integration of varied social values and cultural elements, so did the dramatist's verbal capacities for epiphora. If metaphor, according to Aristotle, consists in the process of applying to a thing a word that belongs to something else, that is, an alien word or name, then indeed the potential of application and the range of transference were, in Shakespeare's case, of very impressive dimensions. The dramatist himself was aware of these dimensions and the varied social points of reference, as when he used "Taffeta phrases, silken terms precise . . . Figures pedantical," or contrasted them (through Berowne, at the end of *Love's Labour's Lost*) with "russet yeas and honest kersey noes" (V.ii.407. 414). But Berowne's rejection of rhetoric in favor of "Honest plain words" (l. 761) points to an alternative which is not Shakespeare's own.

It was the poetic *process* and the *result* of verbal transference, its very comprehension, not merely the transposed vehicle, that mattered; Shakespeare did not use, as do some of his latter-day critics, the alien name for its own sake; he was not, so to speak, alienating the process by abstracting the vehicle from the underlying idea or matter. Nor did he abstract the tenor or underlying idea from what would then have become the merely pictorial ornament of his expression. Rather, it was the *link* between tenor and vehicle that constituted and reconstituted the process of poetic transference and imaginative recognition. Thus, Shakespeare was in a position to release an absolute host of verbal energies and cultural tensions in the metaphoric process of his language, and, ultimately, these drew on more than a supreme moment in the history of the English language: they

[57]See Norman Rabkin's somewhat different but highly illuminating approach to this concept in *Shakespeare and the Common Understanding* (New York, 1967).

reflected an imaginative dimension as large and as lively as the social organism itself. In an age of transition and contradictions, this was possible from a social and artistic position of discovery and experimental activity. There was a vital interest in making connections and explorations, and in the drama humanist endeavors in the arts of language merged with the irreverence and earthiness of popular speech.[58] Perhaps more than anything else the dramatic practice of punning and the joys of wordplay bear witness to the vitality of the impulse by which the process of transferring a word from one object of reference to another thrived upon a world of mobility, social change, and realignment.

But if the range and quality of the dramatist's mode of verbal transference reflect the cultural mingle-mangle of a transitional age, the element of "Trafficke and travell" and the corresponding attitudes toward discovery and experiment must not be overemphasized. Rather, the new cultural and verbal freedom to "transpose" developed at a time when a large body of traditional thought and imagery still enjoyed the public status of a moral and philosophical language. Shakespeare had *already* begun to share the new sense of social and cultural mobility; but, on these premises, he achieved a metaphoric language "full of devise" when there was *still* a powerful body of traditional images and topoi available for poetic discourse. Here, Caroline Spurgeon's statistical analyses are revealing insofar as they demonstrate that mythology is among the three most widely used subjects of Shakespeare's imagery. Similarly, the metaphors that can be said to be most rewarding in terms of an analysis of their social and historical functions belong to that body of imagery with which Shakespeare's audience would be familiar from homilies and other channels of traditional ideology. For instance, the system of correspondences be-

---

[58] I have discussed this context at greater length in my *Drama und Wirklichkeit in der Shakespearezeit* (Halle: VEB Niemeyer, 1958); there is an English summary, "Soul of the Age: Towards a Historical Approach to Shakespeare," in *Shakespeare in a Changing World*, ed. Arnold Kettle (London, 1964), pp. 17–42.

tween the human body and the body politic or between the macrocosm and contemporary society must obviously have inspired images such as "the foul body of th'infected world" or "sun-like majesty." The world and the traditions that such correspondences still reflected and kept alive was a world in which the language of metaphor fulfilled many of the functions that were soon to be taken over by conceptual modes of expression. By the time Shakespeare began to write, these traditions of preconceptual expression, although still available for public utterance, were already coming to be uprooted. (Within another six decades they were dead.) But the very fact that they were in part uprooted pointed to a transitional area in which it was possible poetically to experiment with them, to adapt them, and dramatically to make them conflict with the nonmetaphorical language of the "law" of "nature" which so obviously defined itself beyond "the plague of custom" (*King Lear* I.ii.1–3).

In this sense the historical dialectic of Elizabethan figurative language is well adumbrated by Lyly's "Time hath confounded our mindes, our mindes the matter." The metaphorical imagination projects the form and pressure of "Time" upon its own subject matter. Imaginative attitudes toward both experience and language, which had "heretofore . . . been served in several dishes," are now "minced in a charger for a Gallimaufrey." One of the results is that Shakespeare in perhaps the most sustained single affirmative speech on "degree, priority, and place" has room for the natural language of dissolution and destruction: "Frights, changes, horrors, / Divert and crack, rend and deracinate . . ." (*Troilus* I.iii.98–99). But these revolutionary changes not only disrupt the estates of the realm ("The unity and married calm of states"); they also "deracinate" time-honored patterns of preconceptual language "quite from their fixture!" (ll. 100–101).

The dramatic language (including the verbal texture of Ulysses' speech) reflects and encompasses this historical

process. The newly quantifying effect of the nonmetaphorical nouns and verbs of natural "commotion" (l. 98),
paratactically arranged, contrasts with the metaphorical
notion of the "heavens themselves." But the resulting tension is not even primarily one between metaphorical and
nonmetaphorical modes of expression; it affects the quality
of the links between vehicle and tenor. The "glorious planet
Sol," although poetically conceived to be "in noble
eminence enthroned," is defined in terms of a highly exploratory kind of experience and is said to possess a
"med'cinable eye" (l. 91), which "posts . . . Sans check, to
good and bad." The impact of the imagery of medicine (a
science) and the postal system (of modern origin in Elizabethan England) upon the central metaphorical notion of
degree is considerable. There is a tension between the
modern associations of the image ("trafficke and travell" enrich the vehicle) and the traditional view of the world as a
divinely created (static) hierarchy. The resulting links
constitute a texture "like Arras, full of devise." They thrive
on the mimetic reference to a world which "is become an
Hodge-podge." And the newly released capacities for epiphora encompass the freedom either to juxtapose, correlate,
oppose, or ignore the existence of the most conflicting
imaginative experiences of the varied social elements and
cultural values.

Among celestial bodies the moon, even more than the
sun, is a "matter" which is affected by imaginative "mindes"
which "time hath confounded." There is, on the one hand,
the moon as the traditional image with a mythological
meaning, as "governess of floods" (*Midsummer Night's
Dream* II.i.103–4), which in its varied aspects is related to
either the peace or the "dissension" (l. 116) among mortals.
But at the same time the matter of "the sun, the moon, and
stars" could be divested of all mythological or hierarchical
correspondences; in fact these traditional symbols of order
could be scornfully opposed to a new "law" of "nature" by

which the metaphorical association might be dismissed as
some "excellent foppery of the world":

> we make guilty of our disasters the sun, the moon, and stars; as if we were
> villains on necessity; fools by heavenly compulsion; knaves, thieves, and
> treachers, by spherical predominance; drunkards, liars, and adulterers,
> by an enforc'd obedience of planetary influence.
>
> [*King Lear* I.ii.108–17]

The simultaneous availability of preconceptual and
naturalistic perspectives released that spiritual-material exu-
berance of the metaphoric process that we associate with
John Donne's self-conscious, witty conceit and such com-
parisons as, say, of the souls of the lovers to the two legs of
the compass. Shakespeare's much more spontaneous and less
elaborate figures draw their vigor from a historical context
that is not so far removed from Donne. What, for instance, is
the metaphorical function and poetic status of the moon in
Hotspur's famous

> By heaven, me thinks it were an easy leap
> To pluck bright honour from the pale-fac'd moon;
> Or dive into the bottom of the deep,
> Where fathom-line could never touch the ground,
> And pluck up drowned honour by the locks. . . .
>
> [*1 Henry IV* I.iii.201–5]

Again, the highly experimental quality of the image is related to a vision of the world which by itself involves both a
traditional metaphor of honor and (built into the apprehension of the traditional image) a counter-perspective on
unheard-of explorations and connections. There is a zest for
making poetic discoveries beyond the point "where fathom-
line could never touch the ground." Or, take Hermia's
speech:

> The sun was not so true unto the day
> As he to me. Would he have stolen away
> From sleeping Hermia? I'll believe as soon
> This whole earth may be bor'd, and that the moon
> May through the centre creep and so displease
> Her brother's noontide with th'Antipodes.
>
> [*Midsummer Night's Dream* III.i.50–55]

The imaginative dimension of this language is so striking because the poetic assertion of steadfastness and constancy is
achieved by an image of the impossible, an image that encompasses the highly experimental vision of an earth which
"may be bor'd." (As J. U. Nef has shown, the Elizabethan industrial revolution was especially marked in mining and coal
production.)[59] As in the case of "order," the traditional tenor
is *still* very much available, but it is *already* imagined
through associations that are not so traditional any more. If
the meaning is "constancy" or, for Percy, "honor," the
traditional element in the figure is again affected by a new
imaginative experience of "trafficke and travell."

The resulting link between notion and picture involves
an almost imperceptible tension and a dynamism which is
both verbal and historical and which reflects and constitutes
the immense energy sustaining the range and vitality in the
process of poetic transference. If this process is seen as both a
social and an artistic one, then indeed it cannot be reduced
to a spatial pattern of autonomous verbal interplay, but will
be seen in its mimetic and expressive dimensions as a process
in time and of the times. In this direction, it is submitted, the
study of metaphor has insufficiently been developed. As
these few examples may suggest, metaphor can (at least
tentatively) be related to the total meaning of Shakespeare's
poetry in the theater. This may point the way (although,
admittedly, it does no more) to the critical attempt at an integration of the study of imagery into a renewed and more
comprehensive vision of literary history.

[59] *The Rise of the British Coal Industry* (London, 1932), I, 19 ff., 123 ff., 165;
the shipping and transport of coal to London almost quadrupled in the eighties
and early nineties.

VI

Structure and History
in Narrative Perspective:
The Problem of Point of View
Reconsidered

THE modern critic's growing interest in point of view, like the modern fiction on which it is largely based, reflects a changing and increasingly complex world in which the artist, in order to create, can no longer take wholeness for granted. From one important aspect, the history of modern literature can be described as a process in which the breadth of the object is supplanted by the precision of the subject, pattern by texture, the narrator's whole vision by the functional point of view of fictional characters. In the past, as long as the artist's position vis-à-vis his world informed the characters' imaginary reactions to the world of his fiction, the relationship of author and point of view was more direct and self-evident, and less self-conscious; the subjective experience of the writer was more obviously part of the objective social whole that he set out to explore and to tell tales about. Thus, for the early modern novelist, such as Cervantes and Fielding, as well as for Scott, Balzac and Tolstoy, the mode of representation was more organically related to the means of evaluation; for the narrator's wide angle of selection corresponded to the freedom and (relative) security with which he evaluated in terms of character, incident, and direct or stylized commentary. In the structure of the eighteenth- and nineteenth-century novel, incident and character themselves served more efficiently to define a way of looking at the world. Hence, the narrator's real world and the imaginary world of his creations, the actual and the fictitious points of view, could be brought into a meaningful (if sometimes verbose or slipshod) correlation, and from this emerged, in the great novels of the past, a remarkable unity of objective representation and subjective evaluation.

But in a world of international class divisions, growing technical and educational specialization, and an ever-increasing flow of information and communication, the modern writer's achievement of wholeness can no longer be that of Cervantes or Fielding. On the one hand, the comprehensiveness and the abstract nature of the social process is much less within his reach; accordingly, his subject matter can no longer be approached in terms of the Hegelian concept of totality that Georg Lukács has somewhat dogmatically used as a criterion for realism. On the other hand, and precisely because the "total" world is out of reach, the writer's wholeness of perception will acquire an increased functional status within his narrative method. Here, clearly, a major social function of the novel is at stake, and it is one that a Marxist approach (which is hostile to any apology of alienation in whatever form it appears) will consider as a supreme criterion of value. As Goethe said, the true work of art will correspond to a human unity of thinking and feeling, the whole nature of man. Its understanding of the world is not merely of a logical or abstract nature, but— as Marx remarked—amounts to a "practical-spiritual appropriation of this world" (*praktisch-geistigen Aneignung dieser Welt*).[1]

When, therefore, the novelist's panoramic view of the whole of society has become difficult or even impossible to achieve, the novelist himself can still attain to a view of man and society from which a more functional kind of wholeness is within reach of his poetic perception and his expression. For the novelist the narrative angle of vision may no longer be so wide as Rabelais's or Fielding's, but it can still achieve an element of integrity through the linking of representation and evaluation. If today point of view is to be more than the

[1] *Goethes Sämtliche Werke* (Jubiläums-Ausgabe), XXXIII, 175; Karl Marx, *Zur Kritik der politischen Ökonomie*, Marx and Engels, *Werke* (Dietz Verlag) XIII, 633.

strategy of first- or third-person narration, it must involve the structural correlation of these two basic functions. Both are part of the specific "practical-spiritual" achievement of art: *one* (representation) relates the novel to the objective nature of the world; the *other* (evaluation) to the subjective nature of the viewer. Through this correlation of the world and the self, the narrative point of view functions as a connecting medium between representation and evaluation, and it is as a means of achieving and communicating their unity that point of view must be seen as being at the heart of the narrator's method.

If point of view can thus be seen as both a fictional and historical means of "appropriation" of the world, it has once more become part of the wider context of art and society against which the aesthetics of the novel can be developed. But today this involves a critique of some of the predominating critical concepts and approaches to the novel which, in England and America, are still formalist. The New Critics believed that the novel had to be described and evaluated in terms of its intrinsic categories. Their primary methodological contention about point of view in fiction was that it had to be derived from the text alone. In suggesting that, these critics overlooked the obvious, which is the historical connection of the text: namely, that the texts themselves derive from, and act upon, contexts. To reinstate the context in its reciprocal relation with the achieved art work must be the first step in reopening the problem of point of view in historical criticism. And here perhaps it can be shown that the question of function in literary history can be rewarding historically as well as critically: for the concept of point of view (or structure in general) is as broad or as narrow, as dynamic or as static, as the sphere of activity in which the structural part is conceived to function. The critics who conceive that sphere too narrowly correspondingly impoverish their conception of structure. There is, after all, a point beyond which limitation becomes inaccuracy.

All this calls for a new approach to narrative method,

toward which the present essay can make no more than a few
suggestions that—as mere prolegomena—are mainly based
on the theory and the early history of narrative perspective
in the novel. Even so, these suggestions will involve more
than sociological criteria or the consideration of society as
subject matter that is "mirrored" or "reflected" in the work
of art. Rather, literature and society are seen to be interrelated in the sense that literary values *are* social values and
that social values, if they are to be values, will in the last
resort come to terms with the workings of the imagination
and the telling of stories. In the act of telling his story, the
teller of the tale is faced, not simply with a series of technical
problems and not only with the rhetorical task of communication, but with a world full of struggle and change where
the writer, in order to transmute his experience into art, has
constantly to reassess his relations to society as both a social
and an aesthetic act. In the process of doing this, he will find
that his own experience as an artist in history is so related to
the social whole that the flexibility (which involves the
precariousness) of this relationship itself is the basis on which
representation and evaluation are integrated through point
of view.

Definitions of Point of View

From this approach one would wish to challenge some of the
current and widely accepted definitions in the literature on
point of view. Admittedly, any approach to narrative
method will feel indebted to the important contributions,
from Percy Lubbock to Wayne C. Booth. Also, it is easy to
agree with such statements as Wellek and Warren's that in
the structure of point of view we have before us "the central
problem of narrative method," or that, as Norman Friedman
remarked, "the choice of a point of view in the writing of
fiction is at least as crucial as the choice of a verse form in the
composing of a poem." But as soon as one begins to inquire

into the underlying assumptions or even into the meanings of
the terms so used, one is struck by an element of confusion
and formalism, and sometimes impressionism, which is in
many ways a curious and unexpected phenomenon in one of
the most highly debated areas of recent English and
American criticism. In summing up the discussion of almost
half a century, Wayne C. Booth writes: Percy Lubbock
"could hardly have predicted that his converts would
produce, in forty years of elaborate investigation of point-of-
view, so little help to the author or critic. . . . We have been
given classifications and descriptions which leave us
wondering why we have bothered to classify and describe.
. . ."[2] Hinting at the merely descriptive and typological approach of formalism, Booth stresses its frustrations, but he
does not (though his *Rhetoric of Fiction* goes some way in
this direction) draw attention to the inherent contradictions
within the theory of the concept itself.

There is an uncontrolled element of ambiguity that
besets the current definitions of point of view; lest my own
use of the same term appear to blur this over, it is important
to look more closely at some of the accepted formulas. Most
of them, no doubt, derive from Percy Lubbock's well-known
statement: "The whole intricate question of method, in the
craft of fiction, I take to be governed by the question of the
point of view—the question of the relation in which the narrator stands to the story."[3] This reached the textbooks and
the dictionaries long ago; to take only J. T. Shipley's *Dic-
tionary of World Literature: Criticism, Forms, Technique,*
where the echo of Lubbock's formula is quite distinct: there,
again, point of view is "the relation in which the narrator
stands to the story, considered by many critics to govern the
method and character of the work."

----

[2] René Wellek and Austin Warren, *Theory of Literature* (London, 1955), p.
251; Friedman, "Point of View in Fiction: The Development of a Critical Concept," *PMLA,* 70 (1955), 1180; Booth, "Distance and Point of View: An Essay in
Classification," *Essays in Criticism,* 11 (1961), 60.

[3] *The Craft of Fiction* (New York, 1957), p. 251.

But who is the narrator in these definitions? In some of them it is almost certainly not the author. Against the background of the New Criticism, with its distinction between the personal voice and the impersonal text, this should have been (and often was) clear enough. However, Mark Schorer, in his repeatedly anthologized essay "Technique as Discovery," widely regarded as "the really significant advance in the theory of point of view which occurred in the forties,"[4] considered point of view as a technique; he defined it as the writer's "only means ... of discovering, exploring, developing his subject." Rejecting all "blunter terms than those which one associates with poetry," Schorer could easily dispense with "such relatively obvious matters as the arrangement of events to create plot; or, within plot, of suspense and climax; or as the means of revealing character, motivation, relationship and development." But what, then, had become of "the relation in which the narrator stands to *the story*"? (my emphasis). If his approach to point of view as "thematic definition" had very little to do with plot, character, relationship, and development, as a matter of course Schorer also had to belittle the concept of point of view as a "narrowing or broadening of perspective upon the material"[5]—the "material," that is, as something outside the autonomous status of the art work.

As most of the elements which might possibly infringe upon this alleged autonomy of the art work were rejected or minimized, the new critical definition of the relation of the narrator to the story left no room for a relationship so grossly untechnical as that of the writer to the society in which he, simply as a human being, lived as a character in history. Consequently, the New Critics would use the term *narrator* to indicate a technical or imaginative medium, so that the narrator's relation to the story was, say, Zeitblom's relation to

---

[4] Friedman, p. 1167.
[5] Mark Schorer, "Technique as Discovery," in *Critiques and Essays on Modern Fiction: 1920–1951*, ed. John W. Aldridge (New York, 1952), pp. 67 ff.

the story of *Doktor Faustus*. Or was it still Thomas Mann's attitude to his times and materials as transmuted into the whole meaning of the novel? This question hardly received a straightforward answer, but the full extent of the underlying ambiguity emerged when, in Wellek and Warren's *Theory of Literature*, "the central problem of narrative method" was defined as "the relation of the *author* to his work." Here, "author" must needs refer to a person in history; "his work" would—from René Wellek's position—mean the work of art as "a stratified structure of signs and meanings which is totally distinct from . . . the author."[6] The resulting relationship, the suggested basis of point of view, involves a singular incongruity from which the actual connection between the world and the author-narrator cannot be seen in any meaningful correlation with that of the story and its medium.

This correlative function of point of view (which I hold to be perhaps its most essential aspect) is equally ignored in the German *Stilkritik*, although here, in the work of Wolfgang Kayser, there is at least a hint that narrative perspective faces two ways and that it exists in both the real world and the imaginative world of the art work: the term *Perspektive* (although never sufficiently defined) is *either* used in the fictitious sense of an "optischen Standpunkt" *or* as a "Manifestation des Stilwillen," which would link it up with the historical background of the writer and his society.[7] This twofold aspect is most clearly brought out in an American textbook which is more than ordinarily aware of the "two different connections" of narrative perspective. As Cleanth Brooks and Robert Penn Warren remark in *Understanding Fiction*, point of view

is used in two different connections. First, it is used in connection with the basic attitude or idea of the author, and second, it is used in connection with the method of narration. In the first meaning, one refers, for

---

[6] *Theory of Literature*, p. 231; René Wellek, *Concepts of Criticism*, ed. Stephen G. Nichols, Jr. (New Haven, 1963), p. 293.
[7] Wolfgang Kayser, *Das sprachliche Kunstwerk* (Bern: Francke, 1951), pp. 209 ff.

instance, to the author's ironical point of view, or his detached point of view, or his sympathetic point of view, or the like. Or one might say that a certain piece of fiction embodies a Christian point of view. In the second meaning, one refers to the mind through which the material of the story is presented—first person, first-person observer, author-observer, and omniscient author. Confusion will be avoided if the use of the term *point of view* be restricted to the first meaning, and if the term FOCUS OF NARRATION be used for the second meaning.[8]

The differentiation is extremely useful, but as a purely descriptive definition it seems to ignore the fact that these two aspects of narrative perspective, although distinct, also form some kind of unity and that criticism (if it is to work within the same wider context of history and aesthetics, social function and narrative structure that the novel itself is related to) would find its most rewarding task in discovering and interpreting the very crossing-points and links between the two aspects. Again, if "the basic attitude . . . of the author" and "the method of narration" are anywhere related, criticism would have to examine the degree and the nature of this relationship in order to see the historical as well as the structural elements in any given narrative perspective. Not that their unity will always be achieved, but in the completely integrated narrative work of art, the historical and the technical, function and structure, have become irretrievably fused, and the tensions and the correlations within this whole fusion form the dialectics of narrative method.

From this approach, then, recognizing the "two different connections" of narrative perspective can be helpful only if the differentiation between the terms makes room for a consideration of both the tension and the unity of the historical and the structural aspects in point of view. In order to stress the possible degree of unity, one would wish to incorporate the two aspects in one comprehensive term for which *narrative perspective (Erzählperspektive),* or simply *comprehensive point of view,* is perhaps best suited.

[8] *Understanding Fiction* (New York, 1943), p. 607.

This narrative perspective, or comprehensive point of view, comprises both an author's actual *and* his technical points of view. The author's actual point of view—his achieved attitude toward the actual world of history—may conveniently be called his standpoint; the author's technical point of view will simply indicate his medium or focus of narration (unreliable, omniscient, and so on). Both elements form an infinitely variable synthesis, but the synthesis of this wider narrative perspective is extremely complex and never the result of any one determining factor. It is a relationship that cannot be deduced from any fixed formula, but can finally be studied only within the infinite particularity of each individual story or novel.

In order to illustrate the theoretical nature of this relationship, one might say that technique and sensibility, though never identical, possess areas of interaction and that this interaction informs the dialectic of narrative perspective. The author's narrative standpoint is itself not simply a biographical category, which a prose writer, when interviewed, might sum up into a neat statement. The author's point of view, when transmuted into a work of art, cannot be deduced from his private or political opinions or from anything less than the writer's total weltanschauung, or sensibility. The artist's opinions, whether expressed privately or publicly, are relevant mainly insofar as they reflect or inspire his sensibility or his all-round apprehension and comprehension of things. This is a point that Arnold Kettle made when he remarked that if "we refer to a writer's point-of-view in the artistic sense we are referring to his sensibility rather than to his opinions or intentions."[9] Consequently, the achieved standpoint of an author is not identical with his declared position as, say, scholar, journalist, or politician, but may by itself be the means of defining his weltanschauung more conclusively.

    [9] Arnold Kettle, "Dickens and the Popular Tradition," *Zeitschrift für Anglistik und Amerikanistik*, 9 (1961), p. 230.

If the author's standpoint makes sense only insofar as it is achieved through form, the technical point of view, or focus of narration, is meaningful only as long as it helps to create content. In the light of this functional approach, the technical focus of narration can never entirely be abstracted from the ultimate meaning of the novel and what it symbolically, metaphorically, or thematically, through plot, character, and description, has to say about the world as it is. While constituting a reciprocal relationship, the real and the imagined points of view will hardly ever synchronize; there is room for all sorts of tension: ironical, satirical, humorous. Consequently, the imagined point of view, or medium (say, that of Moll Flanders, Jonathan Wild, or Felix Krull) will appear to be worlds apart from the standpoint of the author. But this tension between the imagined positions of Moll, Wild, or Krull and the actual sensibilities of Defoe, Fielding, and Mann, is the very stuff from which the method of narrative derives its form and pressure. To try to understand this method merely in terms of the narrator's relation to his *story* (and not also to the world from which the raw materials of his story are taken) would be as one-sided as considering Jonathan Wild or Felix Krull without reference to the art work's overall comprehension of things against which the character's point of view (satirically, ironically) falls into place.

Thus, the need for a more comprehensive historical-structural angle of reference becomes apparent. To reinstate the contexts in their reciprocal relations with the achieved art work is to ask the larger question of function; it is finally to correlate the function of technique to the social and individual quality of consciousness. The resulting concepts of structure are as dynamic and as wide as the functioning correlations of literature and society that they reflect and promote. Again, the concept of structure is as meaningful as the contextual sphere of relationships in which the structure potentially functions. In this sense, there is a need for a more comprehensive definition of point of view. Once narrative perspective is seen in its widest connections, it can comprise no less than the sum total of the author-narrator's achieved attitudes to both the world (which includes his readers) and the story as a generalized image of what the novelist wishes to say about the world through his art.

Rhetoric: Structuring Function and Functioning Structure

To stress the reciprocal quality of the relations between text and context is to raise, and to be more deeply aware of, the problem of rhetoric in fiction as a problem of both structure and function, genesis and effect. The first point that should be made in any approach to this problem concerns the changing modes of communication in the living novel—a fact that makes any generalization about narrative structure in fiction hazardous and precludes any normative poetics of novelistic form. The impact of photography, film, psychology, and reportage have turned the novel into a mixed genre where there is plenty of room for dramatic and, perhaps to a lesser degree, lyrical conventions. Nevertheless, the rhetorical function of point of view has much greater structural consequence in the epic or the novel than in the drama or lyric poetry. Why this is so is certainly worth pondering; but an answer to this question will have to go beyond Wayne C. Booth's important contribution and at least attempt to sketch some of the problems arising out of the special relationship between the teller, his tale, and his audience.

Storytelling is an ancient convention which, in contrast to the even older art of miming, has a nonmimetic time structure and a rhetoric distinctly its own. Although (let me repeat) the modern novel, so much influenced by drama and film, has largely dispensed with the traditional conventions of storytelling, the structure of the narrator's relation to time and the nondramatic character of narrative illusion have a tradition that is relevant even today. The original process of telling a tale and the ordinary social function of all storytelling involve an act of direct communication. It presupposes an audience in a way in which the ritual origins of drama originally never required an audience, only participants.[10] In the novel the potential mode of participation is more indirect; it is more a *result* of communication, and it is the communication, not the participation, that is a condition of its earliest social functions. Consequently, the object of communication is never in the present, but is always a matter of the past. For the narrator there is no point in telling about things that, in his presence, his listeners themselves are witnessing. Storytelling at its beginning, and much after, is the telling of things that have (or are said to have) already happened at the moment of their telling. To relate or to report something is never identical with what is so related or reported. It is probably this aspect that Goethe and Schiller had in mind when, in their correspondence, they attempted to define "the great essential difference" between the epic poet and the dramatist: while the former renders an event that is "completely past" (*vollkommen vergangen*), the latter represents something that is "completely ongoing," or present (*vollkommen gegenwärtig*).

Consequently, the conventions of illusion, or verisimilitude, in the two genres are quite different. While on the traditional proscenium stage the actors aim to represent an imaginative world by pretending to be that world and thus ignoring the audience, the criterion of narrative illusion is, and was originally, the narrator's act of recollection and the convincing tone of his address to the audience. The dramatic assumption of the picture-frame stage (that a story or plot renders itself) is quite alien to the narrator, whose

---

[10] I have explored the concept and practice of audience participation in terms of a reconsideration of the ritual origins of the Elizabethan drama in my *Shakespeare und die Tradition des Volkstheaters;* but see my critique of some of the basic positions of myth criticism, including Northrop Frye's, in *Literaturgeschichte und Mythologie,* pp. 342–427.

recollection is the source of his reliability and who reviews the things he thinks are worth telling others about. To expect the narrator to render an event *telle qu'elle est* is a contradiction in itself.

Since the act of narration involves selective communication more than mimetic participation, and since, therefore, the narrative is so obviously not identical with its subject, it already contains an unashamed element of perspective and evaluation. Without it, no narration is possible: how else could the narrator in real life hope to comprehend and arrange the multitude of details that he—in summary or silence—thinks fit to condense or pass over? But to achieve the necessary selection and evaluation is impossible without a point from which to select and evaluate, and this view point (whether consciously or unconsciously taken) is indeed the absolute prerequisite of all narrative activity. It is true that to a certain degree any representation of reality is unthinkable without some such selective and partial view point; but only in the narrative genre does this seeming limitation assume a positive structural equivalent. Here, the social function of verbal communication provides a usable mode of artistic structure. Thus, in contrast to the dramatist, the narrator may incorporate the *process* of his evaluation (which already means organization) and his selection (which also means partiality) into the work of art itself. While the traditional dramatist cannot very well articulate or stylize the mode and rhetoric of his perspectives, the novelist may transform the simplest prerequisite of ordinary storytelling into a highly effective convention of his art. Thus, as in Jean Paul or many first-person narrations, the activity of storytelling itself, its difficulties and triumphs, are transmuted into the narrative activity of some fictive medium. The actual effort of the author's communication and organization can be recreated in a stylized or ironic form; it can find a fictional correlative in the communicative mode of narrative representation in the work itself. The process of this transmutation assumes myriad forms and many stages of distance, counterpoint and irony, but eventually it can achieve a meaning which, although not identical with the author and his world of history, sheds some new and generalized significance upon it.

When I suggest that point of view is a potential link between the actual and the fictive modes of narrative communication and representation, there is no need to ignore the fact that the author's omniscient and reliable angle of narration has—as a convention—been increasingly given up. But this tendency, which is already quite explicit in Flaubert's concept of *impassibilité*, is in itself a symptom of the novelist's increased need to come to grips with the changing function of his art form and the changing rhetorical mode of his achieved perspective. Obviously, the structural correlation of the actual and the technical points of view became more difficult when the naive and immediate solution of the omniscient narrator seemed no longer acceptable. But when the novelist, such as Dickens after his early novels, began to abandon the personal narrator, he gave up only a stylized convention, not the real function of the narrator to select and evaluate. By abandoning the omniscient convention, the author surrendered the direct quality of the link between the world and his fiction, but he certainly did not cease to exist. The relationship between the author's real and his technical points of view became more subtle and, as it were, invisible, but it was not simply canceled out.

If the critics of the modern novel believed that it was, their error was partly due to their unquestioning (and largely unconscious) bias toward the standards of drama, to their acceptance of the norms and appearances of "scenic" showing and narrative "objectivity." This bias, of course, was supported by, or even based on, the immense prestige and experience of such author-critics as Henry James or Spielhagen in Germany. But a bias it nevertheless was; it reflected and generalized the new difficulties in finding any fictional equivalent for the actual narrative activity of the author. A fictive medium for the communicative function of storytelling had now become problematic. The subjectivity or, in the Marxian sense, the *Praxis* involved in the rhetorical mode of narrative activity was no longer considered a legitimate part of the novelist's image of the world. Again, this did not mean that the narrator's subjectivity had ceased to exist; only, that the communicative function of his activity had become more indirect. In this sense the demand for objectivity expressed only the changing modes of the relationship in which the novelist's subjectivity found itself vis-à-vis the objective world of his audience.

If, then, the critics of the modern novel accepted the concept of objectivity so uncritically, the direction of their approach to the problem of point of view was affected accordingly. To approach point of view (as Norman Friedman and other critics do) merely as a "*modus operandi* for distinguishing the possible degrees of authorial extinction in the narrative art" will, *nolens volens,* lead the critic to accept the bias of one type of fiction. If the "prime end of fiction is to produce as complete a story-illusion as possible," and if this is indeed "the basic assumption of those who are seriously concerned over technique," then a very questionable concept of illusion is made a criterion of artistic truth. To quote Friedman's deductions in full: "If artistic 'truth' is a matter of compelling rendition, of creating the illusion of reality, then an author speaking in his own person about the lives and fortunes of others is placing an extra obstacle between his illusion and the reader by virtue of his very presence."[11]

This kind of argument—confounding realism with reality—seems to assume that the author's presence (and, together with it, his actual historical point of view) is dispensed with as soon as he decides to suppress "his own personal voice in one way or another." True, since the influence of the dramatic or film scene on modern fiction is very

[11] Friedman, pp. 1163, 1180, 1164.

powerful, there is some justification for using a basically dramatic concept of illusion as a touchstone for the "artistic 'truth'" of the novel. But to make this partially justified argument into an absolute maxim in the theory of the novel, to claim (in the words of Percy Lubbock) that "the art of fiction does not begin until the novelist thinks of his story as a matter to be shown" is to ignore or distort the very bases of the narrative element in fiction.[12] The difficulties in redefining the aesthetic meaning of narrative subjectivity are rationalized into a new poetics of the novel. In this sense the new poetics merely seeks to apologize for the novelist's increasing reluctance to face the rhetoric of his communication. What is behind this reluctance is the modern novelist's desire to dissociate his subjectivity and his authority from the novel's communicative function as part of a meaningful *aesthetic* activity, which indeed it is. The novelist who writes and the critic who interprets have begun to mistrust the aesthetic expression of the artist's responsibility for his own narrative perspective on society.

Although recent American critics have gone some way toward redressing the distortions of the autonomous fallacy, the assumptions of formalism are still widespread and influential. When academic critics such as Mark Spilka felt the need for an alternative solution, they began to plead for a reconsideration of the author-narrator as the one basis from which the style of the novel could more fruitfully be interpreted. But the concept of the "necessary stylist" was designed expressly to repair the absence of the "author" in "new critical terminology." So the critic began to approach the stylist almost as a necessary evil ("If we connect the author *formally* with his works, rather than historically . . .").[13] It was still the cramped logic of *Stilkritik*. From this, even the most fundamental modern contribution to the theory of fiction is by no means free, although, here, as the

---

[12] Lubbock, p. 62.
[13] Mark Spilka, "The Necessary Stylist: A New Critical Revision," *Modern Fiction Studies*, 6 (1960 / 61), p. 285.

title of Wayne C. Booth's *The Rhetoric of Fiction* (1961) indicates, the focus of interest is remarkably shifted and the basic problems of narrative communication no longer ignored. Booth has a new sense of "the implied author" as the comprehensive "core of norms and choices," a "choosing, evaluating person," and he sees the most basic problems of method as resulting from the author's attempt, "consciously or unconsciously, to impose his fictional world upon the reader." This is a far cry from the formalist ghost of the "affective fallacy"; the dogma of the self-contained autonomy of the art work as "a stratified structure of signs" is pretty much shattered when Booth with no more than common sense acknowledges that although the author can to some extent choose his disguises, "the author's judgment is always present." But the author's judgment (one would assume) is surely affected by historical, social, and psychological forces; and without reference to them the nature and the functions of his judgments can hardly be subjected to criticism. Booth, however, mentions these social and psychological forces that affect authors and readers only in order to dismiss them *expressis verbis* in favor of "the narrower question of whether rhetoric is compatible with art."[14]

This question is not merely narrow—its assumptions are simply wrong. Apart from the fact that the author's relations to his readers cannot be subsumed solely under rhetorical categories, the whole way of posing this question makes wholesale concessions to the formalist tradition. Perhaps Booth's concept of rhetoric reflects the climate of the early sixties, when daring to smuggle the idea of the "impurity of great literature" into the domain of critical purists still required some caution.[15] With this kind of strategy, Booth did indeed score an immense success, but he had, ironically enough, not merely to use the terminology of formalism—he had to get himself entangled in its contradictions. As if it

---

[14] Wayne C. Booth, *The Rhetoric of Fiction* (Chicago, 1961), pp. 74, [ii].
[15] Ibid., pp. 98–109.

were at all possible to narrate without rhetoric! To conceive of rhetoric as something "impure" makes (despite Booth's expressed intention) a vital concession to the old sterile opposition between "mere" rhetorical telling and "artful" showing. Thus, an uneasy element of ambiguity remains in his ironic protests against "cleaning out the rhetorical impurities from the house of fiction." Says Booth: "If the most admired literature is in fact radically contaminated with rhetoric, we must surely be led to ask whether the rhetoric itself may not have something to do with our admiration."[16]

The argument may point in the right direction, but this line of reasoning still seems unsatisfactory. If we are told repeatedly that "even the greatest literature depends on 'impurities' for its greatness," there is something wrong with this whole system of reference. The art of the novel is not (as the ambiguous phrase goes) *contaminated* with rhetoric, for rhetoric *is* a means of narrative *structure*. The (allegedly) "impure" world cannot be opposed to an (allegedly) "pure" structure any more than the actual point of view can finally be abstracted from the technical one. To the degree that both are correlated in the larger historical-structural dimensions of perspective, the social purpose and material of narration and the aesthetic method of narrative interact. This interaction and this integration are achieved through point of view.

Social and Technical Points of View: Toward Their Integration

However, my critique of some of the basic and most widespread conceptions of narrative method and rhetoric must remain somewhat abstract, not to say schematic, as long as the suggested relationship of consciousness and

[16] Ibid., pp. 98 f.

structure is not approached historically, in terms of the concrete modes of correlation between the actual and the technical points of view. In order to illustrate at least one aspect of the historical nature of this correlation more clearly, I propose to look at the origins of the modern point of view. Although space forbids more than a few, necessarily incomplete remarks (which, again, run all the risks of oversimplification), even a tentative sketch may perhaps suggest the extent to which narrative perspective in the novel constitutes itself through the interplay of social and technical modes of viewing. This is probably most obvious in the changing angle from which the narrator implies or expresses his attitudes toward his audience as the—to him—most relevant section of society. It is here that the perspective of the epic poet differs most radically from that of the early novelist, and the degree of this difference provides the best index to the changing social and rhetorical functions of the narrator. The corresponding change in point of view (far from being anything impure or external to the art work) manifests itself in tone and structure and thereby helps to explain why, at the outset, the modern novel is so vastly different from both the heroic and the courtly epic.

As we see in *Beowulf* or the *Nibelungenlied*, the epic poet employed a frame of reference that was taken for granted by an audience with which he shared "some unity of sentiment, some common standard of appreciation."[17] In a society where the division of labor was undeveloped, the poet did not—in his individual point of view—radically dissent from that of the society to which he belonged. The opening lines of the epic stressed this community of perspective:

> Hwæt, wē Gār-Dena in gēardagum,
> þēodcyninga þrym gefrunon . . .

> Uns ist in alten maeren wunders vil geseit . . .
> Von küener recken striten muget ir nu wunder hoeren sagen.

[17] W. P. Ker, *Epic and Romance: Essays on Medieval Literature* (London, 1908), p. 21.

The *wē* and the *uns* comprised the audience *and* the poet in their common attitudes toward both the actual world of experience and the imaginary world of the epic. The distinctive function of the poet was to recollect and to report, and to relate the past world of the epic to the real world of his audience. As "the mediator, the messenger, the guide . . . the knower of the names,"[18] he knew best about the "þrym" and the "wunder" of the past; but the degree of his individual excellence lay in his capacity for mediation, not invention. More than his audience, he had *heard* of the "alten maeren," and from this mediating and interpretative capacity alone, the point of view of his "I" was justified (as in the characteristic *ne hyrde ic* and similar first-person phrases in *Beowulf*.

Thus, the epic poet built up a narrative perspective that was—for his audience—in many ways valid, not relative; real, not fictitious. For Homer, the muses served as an unchallenged source of inspiration. For the audience who applauded, and the poet who cherished, such inspiration, there was no need for an *indirect* medium of narration; the poet himself was already mediating, and an indirect narrator would have interfered with the direct nature and the helpful pathos of his inspiration. As the ancient epic poet did not self-consciously hold any particular perspective, he was in no position to wish to stylize it. Accordingly, the individual modes and, partly, the technical forms of point of view remained undeveloped. The narrator's focus of narration was wide enough to leave room for summary and scenes with dialogue, but as a rule the epic point of view was inseparable from the poet's actual function as the mediator and the knower of the names. There was an indispensable correlation between the poet's actual attitude toward his society and audience and the imaginative perspective of his narration, and from the security and the stability of this correlation the epic point of view drew the strength of its peculiar restraint and dignity, but also its limitations.

[18] T. Greene, "The Norms of Epic," *Comparative Literature*, 13 (1961), 206.

Against the background of the epic, point of view in the novel may be seen more clearly in the historical nature of its origins and functions. Right from the beginning, from Cervantes onwards, narrative perspective presents itself as an individual problem of approach and attitude, for which the early novelist (who is remarkably aware of it) has to find a solution all by himself. Between novelist and reader the unity of comprehension, if not entirely broken up, can no longer be taken for granted; and the narrator must tap all the springs of his individual *humor* (in the ancient physiological sense) and his good humor in order to make his own temper consonant with the multiple tastes and pleasures of his readers. Cervantes, Defoe, and Fielding no longer make a collective address to their audience as a whole, but speak, as it were, man to man, expounding to the individual reader their own equally individual points of view. In doing so, they take up this kind of attitude:

Pero yo, que, aunque parezco padre, soy padrastro de D. Quijote, no quiere irme con la corriente del uso, ni suplicarte casi con las lágrimas en los ojos, como otros hacen, lector carísimo, que perdones ò dissimules las faltas que en este mi hijo vieres; y, pues ni eros su pariente ni su amigo, y tienes tu alma en tu cuerpo y tu libre albedrio como el más pintado, y estás en tu casa, donde eres senor della, como el rey de sus alcabalas. . . .

(But I, who, though seemingly the parent, am in truth only the stepfather of Don Quixote, will not yield to this prevailing infirmity; nor will I—as others would do—beseech thee, kind reader, almost with tears in my eyes, to pardon or conceal the faults thou mayest discover in this brat of mine. Besides thou art neither its kinsman nor friend; thou art in possession of thine own soul, and of a will as free and absolute as the best; and art, moreover, in thine own house, being as much the lord and master of it as is the monarch of his revenue. . . .)

The world is so taken up of late with novels and romances, that it will be hard for a private history to be taken for genuine, where the names and other circumstances of the person are concealed; and on this account we must be content to leave the reader to pass his own opinion upon the ensuing sheets, and take it just as he pleases.

An author ought to consider himself, not as a gentleman who gives a private or eleemosynary treat, but rather as one who keeps a public ordinary, at which all persons are welcome for their money. . . . . Men, who pay for what they eat, will insist on gratifying their palates, however nice and whimsical these may prove; and, if everything is not agreeable to their taste, will challenge a right to censure, to abuse, and to d——n their dinner without control.[19]

This is a different kind of rhetoric, and it reflects a different kind of society: both would be alien to the traditional epic. The society is that of burgeoning "free competition," where the individual, as Marx says, is outside of older "natural bonds" and no longer "part of a definite limited human conglomeration" ("Zubehör eines bestimmten, begrenzten menschlichen Konglomerats").[20] The structure of this new society is reflected in the nature of the narrator's address to his audience. It is an address that—although obviously made to the real world of history—has profound consequences for the structure of the rhetorical and technical focus of narration and—beyond that—for the composition of plot and character. There is a complex sense of the individual as being *a part of* the community as well as *apart from* it. The new consciousness of the "I" stimulates the interest in a person's "own history." This leads to a new freedom of perspective, but not to an opposition of the author's self to the social. As Cervantes shows, the narrator is much concerned with his relations to the *lector carísimo,* but he no longer thinks of the reader as his "relative"; for he, too, has a "mind of his own" and a "free will," and he is master of his own "house" (and property) no less than the sovereign monarch over his revenues! The bourgeois element in the structure of this rhetoric could hardly be more emphatic. From this, Defoe's appeal to the reader's "own opinion" as the final and legitimate verdict on his work is very much in line with Fielding's

[19] *El Ingenioso Hidalgo Don Quijote de la Mancha,* ed. Clemento Cortejon (Madrid: Suárez, 1905), I, 16; trans. Charles Jarvis (London, 1892), p. iii; Daniel Defoe, *The Fortunes and Misfortunes of the Famous Moll Flanders,* Everyman ed. (London, 1930), p. 1; Henry Fielding, *The History of Tom Jones,* Tauchnitz ed. (Leipzig, 1844), p. 11.
[20] Karl Marx, *A Contribution to the Critique of Political Economy,* trans. N. J. Stone (Chicago, 1904), p. 267. Cf. Marx and Engels, *Werke,* XIII, 615 f.

respect for the readers' "right to censure" and the gratifi-
cation of their "palates, however nice and whimsical these
may prove." The narrator's attitudes (no less than those he
imputes to the reader) reflect the structure of a society where
"the different forms of social union confront the individual
as a mere means to his private ends, as an outward
necessity."[21]

But it is not merely the reader who is seen as using the
novel (like all art) as a "means to his private ends"; and it
is not simply the narrator's personality which—as a
biographical fact—is now much more outside the social
nexus. More than that, it is the narrator's work itself which
now, as it were, is considered as his own product or even his
own property, so that Fielding, in a characteristic simile, can
liken his attitude to that of an innkeeper or host "who keeps
a public ordinary." As a kind of entertainer who is free to sell
his fare, he may quite deliberately approach his narration as
the product of his own comprehension of things: *como hijo
del entendimiento,* as the "offspring of my brain," in Charles
Jarvis's translation, which Tobias Smollett in his translation
more literally renders as "the child of my understanding."

This phrase reveals more than the sociological and rhetorical context in which the novelist now communicates with
his readers: the work itself is seen as the intimate product
and the immediate result of the individual artist's apprehension of the world. The modern novel is born in the consciousness of its narrative perspective. It is the perspective of the
individual artist who knows his work to be the direct product
of his own personal sensibility and understanding. In the
words of Goethe, the novel emerges as a "subjective epic, in
which the author asks for the freedom [*Erlaubnis*] to treat
the world according to his own manner [*seine eigene Weise*].
The point, therefore, is if he have such a manner. . . ."[22]
Since the early modern novelist can no longer fall back on
some collective standard of evaluation, this indeed is the first

[21] Marx, *A Contribution*, p. 267.
[22] *Goethes Sämtliche Werke*, XXXVIII, 255.

and foremost problem of his narrative method: to have some distinctive "manner," or angle of comprehension, from which to approach, and hence to impose some unity upon, the myriad details of the world, his material.

Goethe's idea of the world is of course (in new critical terminology) a highly "impure" concept, but the point is that in the last analysis it is the social structure of this world that allows or demands the new personal manner of viewing. What is more, the historical and social foundations of this new manner are connected with the changing structure of the technical focus of narration. At this stage, the correlation between the novelist's social and technical perspectives is still pretty obvious, but this is not primarily (as Booth seems to suggest) a question of communication or rhetoric. Here, to lose sight of the concrete work of art is dangerous, but at the risk of oversimplifying, I would suggest that, basically, the freedom and instability of the novelist's subjective view of the world are correlated to the increasing diversity of his narrative focus which, right from the beginning, is more freely flexible, more subtle, more "relative," and more easily subject to stylization. Hence results the growing breadth of variation among the three obvious forms of narration (the omniscient, the impersonal, and the first-person) as well as the conventional use of the memoir and criminal or picaresque biography. Apart from having to maneuver in the face of the Puritan suspicion of fiction, the early novelist like Defoe, who himself is tossed on the waves of free speculation, enterprise, journalism, and a multitude of projects, has obvious difficulties in imposing some pattern or fictional unity upon his world through the "manner" of his own personality. Unlike Cervantes and Fielding, the lesser personalities in a situation like this are powerfully attracted by the conventions of the picaresque tradition: there, a minimum pattern is established by the point of view of one adventurous individual who, chameleonlike, can reflect all the light and shadow of his ever-changing surroundings. To this, the author's own standpoint would roughly be reconciled if what Defoe calls "the life of the person," the "story", or simply "the wicked part," is brought into some correlation, however tenuous, with "the moral" or "the end of the writer." To pose as editor and to pretend (as in *Moll Flanders*) "that the original of this story is put into new words and the style . . . is a little altered" must have liberated the narrator's vast talent for empirical observation and largely freed him from the frustration of having throughout to sustain his own personal manner. For similar reasons, the convention of the epistolary novel must have been very attractive (although here the Puritan conscience, with its need for introspection and self-analysis, was important). Still, the international success of Richardson's works, like the vogue for the Spanish picaresque novel, can partly be understood in terms of the new needs, possibilities, and frustrations of narrative perspective.

From a historical-structural approach, then, the emergence of the three obvious modes of presentation (omniscient, impersonal, and "I") is indicative of a larger change of narrative perspective. And this change, like every fundamental change in style, reflects a change in the lives of the stylists. Once the three well-known modes of focusing are seen in the wider context of a more comprehensive narrative perspective, their rise and subsequent variations will appear more meaningful than their merely descriptive classification has sometimes allowed. In that case it is, paradoxically enough, the historical approach that alone can bring out their larger structural significance. To sketch the lines of such an approach, I wish, as a kind of summary, to suggest three or four aspects.

First, the novelist's relation to his subject matter. The epic poet, as the mediator of a traditional *matière*, achieved the larger perspective of his community (which includes his own view point) through interpretation and accentuation. The novelist, at the outset, has to create a structural correlative of his individual perspective by himself, through the invention of an original fable, or plot. The traditional *matière* and the epic *Stoffkreise* are too remote from the reality of his society; they seem so discredited and so limited thematically that after Malory no new version or adaptation will ever—as a generalized image—leave room enough for the new narrator's different apprehension and comprehension of the world. To represent the contemporary world more objectively while also expressing his own subjective sensibility more fully, the novelist must find both new subject matter and an original set of images and motifs. The novelty he desires (and the taste for novelty to which he caters) also place new demands on his technical skill: his own creative point of view must become the crossroads where self and society, subjective and social experience, meet.

Second, the new and wider perspective of interpretation and evaluation. The nature of the epic perspective could admit of only a limited range of variations; the pathos and the personal restraint of the narrator encouraged the use of fixed formulas and certain paratactic patterns (such as Malory's "And then . . . Then . . . And then . . . And then . . .": "And then the king let search all the towns. . . . Then much people drew unto King Arthur. And then they said that Sir Mordred warred upon King Arthur with wrong. And then . . . and there was. . . . Then Sir Mordred . . ." [XXI, iii]). This by itself left little room for, and reflected the absence of, the endeavor empirically, causally, and morally to understand, connect, and evaluate. But the novelist, who can no longer fall back on accepted images of description and formulas of traditional interpretation, is almost everywhere called upon, as an individual artist, to suggest motives, to make connections, and to assert values. Faced with an original plot largely of his own making, he is at every turn of the story confronted with an unprecedented need for selection, interconnection, and appraisal. As the range of his objective materials is so much wider and the potential of his subjective reactions so much more subtle and stratified, his point of view, in its supreme correlative function, must ever be alert in its structural, atmospheric, and stylistic dimensions. And although the early novelist still had a public sense of significance and accepted norms of evaluation, such as Fielding's concept of "charity" (*Joseph Andrews*, III, 13; *Tom Jones*, II, 5) or Dr. Johnson's "Truth indeed is always truth, and reason is always reason," the empirical, exploratory, and critical nature of the modern novel soon had to develop a more complex and less secure perspective of reference and value.[23]

Third, the increased variability of perspective. The social, spatial, and temporal structure of point of view in the novel is much less fixed by tradition or convention than the narrative perspective of the epic. In bourgeois society, the more "accidental nature of the conditions of life for the individual" (Marx) is indirectly reflected in the greater imaginative capacity for shifting the narrator's view point; in the novel (as in contrast to neoclassical tragedy) this is not inhibited by decorum or any conservative code of poetics. The greater variability of perspective opens for inspection a wider view of society, and at the same time it assumes new spatial as well as temporal dimensions: the telescope can easily be exchanged for the microscope, and neither distance nor introspection is a problem. The new mobility of the narrative medium is closely linked with a more conscious control of the tempo of movement. The author, as Fielding remarks in *Tom Jones* (II, 1) can leave a scene or a long period of time "totally unobserved," but he can also "open it at large to our reader," and he is quite conscious of doing so. The more variable relationship between the time of the telling and the time of the tale can assume a conscious function of structure, and it usually serves as a means of emphasis and evaluation. The corresponding alternation of summary and scene, with its respective modes of focusing, marks an essential process of narrative method in which the actual sensibility of the author (as a character in history) is

[23] Samuel Johnson, *Lives of the English Poets*, ed. G. Birkbeck Hill (Oxford, 1905), I, 46.

transmuted into the purely fictional focusing of the work of art.

Finally, the ironic use of perspective as a means of distancing or disapproval. The greater freedom and responsibility in the choice of subject-matter, the wider range in interpretation and evaluation, and the increased spatial and temporal variability of perspective—all contribute to the more subtle use of point of view as a deliberate means of stylization. But the process by which the author's true meaning can increasingly dissociate itself from the view point of his medium is ultimately based on the growing separateness and relativity of the individual consciousness as opposed to that of the whole of society. As the freedom and independence of the bourgeois individual are eventually linked with the subjective relativity of his norms and standards, the author finds it increasingly difficult to create a medium whose attitudes and values are neither relativistic in comparison with, nor isolated from, the norms and relations of society. The emergence of the ironic or irresponsible focus of narration reflects this, but at the same time it can be turned into a source of strength: the author can dramatize an attitude which, even while revealing its fullest details and consequences, he can morally disavow through the irony of his whole perspective. The stylized use of perspective for moral distancing greatly enlarges the novelist's capacity for social criticism. Thus, the artist vis-à-vis his society is not simply confronted with an increased relativity of standards: he can avail himself of a critical position that is no longer part of, but is more or less opposed to, the ruling norms of society. In this unique position he can repudiate the excesses of individualism without himself surrendering the achievement of the consciousness of man as an individual. Consequently, the new variable and "accidental" nature of perspective, its increased instability and flexibility, do not rule out a more profound insight into the empirical and causal mechanism of the individual's relation to society. On the contrary, the increased particularity of point of view can help achieve a greater universality and validity. This, perhaps, is the distinction of the eighteenth- and nineteenth-century novel as a "prosaic" image of the world: the individual and quite particular nature of the narrative perspective does not preclude a more general insight into the objective world as it really is. Through the supreme correlative function of point of view, the subjectivity and variability of the author and his medium are perfectly congruent with the greater universalizing meaning of the novel's image of reality.

Structure and Society: A Methodological Epilogue

For a reconsideration of the relationship of structure and society in the literary history of the novel, the paradigm of Cervantes and the eighteenth-century novel has obvious limitations. For one thing, the early modes of narrative perspective cannot account for the changing structure of the more recent novel (up to and including the *nouveau roman*), and they must not furnish us with any preconceived criteria of evaluation. For instance, the eighteenth-century and, partly, the nineteenth-century novel has certain preferences for personal telling as against impersonal showing. The dramatically presented scene is not so dominant, and "objectivity" not yet identical with *impassibilité*. To object to the critics' identification of the former with the latter is one thing; but it is quite a different (and problematic) matter for the critic to base value judgments on his preference for this or that focus of narration. This is a point that has to be made quite strongly: to reject critical preferences for dramatic showing is not to advocate a preference for personal telling. Since the focus of narration is not determined by, but is correlated to, the narrator's standpoint, any evaluation of point of view will have to be based on functional, not on genetic, criteria (even though an examination of the latter can provide an important clue in deciphering the quality and direction of the former). In other words, the historical origins of any particular mode of focusing must be viewed critically: they cannot provide us with any normative standards. Function is related to origins, but it is never dictated by it: the past significance of a narrative form (such as impersonal showing or personal telling) does not *prescribe* its present meaning.

Here, to refuse to *equate* historical analysis and critical evaluation does not mean, however, that the history of any one mode of perspective is meaningless in a critical or theoretical approach to narrative method. Far from it; any given structure, although it can survive the context of its genesis, will stimulate the process of its own reception to the degree that this reception can realize a *genetic potential* of meaning that may or may not be explicit at the time of its creation. For example, the recent renaissance of the picaresque "I" in modern fiction is a case in point. The image of the aimlessness of the modern antihero is certainly not identical with that of the patronage-seeking Lazarillo or the moralizing Guzman; the function of the modern picaro is neither determined nor anticipated by his literary genealogy. Yet the meaning of the modern picaresque, just like the modern meaning of *Lazarillo de Tormes,* draws on a hermeneutic potential that cannot be dissociated from the history of its creation. In this sense the past origin is interrelated to the present meaning which, in its actual functioning, revives and modifies some narrative correlation between the standpoint of the humanist conscience and the drifting existence and the bewildered point of view of some chameleon-like "I."

Just as function (and the evaluation of functioning structure) need to be related to origins, so genesis to function. Once the quality of point of view is defined in terms of both the narrative modes of representation as evaluation *and* the rhetorical as the communicative achievement of the novel, the writer's perspectives and the reader's attitudes can be related. For that, again, the paradigm of the eighteenth-century novel must be seen in its limitations, but it does show the degree to which the changing representational and rhetorical structures are formed in the *Praxis* of their aesthetic, moral, and communicative functions. The eighteenth-century novel is so related to contemporary society that both the intrinsic and the extrinsic aspects of point of view, the narrative focus and the narrator's standpoint, can be seen together in the unity of their aesthetic and their social effects. The emerging forms of representation and rhetoric are related to new, and sometimes experimental, modes of writing and reading which, in their turn, reflect increasingly complex and flexible patterns of social relationships. Here, it must suffice to refer to the comic epic tradition in prose, the new novel in letters, the many private histories, the criminal biographies, and the picaresque stories of adventures and travels. The rise and development of these diverse forms reflect rapidly crystallizing attitudes toward the new experience of public significance through the private reading of individual "history." The early modern novelist is profoundly aware of, and much concerned with, the changing cultural needs and the new self-conscious identity of his reader, so much so that he tends to write the potential reader's responses into the narrative. Hence, in novels like *Don Quixote* or *Jacque le Fatalist*, the reader's experience is explicit, and in many other novels at least implicit, in the structure of the work itself.[24] In *Tom Jones* the reader is made a partner in the exploration and discussion of the mode and organization of omniscient narrative. In *Robinson Crusoe* and *Moll Flanders*, but also in *Roderick Random*, the hero's first-person singular offers the reader the most intense and empirical mode of the dissociation and (final) association of self and society, and the sorrows and triumphs of self-made identity. As noted above, the point of view of the "I"

[24] For a discussion of the reader in the English novel, see Wolfgang Iser, *Der implizite Leser* (Munich: Wilhelm Fink, 1972). For a "classification of narratives according to receivers" (p. 121), see Gerald Prince, "On Readers and Listeners in Narrative," *Neophilologus*, 55 (1971), 117–22.

(in both the picaresque and the epistolary traditions) may have reflected the absence of the novelist's own manner; but at the same time, the first-person singular provided the kind of representation and the type of rhetoric that, perhaps, catered best to the middle-class reader's own bourgeoning manner of self-projection and self-analysis. In this sense the new mode of reception is built into the form itself, rhetoric into structure: function itself is one of the factors constituting the new forms of narration.

To be aware of the historical context of the novel's past function is one way of establishing a critical perspective on its present meaning and, potentially, the new reception it can hope to attain. This, however, is the task of the practical criticism of individual works, the results of which I can here neither anticipate nor repeat.[25] As for any further conclusions, these incorporate some of the answers to the questions asked in the Introduction to this book and the opening of this essay. The need for the correlation of the genetic, aesthetic, and functional approaches and the interrelatedness of the aesthetics of representation and the aesthetics of reception has been confirmed. It can again, and finally, be suggested that this correlation and this interrelatedness are more than a theoretical postulate. They reflect the actual complications in the literary history of the novel, among which point of view assumes a central role for both the writer and the reader. As related to the history of the genre as a whole, narrative perspective is both a product of its literary past, but also a "producer" of the future of fiction. It is the achieved form and content of the writer's sensibility and subjectivity as they confront both the story and the world as its material. Point of view reflects this past confrontation, but it permanently calls for that imaginative

---

[25] For some applications see my study of *Robinson Crusoe*, in *Phantasie und Nachahmung: Drei Studien zum Verhältnis von Dichtung, Utopie, und Mythos* (Halle: Mitteldeutscher Verlag, 1970), pp. 13–67, esp. pp. 50 ff., and "*Jest-book* und Ich-Erzählung in *The Unfortunate Traveller:* Zum Problem des *point of view* in der Renaissance-Prosa," *Zeitschrift für Anglistik und Amerikanistik*, 18 (1970), 11–29.

recreation and realization by the reader without which the novel has no future. For the reader's most basic task in reading a novel is to resolve the irony in the meaning of perspective and to recover that element of wholeness to which point of view is the counterpart. In this direction, the reader has to appropriate the world of the novel, just as the novelist has to appropriate the world through the novel. But the reader (or the author) can finally do so only insofar as he comprehends (or achieves) the relatedness of the narrating consciousness of form to the narrated form of consciousness, the scene to the sense, focus to perspective. To comprehend the connection, or to achieve it, is one way to socialize the individual experience and to personalize the social. It is to particularize the generality of class and type and to universalize the particular and the individual. In this sense, to connect the writing and the reading of point of view as functioning structure involves both history and value. It can and must be related to that elusive contribution that literature can make to the history-making, infinite process of society and its *absolute Bewegung des Werdens,* thus helping to realize the whole nature of man in history.

VII
Text and History:
Epilogue, 1984

HOW does a historical critique of modernist formalism (such as this book attempts) fit into the picture of today's postmodernist critical discourse? The New Criticism is obviously dead, but the specter of formalism is slow to vanish. It continues to hover over the critical scene like "an imposing and repressive father-figure," of whom it may be said that he has left behind "many traces (perhaps 'scars' is the word)" and that these are found, more than anywhere else, "in the repeated and often extremely subtle denial of history by a variety of contemporary theorists."[1] If the continuing impact of formalism especially affects contemporary critical historicity, then the links between the literary theories of modernity and those of postmodernity may well be particularly strong in the area where text and society in literary history relate as an ensemble of discursive and nondiscursive formations.

But while some of the differences "between the older New Critics and the newer new critics" may be viewed as "differences between factions of the vanguard,"[2] the rupture between them must not be underestimated. Moreover, the rupture as well as the area of concurrence cannot be accounted for (let alone criticized) on the grounds of common-sense objections to the decentering of traditional norms of reality and humanity. The critique of modernist repressions of history can be helpful in a postmodernist context only if the changing premises on which the status of the subject in the text, authority in writing, and the whole

[1]Frank Lentricchia, *After the New Criticism* (Chicago, 1980), p. xiii.
[2]Gerald Graff, *Literature against Itself: Literary Ideas in Modern Society* (Chicago, 1979), p. 6.

concept of tradition have come to be dismissed or reformulated are themselves acknowledged. Nor are these changes operative on a purely theoretical level. Since the demise of the New Criticism the liberal inspiration in the educational function of American criticism (and at least part of its traditional humanist context) has been considerably eroded. In this connection the distinction made in my Introduction, between the dominant and the adversary cultures has largely been undermined, just as the social protest and struggle of the 1960s now seem strangely remote, objects of theoretical definition and, perhaps, ideological recovery rather than practical forces in cultural politics.[3] At a time when, as never before in the history of mankind, the sheer threat to the survival of human life on this planet has become *unspeakable*, the cultural self-definitions of humanism may have to be reassessed on a broader and more realistic plane than humanism's classical principles and idealistic premises ever allowed for.

It seems obvious that these changes involve not only postmodernist strategies in literary criticism but their alternatives as well. Even though the antihistorical impulses of formalist theories persist, the ground for confronting them has shifted. This, indeed, is the most stringent raison d'être of the present postscript: As I contemplate the differently situated levels of, first, the past writing and, second, the present reading of my own text (written intermittently between 1968 and 1974), the relationship between the two is one of interrogation rather than confirmation. This does not mean that the obvious gaps (filled, in retrospect, with pain and ignorance) preclude some fundamental propositions in historiographical method which—in view of the current repressions of history—seem more to the point than ever before. In particular, the central theme of this book has gained rather than lost its urgency: the attempt, that is, to

---

[3] See Fredric Jameson's forthcoming essay, "Recovering the Sixties," *Social Text*, which I have seen in manuscript.

inquire into areas of both reciprocity and contradiction between the literary history of the past and its uses in the present, between the past writing and reading of literary texts and their rewriting and new reading in the world today. If the writing and reading of literary criticism, moving beyond its necessary self-reflexivity, are to serve some social and cultural function, this theme of the book continues to provide plenty of provocation. It points to what, in the United States today, has become an even deeper contradiction between the past functions and the present uses of literature.

Hence the question, far from being dated, must be rephrased at a more radical level: Is there still, within this contradiction, a viable mode of correlation between the writing and the reading in the past and the rewriting and new reading in the present? Or has the gulf between the historicity of the texts of the past and their reception in the present become so deep (and, perhaps, so useless) that it can be coped with only from, say, a deconstructive point of view? The question must be faced, since the loss—between then and now—of existential identifications, the gradual depletion of authoritative norms, the final threat to signification itself, have become such heavy liabilities. Since the deconstructionists are prepared, indeed are eager, to transcribe this situation, they must admit the question: Which, as distinct from their textual (and historical) objects, is the actual function of their transcriptions, the function behind their refusal to face, and to do their work within, the links and gaps between life and historicity?

Even to ask this question is to reaffirm that this book has a point of view and that the peculiar *Erkenntnisinteresse* behind this point of view is, although in permanent dialogue with English-speaking literary theory, rooted in an altogether different social, cultural, and national context. Ideally (or so I believe) the moment of dialogue and *Auseinandersetzung* does not contradict but rather thrives

on the distance from which I approach literary criticism in
North America. In any case, both the distance and, through
critical dialogue, its suspension are inseparable from whatever provocation this epilogue can effect.

In what follows I can do no more than survey some of
the more prominent areas in which the dominant criticism
has attempted to redefine (or obliterate) the relationship of
text and society in literary history and criticism. In doing so,
I propose to reconsider some of the poststructuralist revisions
insofar as these involve the use (or rejection) of historiographical perspectives on the text and the world in which it
is written, circulated, and read. Here the most obvious and,
perhaps, urgent emphases are on (1) the new problematic of
"tradition," (2) the troublesome relationship between textuality and historicity, (3) the deconstructive critique and (4)
the discursive *episteme* of representation, (5) modes of correlation between mimesis and (re)production, and (6) mimesis
and appropriation—critiques and counterperspectives. If,
finally, mimesis can so be redefined that, as some mode of
either reproduction or appropriation, it precedes the problematic of the sign and the process of signification, then,
indeed, theoretical concepts of production and appropriation themselves need to be reconsidered historically, in relation to the act of writing and reading and its changing
spectrum of discursive and nondiscursive determinants.
These points can neither be exhaustively discussed nor claim
to provide anything approaching a representative segment
of postmodernist revisionism in literary criticism and historiography, yet the order in which I take them up here aims to
suggest the desirability as well as the overall direction of
some consistently historicizing counterproposal.

"Tradition" as Closure of History?

If the contradiction between the past functions and the
present uses of literature is at the heart of the historiographical impasse of the newest criticism, then it seems doubly

justified to say that the *issue* of history may "determine the direction of critical theory in the years just ahead."[4] It is not a question of salvaging or recovering historiographical standards of the past. As against the traditional concepts of conservative-liberal historiography (the concept of tradition, the history of ideas, literary sociology, etc.), the more recent criticism has raised a number of profound and thorough-going theoretical objections, in the face of which some of the more rudimentary questions in historiographical method may have to be reformulated. Take, for instance, the concept of tradition, whose metaphysical premises (as in T. S. Eliot's "ideal order") cry out for deconstruction in the form of a sustained critique of the assumed presence of such "order." But how does a more stringently historical counter-proposal (such as the one I have submitted in this book) relate to this critique and, more generally, to the deconstructive treatment of the literature of the past? Among the deconstructionists, any notion of tradition would probably be regarded as an illusory project by which reason (or consciousness), in its presumed autonomy, hopes to extend its sense of sovereignty and continuity to the events and figures of the past. And despite the proposed emphasis on discontinuity and the suggested links between literary tradition and social *Praxis*,[5] "tradition" in these critical quarters would still be dismissed as some version of the void on which the false plenitude of history is grafted. But if—as in Harold Bloom's work—the question of textual origins is suspended in a series of rhetorical encounters, a process of perpetual displacement through defensive tropes and strategies,[6] then an understanding of this process of repression and anxiety need not contradict but may well enrich the historical premises of a dialectical theory of tradition. This is especially true when a concept like "repression" helps to convey the

[4]Lentricchia, *After the New Criticism*, p. xiii.

[5]In addition to the essay in this volume, see my *Literaturgeschichte und Mythologie* (Frankfurt a. M., 1977), pp. 79 ff.

[6]See Harold Bloom, *The Anxiety of Influence: A Theory of Poetry* (New York, 1973), and *Poetry and Repression* (New Haven, 1976).

Nietzschean (and, of course, Freudian) notion of "the complexity of the act of choosing forgetfulness."[7] This is the *oubliance* that Derrida acknowledges as an active faculty and that, by implication, he relates to the play of knowledge and ignorance which is part of the *différance* in writing. But when "tradition," or *Erbe*, is defined historically not only by what is preserved but also by what is repressed, not only as liberating but, in the words of Marx, also as burdensome,[8] then the notion of "order" or even the formulation of a canon will, as an act of historicity, appear more deeply heterogeneous and contradictory. The nature of this heterogeneity and the source of the contradiction can, I suggest, best be explored as a clash between what in this book has been called "past significance and present meaning." Once this formula is read pragmatically (and not philosophically, as, say, a theory of "meaning"), it should be possible to redefine the underlying contradiction as one between appro-

---

[7]Gayatri C. Spivak's phrase, in her "Translator's Preface" to Jacques Derrida, *Of Grammatology* (Baltimore, 1976), p. xxxi.

[8]"Die Tradition aller toten Geschlechter lastet wie ein Alp auf dem Gehirne der Lebenden" (Karl Marx, *Der achtzehnte Brumaire des Louis Bonaparte*, in *Werke* [Dietz Verlag], VIII, p. 115). But if "tradition" can haunt the living like a "nightmare," the pattern of farcical repetition may not be as scandalous as, for instance, Jeffrey Mehlman suggests in *Revolution and Repetition* (Berkeley and Los Angeles, 1977), pp. 8–23, 33 ff. For Marx to understand "this borrowed language" as some "disguise" is to approach "the recollections" of the past *(Rückerinnerungen)* and "the resurrection of the dead" (ibid, pp. 116 f.) critically as well as functionally, i.e., as serving the purely ideological needs of the present. What then, in *The Eighteenth Brumaire*, is emphasized, is not the *logic* but the *ideology* of representation, the insoluable nature of the *contradiction* between past significations and revolutionary (or conservative) "meanings," the impossibility in history, of replicas and repetitions, the "farcical," i.e., the pseudo-representational character of political resurrections of the past. It is precisely because such "traditions" contain "self-deceptions" and some "superstitious belief in the past" (*Selbsttäuschungen* and *Aberglauben an die Vergangenheit*, ibid.) that Marx's concept of "tradition" goes beyond any assumption of the sovereignty of historical consciousness and contains, at least by implication, the postulate to displace the "incubus" (*Alp*) of past traditions and generations, so as to make room for "the dead to bury the dead" and for future revolutions "to arrive at their own content" (p. 117). Thus, although Mehlman is highly perceptive when he links "the extravagant expenditure(s) of Bonapartism to a crisis of representation" (*Revolution and Repetition*, p. 33), history and historiography for Marx do not "occupy the positions of the repetitive structure" (p. 20).

priation and alienation, between what can be made one's own and what must be disowned.

In so hurried a formulation, any definition of tradition must appear altogether schematic but need not involve a teleological concept of history or one that hinges on the self-authenticating writing of "the individual talent." Nor would such a project collide with the proposition that history cannot ever be read as an unfolding of continuities and that its "meaning" (whatever that may be) cannot possibly derive from some evolutionary or, for that matter, utopian projection of origins or of ends. But if the differential consequences of discontinuity, heterogeneity, and contradiction are (justifiably, I think) emphasized against traditional assumptions of continuity and linearity, does this mean that history as process and product cannot ever be present in the text, since the text itself must be viewed as an unending series of differences, deferments, and ruptures? The question, then, is not simply whether there is any alternative to the idealist concept of tradition (or one conceived in terms of the history of ideas), but whether textuality itself allows for any conceptualization of the process of history within and without the text. In other words, is the textual principle of *différance* compatible with a historical perspective on simultaneous change and temporary permanence? Does it allow not only *for* the contradiction between the forces of heterogeneity and those of homogeneity but also the more profound tensions within the temporal process of fragmentation *and* that of socialization as they both at the same time inform the language of the text itself?

If anything, the proposed contradiction between past significance and present meaning involves a historical (again, not a philosophical) emphasis on *temporal* changes of meaning, that is to say, "meaning" not as some closed or predetermined entity but as a historical mode and result of appropriating or alienating (distancing and forgetting) the literary language of the past. Once such a concept of "meaning" is related to the contradiction between past writing and present reading, between the fictional nature of the past text and its actual function in society, the concept of tradition is unthinkable without the appropriation (or repression) of two contradictory orders of language and temporality within, and through, the use of the text. What, in this connection, "tradition" amounts to is a certain historical constellation between the objects and the determinants of this appropriation. Such a constellation stipulates the absence of either pure continuity or discontinuity, the rejection of closure as some totalizing sense of identity (or, for that matter, the suspension of rupture as a source of nonidentity) between what is past and what is alive. There are no innocent readings of the past, and, as more recent experience has taught us, there is less and less reason to minimize the contradiction between what can be made one's own and what forever remains alien, between the "ownership of meaning" (the appropriation to my own use of the impersonal system of signs) and the absence of its elusive presence, the expropriation of meaning (*"no one* owns meaning.")[9]

Textuality and Historicity

To ignore the historical nature of this contradiction seems unhelpful, especially when the existential dimension of writing and reading as the ultimate substratum of literary historicity is to be acknowledged. It is precisely in this respect that poststructuralist concepts such as "text" and "textuality" leave too many questions open. In the use of such concepts, these critics' existential situation in society is theoretically unreflected, so much so that some "little pedagogy" (Michel Foucault) obliquely and, sometimes, disas-

[9]Michael Holquist, "The Politics of Representation," *Allegory and Representation: Selected Papers from the English Institute, 1979–80*, ed. Stephen J. Greenblatt (Baltimore, 1981), pp. 163 f.

trously enters into their critical presuppositions, helping to obstruct rather than illuminate a historicizing perspective on the literary texts of the past. What seems most questionable about the textualizing alternatives to the traditional modes of literary historiography is that these alternatives tend to situate themselves outside the very determinants of textual production whose (historical) correlatives in the deconstructed texts of the past are explored with so much subtlety and perspicacity. Once all texts are seen to dislodge or displace other texts, and once this dislodgment is understood to be part of a discursive situation in which language, through discourse, is appropriated to social uses, discursive practices cannot be isolated from nondiscursive practices and pursuits of power and desire in the world of history. But even when a good many poststructuralist critics, especially those following Michel Foucault, would grant the validity of such involvement of the text in the world of nondiscursive history, they still tend to ignore or minimize the implication of their own writing in historical acts of social practice and political power.

It is in this connection that the question of the subject must be reopened in a broader context. A text "is never sovereign, always ridden by the absence of the subject, always offering a 'lack' that the reader must fill, as well as the materials with which to begin to fill it."[10] But Derrida's concept of textuality (just as Foucault's definition of the author function) goes much further than this: There is supposed to be no subject, because, as J. Hillis Miller puts it, the "act of deconstruction . . . has always already, in each case differently, been performed by the text on itself."[11] Similarly, although in a different context, it is possible to view the author purely as a function of the text, but impossible ever

[10] Derrida, *Of Grammatology*, p. 320 (Spivak's note).
[11] J. Hillis Miller, "Deconstructing the Deconstructers," *Diacritics*, 5 (Summer 1975), 31.

to view the text as the function of an appropriating subject.[12]
But once writing and reading are linked with the production
of knowledge, imagination, and power, this production need
not at all be defined as a sovereign instance of consciousness
or individuality; on the contrary, the question must be
asked—even in a theoretical text: Does "the absence of the
subject" (in the form of a sovereign creator) allow for some
highly mediated and multideterminant individual form of
historical *activity* through which social conglomerates, cultural institutions, ideological apparatuses, etc., can assert
themselves as historical *Subjekt?* Once the determinants of
ideology, power, and desire are acknowledged, how can
these determinants become either inoperative or purely
intrinsic in the poststructuralist text? The critique of some
absolute "meaning" in literary history seems justified; but
can it assume that there is an alternative to the appropriation (or expropriation) of language in and through discourse
and that this act of appropriation is independent of a historical situation and a social activity involving existential constraints and determinants? If, as I have suggested elsewhere,
the act of appropriation itself must be viewed as some form
of historical activity, then the deconstructionist position ("*no
one* owns meaning") does constitute an act of expropriation
(or self-expropriation) which—as we shall see—has a number of striking correlatives in the world of contemporary
history. In practice (and as against their own theoretical
premises), textualizing critics cannot extricate themselves
from a process of intellectual communication, social relations, and political and cultural functions in which they are
implicated at the level of their own existence.

Since the most influential position in poststructuralist
criticism does not acknowledge this implication as a methodological point of departure, the relationship between his-

---

[12]For a definition of the concept of "appropriation" used throughout this
Epilogue, see my article, " 'Appropriation' and Modern History in Renaissance
Prose Narrative," *New Literary History*, 14 (Spring 1983), 459–95.

tory and textuality is highly problematic from the outset. Is it possible, then, to claim, as Michael Ryan has done in *Marxism and Deconstruction*, that there is "a radical concept of history in Derrida"? And that even his renunciation of the "adherence to axiomatic first principles," even "giving up first principles and last truths . . . implies entry into history"?[13] It is true that there are no social norms, axioms, and principles outside the world of history, and that whatever validity we can obtain is not against but through the historical process whose past course we know of mostly through writing, even when we may directly inspect material relics of the past, including works of architecture, paintings, burial sites, mines, factories, and so on. If this is more than a commonplace, then the concept of the text can be used more widely, in reference to the complex interaction among the determinants of any act of historical communication. Moreover, it can be made to connote a certain type of historical event which is "produced by concatenated chains that . . . determine it as a multifaceted, multirooted 'matter' whose truth (in the sense of the revealed presence of the thing itself) could never be fully plotted out or resolved into a presence to which a decisively absolute and all-inclusive meaning could be assigned."[14] But even when it must be granted that, as Derrida notes in *Speech and Phenomena*, "differences . . . could be 'historical' through and through and from the start"[15] (in the sense that, for instance, they help preclude the *stasis*, the linearity, the self-identical nature of events), does it follow that—as the full quotation claims—"differences *alone* [my italics] could be 'historical' "?

What Derrida suggests is not a philosophy that defines thought and being in radically historical terms, but a certain mode of textual analysis which, by analogy, can prove

[13]Michael Ryan, *Marxism and Deconstruction: A Critical Articulation* (Baltimore, 1982), pp. 57, 62.

[14]Ibid., p. 24.

[15]Jacques Derrida, *Speech and Phenomena*, trans. David Allison (Evanston, 1973), p. 141.

potentially helpful in dismantling any monistic, mechanical, or idealist approaches to historical data, events, and gestures. It is from within the logic of deconstruction, then, that the question must be asked whether *différance*, involving some form of temporalization within differentiation, can project objective perspectives in discourse onto a historical alternative to the unacceptable patterns of metaphysical modes of literary historiography. If, according to Derrida, the actualization of reference and the constitution of meaning are *deferred* through the differential of signs (and the nonrepresentational nature of the relationship between signified and signifier), then this moment of temporal suspension or postponement cannot, strictly speaking, be outside larger criteria of temporality and heterogeneity. In other words, Are there historically differing modes (and degrees) of deferment and, if so, How can these relate to nondiscursive modes of temporal determination and concatenation?

The answers are difficult because in Derrida's version of textuality the temporal dimension of *différance* is extremely limited and quite intrinsic. It is true that in one of his early essays (published in *Critique*, no. 193/194, June/July 1963, and reprinted in *Writing and Difference*) Derrida refers to the "historicity of the work itself" in its relation to a concept of genesis which points beyond psychological and sociological origins. This historicity, then, is not to be derived from the pastness of the literary work (out of which—through the author's intention—the writing can anticipate itself); rather, it resides in textual form: in its impossibility ever to be present, ever to be summarized in any absolute mode of simultaneity or immediacy.[16] What Derrida here suggests is an "interior genesis," an intralinguistic state of becoming in which origins and ends are

---

[16]Jacques Derrida, *Writing and Difference*, trans. Alan Bass (Chicago, 1978). Although subsequent references are to Bass's English-language edition, this reference is to the German edition, trans. Rodolphe Gasché (Frankfurt a. M., 1976), p. 27.

unthinkable, just as (and to the degree that) language cannot operate out of itself in order to question its own genesis. Although, in this early context, Derrida still uses concepts such as "value" and "meaning" in relation to this intralinguistic mode of historicity, his main emphasis is already on "language as the origin of history."[17] This emphasis precludes extralinguistic perspectives on language as a means or medium, a product or mode of production of social and cultural history. Nor is this surprising; for, in his mature work, concepts such as difference and deferment are designed to project, first and foremost, a textual strategy whose direction is marked by the textualizing of discursive activity rather than the historicizing of textual function.

In this connection Derrida is almost bound to repress any definition of the existential plane by highly sophisticated strategies of supplementarity and undecidability. However, on the level of its critical transcription, the ambiguity and undecidability of textual meaning do not necessarily imply an undecidability of cultural function. If the text is always ridden by the absence of its author, this absence constitutes a hermeneutic problem (in the sense that the reader must always fill a "lack"), but it does not preclude the historical activity of that text, since the absence of, say, the author's intention does not at all obliterate the social and individual constellation that constitutes discursive practice. Again, Derrida certainly has a point when, in *Of Grammatology*, he notes that "historicity itself [is] tied to the possibility of writing in general," so that a "history of writing should turn us back toward the origin of historicity."[18] But nowhere in his magnum opus does he take this early point of departure further, except when he postulates that, instead of a philosophy of history (or history of philosophy), it is only grammatology that opens up "a history of the possibility of history."[19]

[17]Ibid., p. 4 .
[18]Derrida, *Of Grammatology*, p. 27.
[19]Ibid., p. 28.

The critique of the Hegelian metaphysics of history is surely welcome; but how far does Derrida's own concept of historicity actually transcend the idealist construct? Indeed, historiography presupposes writing; but beyond that, it involves the transcription not only of past texts and records but also of present needs, activities, and relations. To ignore this or even, as a point of methodology, to refuse to implicate one's own time and place in the act of writing and reading amounts to a perfectly hermetic and, in its turn, metaphysical concept of "historicity." Again, a history of writing may indeed be written so as to explore the "history of the possibility of history," but not on the basis of a thoroughly autonomous, textualized concept of history itself. For Derrida to refuse to explore the existential determinants of writing is to envisage a "history of the possibility of history" in which the very act of historiography as discursive practice is repressed.

As a consequence, Derrida's own idea of the history of writing ends up in a typological construct that, in line with its intrinsic presuppositions, postulates the binary "poles" of two abstractions:

> The history of writing, like the history of science, would circulate between . . . two forms of transparence and univocity: an absolute pictography doubling the totality of the natural entity in an unrestrained consumption of signifiers, and an absolutely formal *graphie* reducing the signifying expense to almost nothing. There would be no history of writing and of knowledge—one might simply say no history at all—except between these two poles. And if history is not thinkable except between these two limits, one cannot disqualify the mythologies of universal script—pictography or algebra—without suspecting the concept of history itself.[20]

If this is one of the most extraordinary statements of historiographical principle, it is not because the typological poles[21]—pictography and algebra—appear unrevealing. But

[20]Ibid, p. 285.
[21]Ironically, to assume that "history is not thinkable except between these two poles" is to fall back upon typological abstractions à la Dilthey's *Geisteswissenschaft*.

the methodological strategy is one of reduction; first, history in the form of both recorded (nondiscursive) events and discursive (recording) acts is entirely textualized, and second, *on the basis of this textualization* "the concept of history itself" is made to appear suspect. What the presupposed opposites, the binary "mythologies of universal script" do reveal is not, then, the limits of history "between the two epochs of universal writing," but the two opposite poles in the "consumption" (or "expense") of the signifier. But since the history of writing is reduced to the economy of signification and since this economy is transcribed in the typological narrative of "two poles," the historiographical limitations of the intralinguistic approach appear rather obvious. The question may even be asked: Does Derrida, in the last resort, go beyond the Hegelian position that "the concept of history is therefore the concept of philosophy and of the epistémè"?[22] The answer, at least at the intersection of linguistics and epistemology, is that he does not, and the use of a concept like "economy" turns out to be in the nature of similitude; a mere suggestion of pseudohistorical analogies. ("The visual economy of reading obeys a law analogous to that of agriculture. The same is not true of the manual economy of writing."[23]) It is at this point that the reduction of discursive and nondiscursive practices to textual traces visibly and definitively fails to satisfy as a principle of historiography.

In the light of this failure, Derrida's repeated linking of "history" and "teleology," his talk of "all the historico-metaphysical presuppositions"[24] of historiography, might almost assume an unintended tone of irony (or facility) were it not that the very language of his polemics reverberates with the historical determinants of his own ideological situatedness in time and place. There is good reason to believe that this

[22]Derrida, *Of Grammatology*, p. 286.
[23]Ibid., p. 288.
[24]Ibid., pp. 25, 27.

failure, the obvious limitations in his historiographical language, corresponds to the whole direction and function of his critique of Husserl's phenomenology; it was through this critique in the first place that Derrida moved away from the theoretical premises of structuralism and what he calls its "more or less direct and admitted dependence on phenomenology."[25] This, indeed, is Derrida's extremely successful point of departure; uncovering, as he does, the metaphysical as well as the empirical-positivistic remnants in Husserl's critique of historicism, he proceeds to show how the whole phenomenological project achieves momentum out of a critical response to the philosophical contradictions of nineteenth-century historicism, including Dilthey's version of *Geisteswissenschaft.* (For Derrida, Dilthey ushers in the worst of all the "historicist menaces," since he suspends naturalism and atomism in his attempt to salvage metaphysical norms only by proposing to base them on a more profoundly conceived level of empiricity.) In line with this point of departure, Derrida's critique of the phenomenological approach to genesis is impressive, especially when, in viewing together the "logical," the "egological," and the "historical-teleological" modes of historiography, he brilliantly discloses the phenomenological versions of the *ego* and the *telos* as versions of "genesis itself," the most powerful structural *apriori* of historicity by which the phenomenological critique of classical metaphysics helps to reproduce and consummate the classical historical project.[26]

However, Derrida, in his deconstruction of the phenomenological position, is so obsessed with the object of his critique (and so entangled—through structuralism—in his own philosophical point of departure)[27] that it never occurs

[25]Derrida, *Writing and Difference*, p. 48.

[26]Here, the essay "'Genesis and Structure' and Phenomenology" in *Writing and Difference* is the most revealing text.

[27]As is well known, *Edmund Husserl's Origin of Geometry: An Introduction*, trans. John P. Leavey, Jr. (Stonybrook, 1978), originally appeared in French as early as 1962 and links up with *Speech and Phenomena* (first published in French in 1967).

to him that there may exist extralinguistic versions of history which either precede or transcend Husserl's "monadisch konkretes ego"[28] and his *eidetische Reduktion* toward a *Wesensschau*. Although one hesitates to ask, Can it be that Derrida's repudiation of historiography involves, first and foremost, a rejection of such *ego* and such consciousness? And that his inability to think of extralinguistic history except in terms of teleology reflects some deep-rooted suspicion at the *telos* of such *Wesensschau?* In any case, his counterproposal, in one important respect, does not take further the (cautious) phenomenological critique of "the classical system" of philosophical idealism but, rather, falls back on the kind of methodology and typology which, ironically, is associated with the philosophical tradition of idealism. What we have as a result is a new metaphysics of history which literally and amply confirms the notorious charge that Michel Foucault directed at Derrida when he called him "the most decisive representative of the (classical) system in its final brilliance," only to continue: "I do not say that it is a metaphysics, metaphysics itself or its closure, which is hidden in this 'textualization' of discursive practices. I shall go much further: I shall say that it is a trifling, historically well-determined pedagogy which very visibly reveals itself."[29]

To dissociate discursive from nondiscursive practices is, once and for all, to preclude a historiographical focus on text and society in literary history. Again, instead of historicizing the text through the acts of writing and reading, Derrida textualizes historicity. If this involves "pedagogy" of a sort (not to say ideology), this pedagogy may indeed be "well-determined," though not perhaps "trifling," in its own

[28]Edmund Husserl, *Cartesianische Meditationen*, "Husserliana," (The Hague, 1963), I, 102.

[29]Michel Foucault, *Histoire de la folie à l'âge classique* (Paris, 1972), p. 602; Derrida here is described as "le représentant le plus décisif" of the classical age, his strategy (not to say ideology) as "une petite pédagogie historiquement bien déterminée." The translation above is that of Josué Y. Harari, ed., *Textual Strategies: Perspectives in Post-Structuralist Criticism* (Ithaca, N.Y., 1979), p. 41.

social and cultural functions. As Frank Lentricchia has noted, "American poststructuralist literary criticism tends to be an activity of textual privatization, the critic's doomed attempt to retreat from a social landscape of fragmentation and alienation. Criticism becomes, in this perspective, something of an ultimate mode of interior decoration."[30] Even though a word like *retreat* may not adequately (or even justifiably) describe the poststructuralist project, the self-cancellation of a good many of the social and cultural functions of criticism must be viewed as a phenomenon of great consequence. If, as I have suggested, the contradiction between past and present uses of the literary text has become depleted as a source of energy in the cultural language of criticism, such depletion now appears as a syndrome of the narrowing function of literary criticism, as part of literary criticism's decline in social and cultural representativeness. The poststructuralist critic's refusal to implicate his or her existential situation in the act of writing and reading involves a failure to relate, a repudiation of connectedness, the inability finally to revitalize the representative functions of the writer in reference to his or her society as an ensemble of cultural relationships and communicative possibilities. As these critics are determined practically as well as theoretically to shake off the burden of representation, they repress the need for a transcription of the crisis in their own social relatedness, in which the writing of criticism itself is existentially involved.

Representation (I): Vulnerability and Resiliency

The argument against representation is so much a part of a whole close context of poststructuralist theory that the crisis in poststructuralist critics' cultural representativity must not superficially, not from without their own conceptualiza-

---

[30]Lentricchia, *After the New Criticism*, p. 186.

tions, be linked with their antirepresentational position in linguistics and aesthetics. More importantly, these critics have made a virtue out of necessity: Their critique of the classical structuralist approach to the sign is profoundly revealing and highly suggestive. The breaking up of any facile logic in the links between signified and signifier, even the attempt to liberate language from its exclusive association with the tasks of representation, must be accepted, I think, as profoundly affecting the redefinition of the aims and methods of historical criticism. However, although the underlying critique of epistemology through language may achieve considerable depth and consequence,[31] the problematic of the antirepresentational position must not be overlooked. What is so contradictory about it is that certain presuppositions (which are basic to its intralinguistic frame of reference) are themselves situated in a nondiscursive context of intellectual production and cultural function. More than anything, the whole textualized concept of writing is embedded in the history and ideology of certain philosophical decisions by which the text is immured against phonocentric, logocentric, and ultimately, anthropocentric standards of discourse as a social act of appropriating language. It is precisely in this wider philosophical context (marked, among other things, by contemporary French receptions of Nietzsche, Freud, and Heidegger and a thoroughgoing critique of Husserl) that Jacques Derrida's revision of the sign is historically situated.

If, as Derrida suggests in *Of Grammatology*, the traditional concept of the sign thrives on the preferential treatment of *logos*, on a metaphysical order in which signification itself, the relationship between thought and language, is affected by the norms of representation, then

---

[31]As has readily been acknowledged by Marxist critics such as Fredric Jameson (*The Prison-House of Language* [Princeton, 1974], pp. 173–186) and Terry Eagleton ("Text, Ideology, Realism," *Literature and Society: Selected Papers from the English Institute, 1978*, ed. Edward W. Said [Baltimore, 1980], pp. 149–73).

one of the most consistent pressures on his project is to circumvent the need to think of language not only in terms of any representational function but also, and even more so, in reference to any act of production and appropriation. But granted that the relationship of signified and signifier cannot be subsumed under the norms of representation, does it follow that the act of signification itself can be abstracted from the existential needs and constraints of appropriation and *distanciation* in which the "interpretant" (Charles Sanders Peirce's term) is *nolens volens* involved? Signs, as Umberto Eco has shown, are no natural phenomena; their uses stipulate a recipient who "even when by himself lives in society."[32] In this sense, the uses of signs in discourse involve social acts of appropriation, production, and consumption: "The production of signs is work, no matter whether these signs are words or goods."[33] And even though the signifier (and, on a different level, basic elements of the signified) is always already given, the act of signification itself cannot be defined outside such discursive practices as relate to (or are correlated with) nondiscursive acts of appropriation and alienation.

In this connection, J. W. Austin's speech act theory has provided cogent (though by no means exhaustive) arguments for the social uses of appropriated language. But if the speech act theory can profitably be applied to a more deeply functional understanding of literary discourse,[34] it must also and at the same time be developed in a historical direction, toward a redefinition of the historically changeful links and gaps between spoken and written language. In this respect, Derrida's grammatology provides a profoundly challenging but deeply problematic reinterpretation. In Derrida's attempt to repress the need to think of language in terms of

[32]Umberto Eco, *Zeichen: Einführung in einen Begriff*, trans. Günter Memmert (Frankfurt a. M., 1981), p. 15.

[33]Ibid., p. 186.

[34]See Mary Louise Pratt, *Toward a Speech Act Theory of Literary Discourse* (Bloomington, Ind., 1977).

discursive practices, the phonocentric medium and the anthropocentric context of the spoken word do indeed present a number of awkward obstacles. Since spoken language is naturally (audibly, empirically) tied to "voice," a human and social existence in history, the most effective mode of abstracting from any such presence (and from the need for recreating this presence through re-presentation) is to move from voice to text, to textualize discursive-practices. Whereas the communicative functions of the spoken word will again and again establish the signifying principle *aliquid stat pro aliquo*, the textualized stratum of language as inscription can more easily be dissociated from the necessary historicity of such significations. What "textuality" presupposes, then, is a self-generating mode of interaction within a system of *différance* to which the scriptor (and reader) can relate in response to some unbearable constraint in the socially representative function of language. In relinquishing this function, the poststructuralist critic suspends the need for continuing to confront the links as well as the contradictions between voice and utterance, life and writing, socio-individual existence and the systematic uses of language. As against the weight of these contradictions, culminating as they do in the triumphs and defeats, the possibilities and impossibilities, of representation, the Derridean textuality shields the inscribed utterance from the historical compulsions of the author in his social acts of cultural representativity.

However, since the textualizing strategy, seeking to undermine representational "meaning" as some metaphysical illusion of presence and plenitude, is itself implicated in certain historically determined functions of discourse, these present functions of critical discourse must be viewed as they collide with (but not necessarily invalidate) the changing modes and uses of representation in literary history. The antirepresentational position refuses to concede literature the status of event: it seeks to cancel out the notion of discursive practice as involving writing and reading in some nondiscursive activity inseparable from whatever signifying process is brought forth and received temporally, through the appropriation of language. To abstract from all this and to refuse to consider inscribed language as an "interception or suspension of speech's worldliness"[35] and, hence, the circumstantial reality through which the text finds itself situated as well as actualized is, to say the least, to obliterate the very foundations on which a nonmetaphysical and nonmechanical understanding of "representation" in history can be redefined. But then, as we shall see, such obliteration involves too much blindness and silence about what Stephen Greenblatt so aptly calls "the cunning of representation," its "resiliency, brilliance, and resourcefulness."[36]

According to its most rudimentary definition (ranging from the dictionaries to philosophers like Pierre Trotignon) "representation" involves (1) the image, portrait, transcription, or reproduction of a speech, text, gesture, thought, situation, i.e., the *represented*, as well as (2) the *act* or *process* of bringing forth, producing, or constituting the image or reproduction of such object ("soit l'image d'un object soit l'action de constituer cette image de l'object.")[37] Once the representational moment in writing and reading is viewed as combining (and interrelating) the *product* and the *process* of representation, this moment can only be thought of as involving an activity that is significant precisely because it enters, as it were, into the text itself from two differing sides and on the levels of two differing functions. On the one hand, representation (when viewed as *product*

---

[35]Edward Said, "The Text, the World, the Critic," in *Textual* Strategies, intro. Harari, p. 164.

[36]Greenblatt, *Allegory and Representation*, p. ix.

[37]Pierre Trotignon, "Réflexions métaphysiques sur le concept de représentation," *Revue des Sciences Humaines*, 34 (1974), 195. The nonidentity between representation and the represented corresponds at least in part to the distinction between what William Wimsatt called "iconicity" and "reference": "Mimesis involves difference." ("In Search of Verbal Mimesis," *Yale French Studies*, 52 [1975], 243.)

or *result* of reproduction) helps to assimilate and to appropriate the image of an object or the transcription of a text; on the other hand, representation (when viewed as *process* or *activity*) helps to project and objectify the pressures, the potentialities, and the interests inherent in the links and gaps between the social mode and the individual act of aesthetic production. But the two aspects are indissolubly linked: representation (as product) constitutes the image or transcription of a social or individual situation, not through the "objective" recreation or repetition of that situation (or that speech, text, thought), but through the assimilation or appropriation of it in terms of the needs, interests, and perspectives of the representing activity or mode of literary production. In other words, the activity behind the process (which need not involve an individual instance of production) enters into a historically changing relationship to the represented through the product of representation itself. It is only by refusing to interrogate these twofold connections (representation as product and process) that the poststructuralist critic can repress the cultural functions and discursive practices in which representation is embedded— functions and practices that range from illocutionary to perlocutionary modes of utterance just as they embrace capacities for appropriation and alienation, assimilation and distanciation. Nor can these social functions of discourse be thought of as being mutually exclusive: It is precisely the historicity and "the politics of representation" which make the appropriation and the expropriation of language so interactive. As Michael Holquist has noted: "I can appropriate meaning to my own purposes only by ventriloquating others. . . . We bend language to represent by representing languages."[38]

It is perfectly true that the literary uses of language, and especially those in late-twentieth-century America, cannot be analyzed in terms of the full spectrum of those tradi-

[38]Michael Holquist, "Politics of Representation," p. 169.

tional functions of representation which, in eighteenth- and even nineteenth-century discourse, were as a matter of course taken for granted. (This, as I have suggested in Chapter 6, deeply affects narrative strategy: we have only to recall the ease and the sense of security and public significance with which, for instance, Fielding in *Joseph Andrews*, III, 13, or *Tom Jones*, II, 5, uses the language of justice and "charity," or the way that Emerson views the poet, of all people, in terms of his human and cultural representativity, namely, as "representative man" par excellence.) But just because the spectrum of representativity is greatly reduced in modernist and, even more so, in postmodernist discourse, the contradictions (between the product and process, the objectifying and the appropriating aspects of representation) have not ceased to exist. On the contrary, it would be much more accurate to say that these contradictions have entered such an impasse and become so painful and unthinkable that postmodern theory has altogether surrendered the endeavor (underlying classical notions of representation) to face the burden of self-identification through relationship, appropriation through objectification.

Indeed, there is no doubt that this burden may seem especially heavy at a time when the avant-garde literary intellectual finds himself at such an exorbitant distance from both the centers of political and economic power and the ordinary pursuits of the huge majority of the population. If anywhere, it is in this context that the politics of representation must be recognized as at the center of what has become the burden of signification in modern American literary theory and practice. But although, in the political and cultural spheres, the postmodern intellectual has become so reluctant to consider himself a "representative" of any larger social situation or practical activity, his activity cannot thereby be defined as being outside the constraints of and responses to situations and activities in history. For one thing, his refusal, through the intralinguistic theory of literary production, to relate to the referents of his own discourse, must not be dismissed as yet another version of the ivory tower. If the antirepresentational position involves blindness and areas of silence, this silence must not be oversimplified as a strategy of escape or intellectual surrender.

On the contrary, to challenge the logocentric orientation of literary activity does involve responses to a social and cultural situation, but a situation with which the activity inside the text does not care to associate itself. What, among other things, this textual activity questions is a good many illusions dear to the liberal educators of the not-so-distant past. Underlying these responses may well be an awareness of the anonymous impact of huge corporate powers of mediation and circulation upon the writing and reading (and viewing) activities of the individual. (Their sheer pressure must be more formidable than Marshall McLuhan's belief in the totalizing consequences of the technological "implosion" suggested.) Under these conditions, the refusal of the latest avant-garde to serve in any *re-presentative* function, the determination of the individual not to lend his intellectual voice to invisible arrangements of mute power, need not amount to that gesture of "self-abasement" or that "compensatory self-adulation"[39] that the self-cancellation of the articulate subject might under different circumstances involve. At this late date there is no point in ignoring the disruptions suffered by the liberal imagination and the forlorn stand of the traditional humanistic education vis-à-vis the anonymity of the powers that be (not to mention the threats to the survival of human life, which are, literally, *unspeakable*). In a situation like this, the urgency of the issues raised by the antirepresentational direction of poststructuralist thought must not be underestimated, especially when so many forms of interpretation and representation (including their political correlatives) can be shown to constitute "a technique of

[39]Graff, *Literature against Itself*, p. 181.

power," a form of "reduction, repression, obliteration of fact."[40]

To view the argument against representation as a deliberate self-destruction of cultural identity through the preclusion of unwelcome relationships is to point to a surging contradiction, ever present in the existential domain of function, which of course is not visible (is in fact made unrepresentable) in the textualized logic of deconstruction. Since, on the level of social function, the very self-destruction of identity still performs, against all disclaimers, an act of negative representativity (of re-presenting the muteness and the fury of a certain intellectual activity transcribing, into privileged gestures of repudiation, a circumstantial situation in history), this self-destruction of identity is, despite itself, deeply revealing, and especially so as it subversively affects the poststructuralist stance on signification. How consistent is the poststructuralist critic's refusal, through the self-deconstruction of his or her own text, to signify? It is true that this refusal presupposes the ambivalence of *brisure*[41] ("break" as well as "articulation") and a recognition that neither the diacritical nor, for that matter, the ideological constituents of signification can be subsumed under metaphysical presuppositions of reason, truth, or similitude. But once we perceive the inadequacy of such idealistic constructs, the deconstructive counterproposal may appear neither consistent in itself nor, indeed, radical enough. What we have to look for is a deeper level of activity, one preceding the deconstruction of purely differential relations in language or transcending a purely textual concept of production. As against that, activities such as the appropriation of language in the world and the appropriation of the world in and through discourse can be linked to other (and no less existential) modes of production. As soon as such a link is established, the limitations of the poststructuralist position

[40]Alan Sheridan, *Michel Foucault: The Will to Truth* (London, 1980), p. 221.
[41]Derrida, *Of Grammatology*, pp. 65 ff.

become obvious. Instead of *arresting*, through textualization, either the break or the mediation between thought and
language as always already given, the appropriating strategy (which is not identical to any proprietory or acquisitive
stance) will simultaneously have to relate to both the signification of the process and the process of signification: the
"meaning" of the function (of the activity behind the process) and the function of the meaning (derived from interrelating process and product). In Derrida's terms, this
involves the articulation of (and within) the break, and the
break as part of the articulation itself. Once such interaction
between writing and *Praxis* is accepted, the need to face our
own existence in the world of history should make it possible
at last to attempt to confront the links as well as the gaps
between past discourse in history and history as something
present in our own discourse on the past. In other words,
representation can then be seen not as establishing a privileged content within the relationship between sign and
significandum but as one possible strategy of discourse: not
as a metaphysical or aesthetic norm but as a strategic position vis-à-vis a wider spectrum of functions, ranging from
appropriation to alienation of language (and its referents) in
discourse.

Representation (II): Collapse
of a Discursive *Episteme*

Whereas the Derridean critique of representation appears
to be based on the textualization of historicity within discursive practices, the work of Michel Foucault suggests that
the argument against representation itself can be couched
in a historical narrative. Having at an early stage rejected
Derrida's textualization of discursive activity, Foucault in
his more recent writings has come to view discourses as
subsumed under the genealogy of power. It is precisely

through changeful discursive practices that language, according to Foucault, constitutes the varying modalities of the order of things by providing certain categories of perception and also the respective patterns of order established upon its objects. Thus, the underlying modes of discourse assume the function of an intractable, almost uncontrolled paradigm by which the free agent of *parole* is replaced by the historical specificity of language usages as a determination of semantic processes. Once these are accepted as forcefully operative, there remains in the present world little room for any representational relationship between "the order of things" and "the order of words." In fact, even the tentative assumption of any fixed correspondence between them reveals itself as some anthropocentric illusion. The collapse of all representational concepts of linguistic function is at the heart of whatever the archaeology of knowledge can transcribe about the phenomena of "labor," "life," and "language."[42]

Again, on a certain level this critique of a positivistic approach to language (language as a reservoir of value-free vehicles of representation) seems altogether salutary. To be sure, the relationship of language and thought is more complex than the conception of the word as transparent icon or, indeed, as neutral material for some *signifié* would ever allow. In this sense, the limitations of language, hidden in the predetermination of discursive usage, to serve as reliable tools of knowledge seem persuasively argued, especially when the function of discourse—as opposed to its rationalistic definitions—is defined "not by what it permits consciousness to *say* about the world, but by what it prohibits it from saying, the area of experience that the linguistic act itself cuts off from representation in language."[43] From here, and

---

[42]"Travail, vie, langage" inform the three sciences (political economy, biology, philology) which Michel Foucault uses as the major nineteenth-century paradigmata for the dominant code of (historical) knowledge (*Les mots et les choses* [Paris, 1966], pp. 262–313).

[43]Hayden White, "Foucault Decoded: Notes from the Underground," *History and Theory*, 12 (1973), 32.

with considerable consistency, Foucault has moved from the archaeology of knowledge to the discourse analysis of power, according to which discourses are viewed as subjected to certain types of ownership: They are "objects of appropriation"; they have become products, things, "a kind of goods"[44] whose possession is a manifestation of privilege and a source of social control. In this perspective, the concept of the literary "work," like that of the "author," must appear thoroughly problematic, especially when viewed against the institutionalized determinants of discourse (such as, in a different context, Foucault had explored in his studies on madness and the clinic). Nor, at this point, is the notion of writing as *écriture* theoretically tenable, since it tends to serve as one of the means of "subtly preserving the author's existence": "It keeps alive, in the grey light of neutralization, the interplay of those representations that formed a particular image of the author."[45]

By his emphasis on the author's function (as distinct from the author's presence) Foucault attempts to exorcise the ghost of representation from the very premises on which the text is thought as given. The question that must be asked in this connection concerns the status of the author or scriptor. As long as the author's activity is viewed as the "image" of a certain (classical-romantic) aesthetic or social theory, his role as originator can indeed be exaggerated out of all proportion. But this question can be asked from a theoretical position beyond that of the privileged *episteme* of individualism, and it need not be tied to any one aesthetic (or political) *norm* of representation. As I have suggested above, it seems impossible to define the subject in relation to discursive practices without conceiving it in terms of collective activities, as an ensemble of social *and* individual energies. A reconsideration of the function of the author cannot very well abstract from these activities or from those conditions

---

[44]Michel Foucault, "What is an Author?" in *Textual Strategies*, intro. Harari, p. 148.
[45]Ibid., p. 145.

in history (social, cultural, communicative) under which his transcriptions contain changing degrees and differing areas of representational action, and under which the societal and the subjective orientations of this action engage in variegated modes of contradiction and interrogation, inclusions as well as exclusions. As in Derrida's case, the logic of this peculiar theoretical strategy contains an unforeseen element of paradox: To analyze the subject as a function of discourse without, at the same time, analyzing the discourse as a function of the subject, and to insist on this procedure with a view to precluding "the interplay of (autobiographical) representations," constitutes a *repressive* (in the full sense of word) strategy and a *privileged* code serving the inversions (not the destruction) of certain normative hierarchies.

It should come as no surprise, then, that Foucault in his own history of the sign places so much emphasis on the rise and fall of representational action in thought and writing. In *Les mots et les choses* the historiography of signification is subsumed under a wider approach to changing patterns of *les sciences humaines*. But what this brilliant analysis of centuries of thought and signification finally yields is the recognition that the present impossibilities of representation can more sharply be discussed against the historical foil of its past possibilities, and vice versa. It is almost as if—in the teeth of its denial of teleology—Foucault's archaeology of the scientific consciousness maps out a cyclic movement (not to say development) toward the *liberation* of language from its representational functions. In the Renaissance, the relationship of words and things was one of resemblance, and the pattern of similitude "controlled the art of representing" the world. While, at that time, representation "was positioned as a form of repetition" (the theater of life or the mirror of nature providing elements of the dominating code of knowledge), it was only in the classical age—from the middle of the seventeenth century to the end of the eighteenth—that language was wrested free of things, entering into a relation with them in which signs and similitudes surrender their alliance. As a result, language was turned into a pure function of thought: "Its whole existence is located in its representative role, is limited precisely to that role and finally exhausts it."[46] But while, in the classical age, man (for whom and by whom representations existed) was himself absent from the discursive practices of knowledge, at the end of the eighteenth century he made his entry into the historicity of the scientific consciousness. In Kantian philosophy, "the withdrawal of knowledge and thought outside the space of representation"[47] is powerfully projected. Out of the collapse of the classical model of "objective" representation man emerges as a self-conscious projection so that in nineteenth-century science (biology, political economy, and philology) men represent to themselves the subjectivity of their historical *experience* as living, laboring, and speaking beings. But while the self-conscious historicity in which this concept of man was originally embedded appeared to suffuse ever-larger areas of life, labor, and language, in fact a reversal set in: Even as he was bestowing his own sense of historicity upon the order of things, man found himself dispossessed of historical content.[48]

While the profundity of this reinterpretation of the modern consciousness cannot be doubted, from the point of view of historiographical method many more problems are

---

[46]Michel Foucault, *The Order of Things*, trans. Alan Sheridan (London, 1970), p. 79. (Whenever available I have taken quotations from this English edition.)

[47]Ibid., pp. 242 f.

[48]"Les choses ont reçu d'abord une historicité propre qui les a libérées de cet espace continu qui leur imposait la même chronologie qu'aux hommes. Si bien que l'homme s'est trouvé comme dépossédé de ce qui constituait les contenus les plus manifestes de son Histoire. . . ." The resulting paradox is that of positivism and its atomistic concept of history: "L'être humain n'a plus d'histoire: ou plutôt, puisqu'il parle, travaille et vit, il se trouve, en son être propre, tout enchevêtré à des histoires qui ne lui sont ni subordonnées ni homogènes" (*Les mots et les choses*, p. 380). But the dilemma of nineteenth-century historiography does not by itself refute a concept of historicity based neither on "subordination" nor "homogeneity" between men and events.

raised than answered. This becomes obvious when *Les mots et les choses* (defined as an "archaeology" of the human sciences) is seen from the point of view of what Foucault, only a few years later, was to define as a *genealogical* approach to history. Using Nietzsche's concept of *wirkliche Historie*, he rejects the whole idea of *Ursprung* (origins) as "that which was already there" as a vain attempt to capture the essence of things, the inviolable identity of their genesis, "the metaphysical deployment of ideal significations and indefinite teleologies."[49] But although, in *Les mots et les choses*, he does his best to interrogate the processes and products of consciousness and language and to emphasize what in his preface to the English edition he calls "the unformulated thematics, the unseen obstacles . . . the negative side of science—that which resists it, deflects it or disturbs it"[50]—the whole project may well be characterized by saying that it thrives on an inversion of "ideal significations" and a submerged mode of "teleology." At this point it would be easy to trace certain patterns of a facile typology and subject them to the same kind of critique that *idealtypische Geisteswissenschaft* invites. For instance, Foucault's version of the decline of the classical *episteme* is profoundly metaphysical insofar as the archaeology of representation is viewed as self-sufficient and self-contained, so that the actual forces in modern history are either obscured or relegated to a secondary status. (Thus, "the obscure but stubborn spirit of a people who talk, the violence and the endless effort of life, the hidden energy of needs,"[51] are being considered as secondary either in reference to, or as a function of, the history of representation.) But what, in the present context, is more deeply problematic is the way in which the vast and complex construct of Foucault's archaeology is

[49]Michel Foucault, *Language, Counter-Memory, Practice*, ed. and trans. Donald F. Bouchard (Ithaca, N.Y., 1977), p. 140.
[50]Foucault, *Order of Things*, p. xi.
[51]Ibid., p. 209.

finally and ultimately used to project some cyclic anticipation and vindication of the postmodern *episteme:*

> If *this same language* is now emerging with greater and greater insistence in a *unity* that we ought to think but cannot as yet do so, is this not the sign that the whole of this configuration is now about to topple and that man is in the process of perishing as the being of language continues to shine ever brighter upon our horizon? Since man was constituted at a time when language was doomed to dispersion, *will he not be dispersed when language regains its unity?* . . .
>
> Ought we not to admit that since language is here *once more,* man will *return* to that serene non-existence in which he was formerly maintained by the imperions unity of Discourse?[52]

My italics cannot point to the methodological (and ideological) premises of this thought-inspiring construct, but they may perhaps suffice to suggest that the postmodern conception of language regaining its unity at the expense of human activities in history is itself a metaphysical "configuration" when the nonexistence of men and women in social history is thought to be "maintained" by certain patterns of language. *Les mots et les choses* is still the most basic and, no doubt, radical version of "the explosion of man's face in laughter," and it is here that the postmodern message ("that man would be erased, like a face drawn in sand at the edge of the sea")[53] finds its most sophisticated and, perhaps, consequential formulation. Since the book is one of the rare attempts to provide a consistently diachronic foundation for this revulsion from the humanistic tradition, its historiographical principles cannot be taken lightly: man as maintained by language, thought as a function of discourse—these and related conceptions take us directly into the basic strategies of poststructuralist criticism, where the author is viewed as a function of the text, but the text never as a function of the labor or work objectified in it, never in relation to the mode of production and appropriation implicating this labor.

[52]Ibid., pp. 386 f.
[53]Ibid., p. 387.

Again, there is no doubt that Foucault's challenge to nineteenth-century consciousness, for all its methodological contradictions, is as profound as it is directed against the most vulnerable elements in the crisis of the classical traditions of humanism. But the question must be asked whether, as a matter of course, the impasse in the liberal conceptions of humanity by itself invalidates the actual conditions under which men and women continue to appropriate language as a humanizing (or, for that matter, alienating) medium of their social existence.[54] The rupture between discourse and representation may already have reached awesome dimensions; to assess these fully, the historicizing approach to the problem would have to differentiate among variegated types of discourse according to their social function and cultural *Praxis*. In all likelihood, only in certain spheres and under certain conditions of literary production has the gulf between the existence of man and the function of language become so extreme as to justify talking of their "incompatibility." In other words, there is a vast spectrum of socially determined and empirically demonstrable uses of language which poststructuralist philosophy has left out of account. Even more important, if the reproduction and use of signs are, as Umberto Eco suggests, a mode of labor, then the postulated "incompatibility" between the order of language and the order of humanity must be questioned in regard to the possibility of that tertium quid which—through work— may establish certain links (without obliterating the existing gaps) between language and society, the use of words and the activity of individuals.

It is revealing that the concept of "labor" does have a significance in Foucault's scheme of words and things. The classical mode of representation is shown to be upset by, among other factors, that new concept of wealth which Adam Smith develops in his political economy. The classical

---

[54]See Manfred Naumann, *Gesellschaft, Literatur, Lesen* (Berlin, 1975), on "Humanisierungsfunktion und 'Kunstsinn' " (pp. 24–34).

representativity of wealth is threatened when what it represents is no longer objects and objectives but the amount of work invested in its production. There is, then, a new order of things, which cannot be referred to a process of representation through exchange but which ultimately rests on the irreducible condition upon which the producers of wealth have to give their time, energy, and lifeblood in order to produce wealth. But while the underlying relationship between the activities of men and the value of things retained a representational order, it was in Ricardo's political economy that value, ceasing to be a sign, became a historical product.[55]

What is so extraordinary about Foucault's analysis is the rigid compartmentalization of his scheme of *epistemes*, which reflects his unformulated (dogmatic) assumptions about the rupture between past insights and present knowledge, a troublesome relationship between history and value, history and methodology. In other words, Foucault's (historical) analysis, his acts of recognition vis-à-vis the history of political economy, are not accompanied by a corresponding perspicacity in regard to both his own method and his own mode of intellectual production. For how can the production of texts do without (or be independent of) that sacrifice of time and energy which is characteristic of all modes of labor? And since it is not labor as such which changes but the relation of labor to the process of production (and circulation), how can the history of literature be studied beyond this relation?

[55]Cf. Foucault, *Les mots et les choses*, pp. 233–38, 265–71. It is startling to note the facility with which the relationship between signs and values (or, on a different level, between the formation and the representativity of value) is dismissed as a problem of the past—just as the refusal, on the part of Marxism, to repudiate the continuing significance of these problems is ridiculed rather than analyzed with any seriousness ("Le marxisme est dans le pensée du xix° siècle comme poisson dans l'eau" [p. 274]). As against this postmodernist note of intellectual arrogance, the changeful areas of both tension and concurrence between "past significance and present meaning" deserve to be explored even more searchingly.

Although Foucault theoretically advocates the study of the links between discursive and nondiscursive "formations," it is in the (re)production aspect of writing and reading that he most obviously and most consistently fails to do so in practice. Production (political economy) and life (biology) are indeed used as vital points of reference for the scientific consciousness, but only insofar as these are revealed (or transformed) in those rules and codes of knowledge which emerge through the givenness of certain types of discourse. But from such premises, the archaeology of signification leaves open all those points of intersection where the relations of literary signs and social activities most centrally constitute historicity within the writing and reading of literature itself. Again, this is not to deny that conceptualizations in political economy may not be thought of in reference to, or even in analogy with, the changing modes of literary signification; but the irreducible process of labor, which is behind all representational and nonrepresentational modes of writing, precedes (even when it fulfills) the dominant *episteme* with its discursive rules—so much that, historically, these rules can themselves be defined only in reference to previous acts of production, circulation, and reception. Such acts constitute an event that potentially either confirms or helps transform given systems of signification. In other words, since writing and reading are implicated in discursive rules and codes of knowledge as well as in nondiscursive formations of appropriation, power, and politics, the historicity of literary texts cannot be grasped outside the given relationships between signs and activities, grammatology and production, literary language and social existence.

Mimesis: The Challenge of (Re)Production

At first sight, both the philosophical critique of representation and the genealogical analysis of discourse appear curiously incongruous with the renewed and rather intense

interest, in recent years, in the concept of mimesis as formulated by a number of critics, mainly in France and the
United States, whose work is generally associated with a
poststructuralist position. This is not the place to assess their
contributions or to attempt an exhaustive summary of the
main directions of their thought, but we should at least
glance briefly at the larger context in which mimesis is
redefined and rewritten as a major formula of response to
some of the central issues in contemporary literary, philosophical, and cultural-political controversy. If these new
versions of mimesis themselves respond to and help constitute a historical situation in Western literary theory and
criticism, then the question must again be asked and pushed
further: On what grounds and to which purposes has the
concept come to be reinaugurated at a time when the most
persistently central of its traditional definitions (mimesis qua
imitation and/or representation) has been repudiated by
both modernists and postmodernists?

As an answer, the studies assembled under the title
Mimesis des articulations (Paris, 1975) provide a number of
highly revealing suggestions. The book is designed as a collective statement on the subject, even though the authors
neither claim nor intend any unity in their approach to
what turns out to have the status neither of "object" nor of
"theme." Instead, their most general initial understanding of
mimesis is that of "reproduction,"[56] which involves the activity (the mode of production) of these texts themselves. The
individual essays (Sylviane Agacinski, "Découpages du *Trac-
tatus*"; Jacques Derrida, "Économimesis"; Sarah Kofman,
"Vautour Rouge [Le double dans *les Élixirs du diable*
d'Hoffman]"; Philippe Lacoue-Labarthe, "Typographie";
Jean-Luc Nancy, "Le Ventriloque"; Bernard Pautrat,
"Politique en Scène: Brecht") develop this position, if they
do so at all, in a highly variegated manner; yet their general
direction is to aim at an understanding of mimesis which

---

[56]*Mimesis des articulation* (Paris, 1975), p. 5.

transcends not only any concept of imitation and representation but also the level of theoretical conceptualization itself. "If the concept has always been thought as the reproduction of the thing itself, *mimesis* is what in itself undoes the old concept of imitation."[57] In other words, mimesis is thought of as some deconstructive force or energy that "mobilise, déforme et démonte ce système": it dislodges the unity of the work and the identity of the names of those theoreticians who (from Plato, Kant, Hegel, to Wittgenstein, Brecht, Girard) have written on it. At the same time, mimesis affects the status of the textual activities assembled in *Mimesis des articulations*, and it does so "selon la loi d'une *désarticulation* générale."[58]

Such ambivalence, typographically reproduced in the reduced space, in the printing of the title, in capital letters, between *des* and *articulations*, is at the center of this undertaking. These authors aim at an understanding of "mimesis" as undetermined by either its object or the *régime* of the writing in which it occurs. It is a "mimesis" that would be difficult to situate historically, since it precedes the absolute beginning that theory would necessarily presuppose or take for granted. Mimesis so defined would have to be thought of as "before" ("mais que veut dire 'avant', ici?") all language, all theater, all gestures: "Ça, non articulé, mimerait."[59]

Although this summary of the collective self-definition of this project says little, if anything, about the more specific kind of question the individual texts raise, it seems possible even here to notice some of the paradoxical results of the poststructuralist reading of mimetic theory. Insofar as the uses of mimesis in Aristotelian and neoclassical poetics tended to favor the presence of a *mythos*, the identity of an action, the reproduction of thought (and insofar as these

[57]Ibid.; cit. from blurb.
[58]Ibid. The typographical ambivalence is lost when the title is cited as *either* in two words (as, e.g., in *Textual Strategies*, intro. Harari, p. 435) or, more often, in three (for instance, in *Diacritics* [March 1978], p. 12; [June 1981], p. 5, etc.).
[59]Ibid., p. 11.

modes of presence, identity, and reproduction were sustained by representation and/or imitation), the poststructuralist revision can be said to constitute a radical and yet highly ambivalent reversal. To characterize the new departure it is not enough to say that the concept of mimesis is dissociated from its traditional functions—functions that (justifiably or otherwise) tied the mimetic activity to a privileged human *ethos* and *dianoia*, to "action" as an image of certain aspects of human life, relations, and energies. What, over and beyond that, the new approach attempts to do is to trace the trajectory of classical and postclassical theory to the contradictions and obliterations in its own premises, where the unformulated fears of Plato, the repressions of Kant, "la mauvaise conscience" in Hoffman, the "Urzeichen" in Wittgenstein, and the *distanciation* in Brecht preclude identification through representation (and articulation) in mimesis.

Jacques Derrida's reading of the Kantian aesthetic is a particularly rewarding case in point, insofar as his "Économimesis" traces the neoclassical project to the point where it exceeds the limitations of an imitative poetics and involves itself in that "inexhaustible reiteration of the humanist theme" whereby the "pure productivity of the inexchangeable" initiates a sort of immaculate commerce, some universal, infinite, limitless communicability between the divine creator of nature and its humanistic counterpart.[60] Challenging the Kantian distinction between liberal art and mercenary art (*Lohnkunst*), Derrida, in a highly successful operation, refutes the classical proposition that *mimesis* and *oikonomia* have nothing to do with each other. As against the traditional, simplified, and ossified ("durcie") opposition between *tekhnè* and *physis*, this critique starts from what is much closer to a pre-Socratic position, in the light of which the Kantian position is strikingly reread. In rejecting any

---

[60]Ibid., p. 67. In some paraphrases and in a few quotations I have used the English translation in *Diacritics*, 11 (June, 1981).

definition of mimesis as an imitation of nature, Kant had argued that nature, assigning its rules to the artist as genius, asserted itself *through* art. But if, in accordance with this position, the source of mimesis was "une flexion de la *physis*, le rapport à soi de la nature,"[61] then what we have at the center is the metaphysical principle of pure and free productivity, a case of *natura naturans:* mimesis can, through its very independence of nature, hope to imitate it the better: "Moins elle dépend de la nature, plus elle ressemble à la nature. La *mimesis* n'est past ici . . . la reproduction d'un produit de la nature par un produit de l'art. Elle n'est pas le rapport de deux produits mais de deux productions. Et de deux libertés."[62]

But even while Derrida dismantles the edifice of the Kantian aesthetic, there emerges a growing and largely unresolved tension between the level of activity in his own writing and that of its object, a complete failure to historicize (or even conceptualize) the contradiction between what is deconstructing and what is deconstructed in his own text. To begin with, he must almost deplore (or distance his own text from) the repudiation of an imitative concept of mimesis in favor of one that defines itself as "not the representation of one thing by another," "not the relation of two products but of two productions." Having established the political economy of the Kantian mimesis, he again must keep the constraints of his own economy and his own politics in the dark, as somehow categorically distinct from the political economy within the criticized text itself. If this strategy appears unsatisfactory, at least part of the reason is that, in this volume, the collective definition of mimesis as "reproduction" (to which Derrida himself subscribed) can tentatively be taken to sanction a secularized version of productivity in terms of a correlation between the productions of art and the productions of society. But how could such a

---

[61]Ibid., p. 59.
[62]Ibid., p. 67.

correlation, such a version, of productivity comprehend itself as outside those pressures of history to which, in a different period and situation, the Kantian aesthetic is shown to be subjected? The question, then, that remains unanswered is that of the effect of the *brisure* between the destruction and the reconstruction of mimesis as (re)production—an effect whose invisibility in Derrida's text appears quite deplorable.

Underlying these difficulties in Derrida's own trajectory is some basic contradiction involved in his own theoretical use of words like *production* and *reproduction* and also in the functional context in which such categories of *Praxis* (categories capable of *positively* correlating art and economy) would have to be integrated into his own system of unacknowledged hierarchies and privileges. Only a few years before contributing to *Mimesis des articulations*, Derrida, in *L'Écriture et la différence*, published an essay, "The Theatre of Cruelty and the Closure of Representation," in which the main thrust of his argument was directed against "the imitative concept of art" as one associated with Aristotelian catharsis. Translating his epistemological objections to representation into the empirical realities of theater criticism, Derrida falls back on a heavily normative reading of Artaud as testimony to "the limit of representation": "The theater of cruelty is not a *representation*. It is life itself, in the extent to which life [is] unrepresentable."[63] But while the theoretical *niveau* of this argument seems highly questionable (indeed, it almost explodes in the attempt to integrate the antirepresentational theory into the phonocentric realities of theatrical production), the full extent of the ambivalence becomes clear when the two Derridean texts are made to confront each other. While in his earlier piece "the imitative concept of art" was attacked as a living aesthetic strategy, a menace almost to "life itself" within the theatrical

[63]Derrida, *Writing and Difference*, p. 234.

transaction, the later essay on Kant proceeded (1) to demonstrate the demise or destruction of the imitative concept in late-eighteenth-century aesthetics and (2) to deplore, as it were, the fact that this new, Kantian "kind of mimesis inevitably entails [*requiert*] the condemnation of imitation, which is always characterized as being servile."[64]

Derrida is brilliantly successful in fathoming the depth of the "discrepancy between meaning and assertion"[65] within the Kantian text. But once mimesis is associated with production itself, even the provisional and shifting status of his own textual activity does not permit Derrida to proceed, to the point of an endless supplementarity, on the differential premise of an always already deferred meaning of the term. Again, even when devastatingly deconstructing the whole "organic linchpin of the system," Derrida reaches the point where the *brisure* between the metaphysical idea of "production" and his own diacritical use of the same sign ("production") must involve "articulation" as well as the obvious "break." But for Derrida to articulate the break, even within his own use of the concept of "production," seems almost impossible, notwithstanding his explicit aim "to exhibit the systematic link between" mimesis and *oikonomia.*[66] Is it at all possible, then, to trace this link without ever, in transcribing the limitations of the Kantian "production," breaking through and overcoming the nondifferential contradiction in the traditional signified? If, for Derrida, the answer seems to be no, the decision behind this answer betrays a (self-)repressive strategy. It is difficult to resist the conclusion that a referential and pragmatic (nondifferential) definition of the links between mimesis and "production" (or even theatrical "production") is repressed by a whole privileged system of methodological premises and textual strate-

---

[64]*Mimesis des articulations*, p. 68.
[65]Paul de Man, *Blindness and Insight: Essays in the Rhetoric of Contemporary Criticism* (New York, 1971), p. 110.
[66]*Mimesis des articulations*, p. 58.

gies. The point, of course, is that this is precisely where an opening for a radically historicizing use of "mimesis" would have to be sought.

Obviously, as soon as mechanical and "liberal" modes of mimesis are historically viewed together, and as soon as theater work is seen as a production of mimesis itself,[67] a nonmetaphysical concept of production must present considerable difficulties to the hierarchies within the code of textuality. To produce is to go beyond the eternal circle of deferment, beyond the limitations of the sign and the permanent displacement of meaning; it is, even more, to break through the textualization of experience and to undermine any hierarchical relationship between writing and speech vis-à-vis discursive practice. The person who makes a watch and reads the time, who plants a tree and harvests its fruits, constitutes himself or herself as a subject; the meaning of his or her activity is not deflected by verbal language as a differential system of signification. The theatrical person who knocks at a door or embraces his or her partner may not, through the production of an object, constitute himself or herself as a subject; but neither can that person's activity be subsumed under the depersonalized modes of textualization. The production of his or her "voice" is both a premise and a product of the particular social activity that a theatrical production re-presents.

Thus, the poststructuralist revision of mimesis creates its greatest difficulties from within its own strategies. As soon as "production" or "reproduction" is pushed beyond the limits of textuality, the almost-forgotten connection between the various *artes*, liberal and mechanical, establishes a wider frame of reference, anticipated in the classical

---

[67]Theater production, here, is so much more than a transcription or realization of a script: "The dramatic text is radically conditioned by its performability" (Keir Elam, *The Semiotics of Theater and Drama* [London, 1980], p. 209). Thus, far from preceding mimesis, "theatricality 'reveals' it—which means that it fixes it, defines and 'presents' it as that which, in all events, it never is on its 'own' " (Lacoue-Labarthe, *Mimesis des articulations*, p. 247).

concept of *tekhnè*, which powerfully disrupts any diacritical system, any definition of, or approach to, mimesis through script as the privileged code of difference and deferment. The resulting dilemma is such that, even in its most radical formulation, "production" (as used by critics associated with *Tel Quel*) tends to be reduced to a textual strategy. In the work of Julia Kristeva, the text *produces itself* by developing from some originating or "geno-text" to the apparent or "pheno-text"; as the intersecting elements (semantic and differential) engage in mutual dissolution and decomposition. Textual "production" constitutes itself through the decentering of the sign. As far as such "production" relates to a subject, this subject manifests itself in the psychic negativity, the "scission" and "rupture" of individual "consciousness."[68] Indeed there is, as against this semioclastic and psychographic reading of "production," the notion of the text as an element of *Praxis*, as "a gesture of assault, appropriation, destruction, and construction";[69] but although this type of discursive *Praxis* is defined by analogy with political revolution, the links with economic *Praxis* remain thoroughly problematic. To be sure, there is the fascinating suggestion that the peculiar kind of "labor" invested in the production of the geno-text is a *travail présens*, that—on this level—"work" is a pre-semantic category. Again, it seems perfectly legitimate to study the decomposition of the sign, to go beyond the univocal viewpoint of its surface, to lay bare the constraints resulting from given ideological rules of exchange and usage (and thereby to help puncture the illusions hidden under self-authenticating concepts of truth and authority). And yet, this strategy must remain blind to the essential challenge in the link between production and value, as contained in the Marxian concept of *Aneignung*.

[68]Julia Kristeva, "Sémanalyse et production de sens," in *Essais de sémantique poétique*, ed. A. J. Greimas, (Paris, 1972), p. 221.
[69]Julia Kristeva, *La revolution du langage poétique* (Paris, 1974), p. 14.

Julia Kristeva cannot justifiably dismiss Marx's concept of "labor" as providing no answer to the question of what *travail* "as such" is.[70] To recall our example, the person who makes a watch or plants a tree stands, of course, for an ensemble of social relationships, in that his or her labor is part of a process of organization, mediation, and circulation whereby the social subject constitutes human existence "through his own action." (Thus, *Arbeit* is defined in *Das Kapital* as "zunächst ein Prozeß zwischen Mensch und Natur, . . . worin der Mensch seinen Stoffwechsel mit der Natur durch seine eigene Tat vermittelt, regelt und kontrolliert.")[71]

By referring to this process as *Aneignung*[72] ("appropriation" without its acquisitive connotations) Marx develops his own concept of *travail* or *Arbeit* not, as Julia Kristeva suggests, in reference to the capitalist conditions of exchange-value, but "as independent of any specific social form" or class formation, as the activity involved in "the production of use values, appropriation of nature for human needs."[73] This is certainly not to say that the work process is identical with the process of production (which presupposes a historically determined *Wertbildungsprozess*); but perhaps here the emphasis on the connection between the two is sufficient to suggest that both work and "production" are functionally related to appropriation, and that, in the use of language, such *Aneignung* is unthinkable beyond a critical assimilation of the whole body of historically prevailing signs and significations.[74] The problems resulting today from even some tentative formulation of a humanist perspective on production are formidable enough; but the dissociation between "pro-

[70]See the cogent refutation by Brigitte Burmeister, " 'Produktion,' nicht 'Abbildung.' Zur Literaturkonzeption der Gruppe Tel Quel," in *Literarische Widerspiegelung*, ed. Dieter Schlenstedt (Berlin, 1981), pp. 586 ff.

[71]Marx/Engels, *Werke*, XXIII, 192.

[72]Cf. ibid.: the purpose of man's work is "den Naturstoff in einer für sein eigenes Leben brauchbaren Form *anzueignen*" (my italics).

[73]Ibid., pp. 192, 198.

[74]Cf. Karl Marx, *Grundrisse: Foundations of the Critique of Political Economy*, trans. Martin Nicolaus (New York, 1973), p. 488.

duction" and value, appropriation and its social function, points to no solution. This must appear as problematic as the attempt, so characteristic of *Tel Quel* and a large segment of poststructuralist criticism, to define the products and effects of textual activity per se, as value free. On premises like these, it must appear exceedingly difficult if not impossible to reconsider the relationship between mimesis and production, and they provide no solid ground on which to go beyond the limitations and anachronistic illusions of classical humanist theory.

Mimesis and Representation: Some Counterproposals

Finally, this critique of poststructuralist revisions of mimesis and representation may be expected to go beyond a purely critical stance. As, in this last section, we move from Derrida to René Girard and his own revision of classical and neoclassical versions of "mimesis," the best way to respond to his poststructuralist escalation into mimetology may be to offer, in rough outline, a counterproposal with special regard to the links, as well as the gaps, in history, between mimesis and representation. Some such proposal, involving a historicizing concept of "appropriation," has been adumbrated in the trajectory of this chapter; even so, Girard's work will provide the best (the most provocative) point of articulation. With Girard, mimetic theory enters into a larger context, one far exceeding the bounds of textuality, where the role of mimetic effects in the social process of human interaction and acculturation is described as one of conflict and appropriation and where this role can be studied from outside the constraints of either the structuralist sign or the intralinguistic notion of historicity.

Rejecting the system of binary oppositions associated with Lévi-Strauss and structural anthropology as well as Derrida's antigenetic position of "always already," Girard

proposes a pattern of mimetic rivalry with a sudden transition from reciprocal to unilateral violence culminating in
ritual victimage. The choice of a scapegoat as surrogate
victim marks the point where, at the breakdown of reciprocity, the reconciliation of the community and the rise of
cultural institutions and divisions takes place. If this project—here given the barest of summaries—goes beyond some
of the most basic structuralist and poststructuralist premises,
it also seeks to undermine essential presuppositions in the
classical theories of mimesis. As Girard says in the introduction to one of his more recent books, the classical concept of
mimesis "has always excluded one essential human behavior
from the types subject to imitation—namely, desire and,
more fundamentally still, appropriation. If one individual
imitates another when the latter appropriates some object,
the result cannot fail to be rivalry or conflict."[75]

It seems obvious at the outset, then, that Girard's repudiation of the classical and neoclassical traditions is far more
radical than any purely deconstructive operation can
obtain. His counterperspective on mimesis is clear and consistent enough: the dynamics of mimetic action and response
are rooted in a disputed object; they do not have to do with
any anthropomorphous inclination to play or any intellectual desire for recognition which, in their epistemological
and aesthetic versions, are seen as derivative. What, in the
present context, deserves particular attention is that Girard's
combined critique of classicism and structuralism does not
simply involve the rejections of representation and signification as constituents of the mimetic process; it also entails a
dimension of collective praxis: His emphasis on the acquisitive nature of mimetic action as a symptom of desire and a
source of conflict leads to some correlation between mimesis
and appropriation which—although the author is unaware
of even the possibilities of a Marxist formulation of the

---

[75]René Girard, *"To Double Business Bound": Essays on Literature, Mimesis,
and Anthropology* (Baltimore, 1978), p. vii.

problem as one of *Aneignung*—establishes a fresh perspective on classical theory itself. Among other things, it helps to illuminate a central paradox in the "omission . . . of acquisitive mimesis" by Plato, who, as Girard suggests, "still shares but cannot justify the universal terror of primitive communities for mimetic phenomena."[76] It is this non-Platonic point of departure which makes it possible for Girard to claim not only that mimesis precedes representations and sign systems, that it "exceeds the problematic of signification in all directions," but that there is "a conflictual mimesis before anything definable as human, in animal life itself."[77]

Girard does not arrest his theory on this level of primitive genesis and aboriginal function; he proceeds from what he calls "the disconcerting simplicity and elementariness of that starting point" to show how the escalation of mimetic rivalry beyond the point of no return results in a new and more complex form of social organization. According to Girard, "the same mimesis which is conflictual and divisive as long as it focuses on objects of appropriation must become re-unitive as the very intensity of the escalation substitutes one single scapegoat for many disputed objects."[78]

In moving from a murderous state of mimetic rivalry to a state of cultural differentiation and unification, Girard offers us a historical narrative. But what appears troublesome from a historicizing point of view is that once he has taken a changeful social situation as the premise on which to base the overall genetic scheme of his cultural narrative, his treatment seems to become oblivious to these presuppositions. As the actual objects and processes of mimesis are made to appear static in their isolation from nonritual activities and nonviolent factors of change in tribal society, the historiographical position on cultural genesis, irrevocably built into the mode of his argument, as it were, is lost sight

[76]René Girard, "Interview," *Diacritics* (March 1978), p. 32.
[77]Ibid., p. 34.
[78]Ibid., p. 33.

of and collapses. The function of mimesis in the social process of human interaction, after having been situated at the cradle of social organization, remains uneventful ever after. The primitive pattern of mimetic conflict and rivalry continues to exist virtually unchanged so that, in this problematic methodology, it can be used as a master key to the understanding of prehistoric ritual, Attic tragedy, Shakespeare, and some of the great nineteenth-century novels.[79]

But the paradox within Girard's methodology is that the (for him) all-important passage from mimetic violence and anarchy to some ritualized sociality through sacrifice must involve an absolute host of changes (social, economic, cultural, etc.), and these changes cannot, within the limitations of Girard's argument, be accounted for socially or historically. Instead, the multiple functions of mimesis are being reduced to a libidinous gesture, a static pattern of desire: "Ce que le désir 'imite,' ce qu'il emprunte à un 'modèle,' en deçà des gestes, des attitudes, des manières, de tout ce à quoi on réduit toujours la *mimesis* en ne l'appréhendant jamais qu'au niveau de la représentation, c'est le désir lui-même. . . ."[80] As Philippe Lacoue-Labarthe comments: "Desire, 'imitates' desire. Better, perhaps, it *mimes* desire. Desire, if you like, desires desire."[81]

As Girard engages in increasingly complex and eventful patterns of historical narrative, he is almost forced to displace the temporal dimension of nonpsychological change,

---

[79]This has found an echo in the work of critics like Cesáreo Bandera, who asserts "that literary fiction *would not exist* without mimetic desire that explicitly or implicitly can only be a source of rivalry and conflict" ("Conflictive versus Cooperative Mimesis," *Diacritics* [September 1979], p. 62; my italics).

[80]René Girard, "Système du delire," *Critique* (November 1972), p. 962.

[81]*Mimesis des articulations*, p. 242. Compare Girard's concept of "desire" with that used by Northrop Frye in *The Anatomy of Criticism* (Princeton, 1957), where a perspective on appropriation as *Aneignung* is not precluded: "Desire is thus not a simple response to need. . . . It is neither limited to nor satisfied by objects, but is the energy that leads human society to develop its own form. . . . The efficient cause of civilization is work, and poetry in its social aspect has the function of expressing, as a verbal hypothesis, a vision of the goal of work and the forms of desire." (pp. 105 f.)

transition, and event by a formula of identity and addition according to which he can lump together "a mimetic destructuration or crisis plus mimetic re-structuration through unanimous victimage."[82] Such a formula (note the atemporal "plus"), which effectively obliterates all other sources and attributes of eventful change, is then made to serve as a code by which centuries of cultural development, from prehistoric ritual to twentieth-century fiction, are read. Take, for instance, Girard's declared intention of showing "that the fundamental institutions of mankind, funeral rites, the incest taboos, the collective hunt, the domestication of animals, become structurally and genetically intelligible as products of unanimous victimage."[83] For such a consistently monistic construct the burden of explanation is as immense as the chosen code must be closed to other, less rigidly univocal forces in prehistoric society. It is only when the reproductive dimension of appropriation is left out of the picture that the conflictual mimesis can, through some unaccountable process of intensification, be said to be superseded or sublimated by that contradictory force of social integration which unanimous victimage is supposed to convey. Thus the actual objects of appropriation, the postmatriarchical female, the domesticated animal, the slain deer, the primitive tool, all drop out of the picture to make room for that single scapegoat that "substitutes . . . for many disputed objects." The appropriating function of mimesis is radically reduced. The violence of the instincts is held to stop short of the most powerful challenge of primitive existence: the challenge of survival—which, I submit, must have resulted in a more deeply existential mode of appropriation.

These critical notes certainly cannot do justice to the Girardian theory in toto, but perhaps they suffice to point to a methodological impasse, which has considerable consequences for the proposed concept of mimesis. There is an

[82]Girard, "Interview," p. 37.
[83]Ibid., p. 35.

arresting, not to say atavistic, moment in Girard's cultural narrative by which the appropriating mimesis on the level of instinctive action is unnecessarily made to overshadow or conceal the appropriating activity on the level of social reproduction. Thus, the Girardian construct is closed to the increasing heterogeneity of social conflict and differentiation, which in its turn affects the ritual and magic forms of mimesis. To reduce their increasingly diverse sociocultural functions to the most primordial level of conflict, and to claim that "all subsequent mimetic effects are ultimately brought back to the radical simplicity of that primordial mimetic interference,"[84] seems unhelpful. René Girard has with great success shown the weakness of what he calls "the strangely one-sided definition of the concept" of Aristotelian mimesis. But perhaps it is impossible "to encompass the entire range of imitative behavior" under one formula. Emphasizing the ritual origins of mimesis certainly is helpful (and appears to be amply confirmed by postclassical scholarship).[85] However, to reduce "all subsequent mimetic effects" to the prehistoric simplicity of instinctive action may seem like an impossible undertaking as soon as the assumed simplicity of this process can be shown to explode into a host of complex contradictions, among them the early dichotomy, the continuing conflict and interaction, between the ritual and representational functions of mimesis.

[84]Ibid., p. 32. In the context of this utterance, "all subsequent mimetic effects" refer to modern narrative from Cervantes to Marcel Proust; cf. *Deceit, Desire, and the Novel: Self and Other in Literary Structure* (Baltimore, 1965), p. 52.

[85]See, e.g., Herman Koller, *Die Mimesis in der Antike: Nachahmung, Darstellung, Ausdruck,* (Bern, 1954), who notes (p. 75) that "mimesis" originally refers to ritual dance and, even: "Sein Bedeutungszentrum liegt im Tanz" (p. 119). Cf. Göran Sörbom, *Mimesis and Art: Studies in the Origin and Early Development of an Aesthetic Vocabulary* (Uppsala, 1960), pp. 22–40. But the Girardian scheme has no room for the solidarity function of mimesis in the Dionysian dance and in Orphic communities, as traced deep into the classical Greek theatre by Jack Lindsay, *The Clashing Rocks: A Study of Early Greek Religion and Culture and the Origins of Drama* (London, 1965), pp. 353 ff., 383.

It is at this point that the poststructuralist perspective on mimesis as presignifying ritual and purely instinctual appropriation would have to come to terms with a historical differentiation of eventful and, in the last resort, changeful social activities in tribal and posttribal society. Once these presignifying dimensions of mimesis are projected into the world of early European history, the whole context of mimetic activity can be seen to change. Through the secularization of the cult and the division of ceremonial functions (participants in the rite eventually turning seasonal actors) the ritual context of mimesis tends to contract, and to amalgate with, elements of representation: There are numerous links between ritual release, the *embodiment*, in a dance, of the communal ceremony itself, and, say, the *representation* of fertility, new life, or the spirit of winter in such late folk play figures as, for instance, Father Christmas.[86] As distinguished (but quite inseparable) from the ritual dimension, the reproductive activity within the appropriating context, the mimetic sanction of the seasons, harvest time, and fertility rites, in correlation with the increasing use of tools and instruments of production, will tend to fortify certain social modes of labor, exchange, and property. In other words, the ritual forms of mimesis, without surrendering their impact and the continuity of instinctive action, must be seen to continue to exist in an increasingly heterogeneous and functional context, one that encompasses a growing amount of reproductive and signifying activities.

However, to propose a more dynamic view of the multiple functions of mimesis is not to sanction any evolutionary or progressive scheme of linear development. As my own studies in the early background of the popular tradition in the theater suggest, the ritual and representational contexts

[86]As against these all-too-sweeping generalizations, see my more detailed analysis of the functions of mimesis in *Shakespeare and the Popular Tradition in the Theater* (Baltimore, 1978), on which part of this concluding section draws. Unfortunately, when this book was first conceived and written in German (1964/67), I was unaware of French reinterpretations of mimesis.

overlap and do not at all preclude each other. Nor can the corresponding modes of theatrical mimesis be conceived in terms of the one superseding the other; what the history of the early modern theater reveals is the changing combination and potent interaction of the two functions, by which, on various levels, the one continues to affect and modify the other. Even by the time Shakespeare writes *Hamlet* and *King Lear* there is a tension and interaction between the representational function of mimesis (as in Hamlet's "to hold, as 'twere the mirror up to nature"), on the one hand, and on the other, some vestiges of a postritual function of mimesis. This latter function appears perfectly anachronistic in terms of Renaissance of verisimilitude and decorum, as when the madness and the antic disposition of the two tragic heroes (at least in part embodying, not the images of a fictive role, but the realities of acting out a communal theatrical occasion) both transcend and work upon the neoclassical modes of representation. The figures of Vice and madness or even the carnival impulse behind clown and fool tend perpetually to re-embody the chaos before and beyond representation, whether tragically or as a comic resolution to the unbearable logic of an ordered-disordered world in theatrical representation.[87]

Even so, as representational and nonrepresentational modes of mimesis continue to coexist and affect each other, the historical context of interaction changes. The Dionysian element of carnival laughter and release has to come to terms, in function if not in form, with the indirect (and largely negative) ways in which drama relates to those civilizing and reproductive activities in society through which the purely violent modes of appropriation are suspended in, though not superseded by, emerging relations of property.

[87]On the complex functions of mimesis in the Shakespearean theater, see my study " 'Mimesis' in *Hamlet*," *Shakespeare and the Question of Theory*, ed. Patricia Parker and Geoffrey Hartman, forthcoming. For a recent defense of the representational content of mimesis, see A. D. Nutall, *A New Mimesis: Shakespeare and the Representation of Reality* (London, 1983).

Within these socializing relationships the appropriating activity is able to constitute itself through the identification with either property or the absence of it, with what is his or her own, or with what is to him or her alien. (Hence, the theme of the "beggar," the "poor naked wretches," even the expropriating language of the gravediggers, assume dramatic stature in these plays.) But, again, the passage from ritual victimization to economic exploitation marks no progress, no linear development, in the uses of mimesis. The timeless world of the clan gives way to larger agricultural conglomerations, but the appropriation of the earth does not yet presuppose the appropriation of the means and tools of production. Under these conditions, "property" "means no more than a human being's relation to his natural conditions of production as belonging to him, as his, as *presupposed* along with *his own being;* relations to them as *natural presuppositions* of his self, which only form, so to speak, his extended body."[88] Under these circumstances, as long as the individual's existence is "mediated by his being himself the natural member of a community," the scope of appropriation, of making things one's own, is limited: The land, the soil, the communal activities based on them, are already his; they are "so to speak, his extended body." Under these conditions, mimesis cannot perform much of a representational function. Even in the folk play, the seasonal actor's performance retains strong elements of self-embodiment: There is no need to re-present what is, through his own body, already present.

It is only when the social modes of appropriation change, when property divides the social presuppositions of this communal identity, that mimetic action tends to perform two functions at once: It can re-embody, through Dionysian release, moments of postritual unity and festive equality, and it can represent, that is, confront and mediate,

[88]Marx, *Grundrisse*, p. 491.

the growing gaps between individual action and social circumstance in terms of some mimetic equation or correlative. And although these two functions of mimesis exist side by side in the greatest period of the modern theater, after the Renaissance the ritual function of drama tends either to decline or to live on in the more limited world of the *Volkstheater*, such as the Viennese, or the later commedia dell'arte, and the various carnival traditions of disguise and clowning. But while the growing social area of appropriation involves more and more alienation, while the spectrum of mimetic self-embodiment is finally reduced to the world of Punch, or the German Kasperle stage for children, the theater of illusion so develops the function of representation that it tends to absorb the process of social association and dissociation, socialization and fragmentation.

There is no space here for developing a historical perspective on the changing contexts of theatrical mimesis, but perhaps the final point that suggests itself is the historical complexity of the functions by which mimesis and representation need to be reconsidered in relation to the appropriation of the world in language through discourse. Unless the direction of my argument is altogether mistaken, "representation" on the stage (and in narrative) already presupposes the nonidentity of the self and the social, a considerable amount of tension between what is representing (representation as an activity) and what is represented (as a product). Far from constituting a privileged entity of hierarchical unification, closure, or "presence," once the world of ritual is submerged, representation establishes the possibility of a permanent contradiction between its capacity for identification and its potential for distanciation through irony, parody, satire, and related modes of critical realism.

As a paradigm of the continuing possibilities of such representation, the work of Brecht suggests itself most forcefully. As Bernard Pautrat notes, the Brechtian mimesis is "une mimesis sans identification (ou presque)." The parenthesis suggests the complex quality of the interaction between nonrepresentational and representational modes of mimesis, as in the heroine of *Der gute Mensch von Sezuan:* "On distingue nettement deux personages: *l'un montre, l'autre est montré*".[89] Thus, the contradiction between what is representing and what is represented can be revitalized in a complex stylized production of mimesis, which challenges the poststructuralist argument against "representation" and makes the Derridean objections to both "the imitative concept" of drama and the assumed metaphysical premises of "production" within representation appear rather pointless. What Brecht's representation through *distanciation* involves is, as Terry Eagleton pointedly notes, "a structure of presence-and-absence. The object is indeed represented, but represented in the context of its non-self-identity, shot through with those contradictory possibilities it habitually absents."[90]

Mimesis in the twentieth century, then, continues to constitute an ensemble of representational and nonrepresentational activities in society. Brecht's idea of the social function of the intellectual was to view the theater (and the mimesis in it) as part of and apart from the appropriation of political and economic power. His was a situation, rather like that of the writer in the modern (the premodernist) period, when the particular intellectual activity was poised between its sense of individual isolation and its sense of social relationship. If, in the wake of modern formalism and structuralism, the dynamism in the tension between these poles is held to have exhausted its energies for intellectual production, the modes of representation may indeed be displaced as part of a nonusable past, repressed as an unwelcome challenge, a burden on the privileges of the new scrip-

---

[89]*Mimesis des articulations*, pp. 353, 357.

[90]Eagleton, "Text, Ideology, Realism," p. 164. For the last two sections of Chapter 7 I have used and condensed material that was first written as a contribution to a volume of critical essays on poststructuralist theory, ed. Jochen Schulte-Sasse (University of Minnesota Press, forthcoming).

tor's diacritical senses of intellectual autonomy. But at the same time, and notwithstanding its crisis, the resourcefulness of representation helps to interrogate and, indeed, inspire the triumphs and liabilities of nonrepresentational mimesis.

Index of Names